The Preferential Option for the Poor beyond Theology

The Preferential Option
for the Poor
beyond Theology

Edited by

DANIEL G. GROODY

and

GUSTAVO GUTIÉRREZ

University of Notre Dame Press   .   Notre Dame, Indiana

University of Notre Dame Press
Notre Dame, Indiana 46556
www.undpress.nd.edu
All Rights Reserved

Published in the United States of America
Copyright © 2014 by University of Notre Dame Press

Library of Congress Cataloging-in-Publication Data

The preferential option for the poor beyond theology / edited by Daniel G.
Groody and Gustavo Gutiérrez.

pages   cm
Includes bibliographical references and index.
ISBN 978-0-268-02986-9 (pbk. : alk. paper) — ISBN 0-268-02986-5
(pbk. : alk. paper)
1. Poverty—Religious aspects—Christianity. 2. Church work with the poor.
3. Gutiérrez, Gustavo, 1928– Teología de la liberación. 4. Liberation
theology.   I. Groody, Daniel G., 1964– editor of compilation.
II. Gutiérrez, Gustavo, 1928– editor of compilation.
BV4647.P6P74   2013
261.8'325—dc23
2013031233

We dedicate this book to

MIKE AND LIZ LAFORTUNE

whose generosity, support, and witness to selfless service helped make this work possible.

Contents

Introduction

GUSTAVO GUTIÉRREZ
& DANIEL G. GROODY

Poverty is a complex issue. While its roots are socioeconomic, it affects people on every level of their existence. Understanding its causes and its consequences requires serious and sustained thought across a wide variety of academic disciplines. The principle of the preferential option for the poor has had an enormous impact on the field of theology, but this same principle has had a ripple effect in other areas as well. The purpose of this volume is to begin to look at how this theological notion has influenced other disciplines and the ways scholars have woven the golden thread of this concept into their various walks of life.

Although this volume approaches poverty from a wide range of disciplinary backgrounds, we begin by grounding the discussion in the reality of the world as it is today, particularly for the poor, the vulnerable, and the insignificant of society. While globalization has helped improve the standard of living for some of the world, still 19 percent of the global population lives on less than one dollar per day, 48 percent lives on less than two dollars per day, and, according to the World Bank, fully two-thirds of the human population lives in poverty.[1] But economic poverty is only one dimension of the problem. Transforming the world into a place that fosters the dignity of *every* person challenges *all* people to consider in what ways they can help to promote justice and peace here and now. It will take economists, lawyers, medical technologists, plumbers, farmers, retailers, CEOs, clergy, scientists, construction workers—in short, those in every profession, occupation, and vocation—to make the refugee camps in Sudan obsolete, to continue the rebuilding efforts in tsunami-stricken south Asia and the hurricane-ravaged U.S. Gulf coast, to put an end to corrupt and oppressive governments wherever they exist, to assist struggling economies so that citizens are not forced by need to migrate, to stem the tide of preventable childhood deaths, to replace violence with peace, and to rectify all circumstances of global injustice.

In the 1960s the expression "the preferential option for the poor" emerged, little by little, as a message from numerous Christians from Latin America who were struggling to be in solidarity with those in great need. While this expression was rooted in Christian faith and praxis, because of its humanistic dimension it also appealed to others who shared similar social, although not always theological, convictions.

Instrumental in this process was bringing the insignificant and marginalized of society to the forefront of history. The poor have been, and continue to be, the biggest absentees from the history of humanity, anonymous during their lives and in their deaths. Except sporadically, they pass through existence without leaving a footprint. Their struggles and suffering, as well as their cultural values, dreams, and joys, have forced them to take not the grand avenues but the side streets, the country roads, and the dead ends of the journey of our people. While they arrived with poverty on their back, as Fray Bartolomé de Las Casas would say, a visible germlike change in recent decades has been emerging, and there is a new consciousness of the poor and about the poor.

Various historical events have allowed us to become aware of the causes and contours of the reality of poverty. As a result many groups have started to rediscover the memory of events and tendencies of their own past and of diverse cultural values which, for many reasons, has been omitted from recorded history. When we speak about poverty, we are not merely referring to its economic aspect, although its importance is unquestionable; we must also keep in the forefront of any dialogue about poverty that it is an exceedingly complex reality. In addition to the economic aspect, poverty also has cultural, racial, religious, and gender dimensions. The preferential option for the poor seeks to acknowledge the multifaceted scope of poverty while standing in solidarity with the socially insignificant and excluded.

This solidarity is at the heart of the biblical message and has therefore led to a rereading and deepening of the Christian message. While the expression "preferential option for the poor" is relatively recent, its content is as old as the Scriptures. In it we find a faith perspective but also a profound reflection on what it means to be human and to create a more humane world. Therefore, while poverty is complex, this humane sense of the option for the poor resonates with various disciplines whose research and reflection add a wealth of richness and depth to these initial and ongoing efforts.

This book has its origin in two international conferences held at the University of Notre Dame, one in 2002, the other in 2004. From the first emerged a book entitled *The Option for the Poor in Christian Theology*, and from the second, *A Promised Land, a Perilous Journey: Theological Perspectives on Migration*, both published by the University of Notre Dame Press.[2] In 2012 we also published through Orbis Books *Gustavo Gutiérrez: Spiritual Writings*. This present book is a further contribution to our reflection on the topic of the option for the poor, but from a perspective different from that of previous works. It seeks to examine faith and justice, in light of the global challenges of the twenty-first century, from the platform of disciplines other than theology. In the stories they tell, we see how the contributors have discovered inventive and life-giving ways to live out their own ethics, ideals, and the call to justice.

This volume is about the option for the poor from an interdisciplinary perspective. While it has a reference point in theology, it also goes beyond theology into other ways in which scholars, activists, and practitioners have tried to highlight the needs of the poor in helping construct a better world. A collection of essays by economists, politicians, lawyers, teachers, a physician, and even a filmmaker, this volume contains their reflections on the option for the poor and how it has affected their lives and their work. It is a volume on how these particular people, each in his or her chosen profession, have used the option for the poor as a guiding principle, that golden thread, woven throughout their respective areas of expertise.

Beginning with an essay by a law professor and ending with one by a practicing litigator, this volume is framed by the legal profession, a vital link in the process of identifying and either reforming or dismantling the unjust structures that perpetuate the cycle of poverty. Robert E. Rodes, Jr., writes a compelling essay on how he learned to instill in his law students the desire to prefer the poor as a possible alternative to moving into positions in corporate America and on Wall Street. He writes that when lawyers, at their best, advocate for the poor, they not only improve the situation of the poor in the existing legal landscape but change the landscape itself, and that lawyers committed to the preferential option for the poor must look steadily at the poor people affected by the landscape and keep their concerns always in the forefront of advocacy and negotiation.

Georges Enderle, a business ethics professor, writes that producing wealth is not only "not evil" but necessary and that the poor should be included in the production of wealth, rather than it being one more thing from which they are excluded. In his essay he seeks to bring business ethics into focus and to the forefront of the various responsibilities of business people and organizations. For Enderle, the option for the poor and business ethics need each other to ensure that globalization can eliminate rather than perpetuate poverty.

Javier María Iguíñiz Echeverría writes from a sociological perspective and seeks to define the multidimensionality of poverty, who are the poor, and why are they poor. This is a complex topic including economic and noneconomic variables, capital, values, rights, and freedom. Development, defined as human flourishing and achievement of a good life, is the goal and the metric for measuring progress toward the elimination of poverty.

Matt Bloom takes up the question of poverty and happiness. At its core he invites us to examine some of the premises of a consumerist culture, especially those that equate wealth and status with well-being. At the same time, he dismantles romantic and naïve notions that see the poor as "happier" because they are unencumbered by the possessions that weigh down many of the well-to-do. Most notably he brings out the centrality of relationships in our search for better lives, and especially in light of the theme of this volume, he reminds us that the option for the poor has everything to do with connecting with those who are often socially, economically, and culturally excluded.

Patricio A. Aylwin, former president of the Republic of Chile, and his son, José O. Aylwin, contribute a chapter on the political process of evaluating and changing laws that affect the indigenous peoples of Chile. The dispossession of tribal peoples from their ancestral lands, bankruptcy of their community economic structures, and displacement from rural to urban areas have resulted in situations of poverty and marginalization for the indigenous, and exclusion from participation in the political processes that result in decisions that affect them. Though this is a story of hope, and progress has been made in restoring cultural identity and some political leverage to tribal people, there is still much work to be done.

Stephen Bede Scharper helps us see that a part of opting for the poor is also opting for the earth, as it is the only home we have. He connects the option for the poor with the notion of sustainable development: meeting the needs of the present without compromising the ability of future generations to meet their own needs. Human poverty, a vulnerable population, ecological devastation, and an at risk ecosystem go hand in hand, and the poor are often excluded from conversations and projects about ecological sustainability.

Kristin Shrader-Frechette's essay builds on Scharper's perspective by looking at the relationship between the option for the poor and environmental justice. This essay chronicles the plight of a poor community with no leverage to exert in order to keep a corporate factory from locating nearby, resulting in contamination of air and water, various illnesses, and diminished quality of life. The option for the poor is exercised when college students with science expertise take up the cause of the community and show, through legal channels, why the factory cannot be built in this location. The story widens as we discover that the practice of locating dangerous factories and plants in poor communities is common, and usually the communities lack the resources to protest.

F. Clark Power and Stephen M. Fallon contribute a chapter fundamentally on the dignity of the poor. They tell the story of creating a curriculum based on the great classics of literature offered to homeless adults at a local shelter in an effort to give the poor an equitable share of society's educational opportunities. If the poor are those who lack power and influence as much as they are those who lack material good, this course seeks to liberate those who participate by helping them find their breath and their voice.

Gerard Thomas Straub, a filmmaker, has contributed an essay on his own journey from Hollywood to documenting the life and struggles of the poor around the world. In his efforts to chronicle the plight of those who live the daily grind of poverty and those who are forced to migrate in search of a better life, Straub reminds us that we are all beggars and all migrants in one way or another, and that we must continue to believe that we can make a difference as we live out the option for the poor.

Mary Beckman's essay recalls the dual nature of the preferential option for the poor. She argues not only that institutions and systems must be transformed, but that direct service to the poor and marginalized must be carried out as well. This concept of acting with those who live in poverty as well as acting on their behalf is brought home to students in a practical way through community-based learning: making regular, meaningful contributions in off-campus communities part of formal academic course work. Students are able to enter the life experiences of those on the margins, integrate their experiences with course work, and come to see the multiple and root causes of social issues.

Paul Farmer, a practicing physician and medical anthropologist, provides a chapter that places medicine squarely within the purview of social justice work. He proposes that the poor be offered the highest quality medical care rather than care that is simply "cost-effective." For Farmer the option for the poor invites an analysis of health systems that are "historically deep" enough to remind us of some of the systemic roots of poverty. And, as several other contributors have done, he challenges us to ask whether the benefits that profit us as people of privilege might just have equal and, sadly, opposite disadvantages that are injurious to people in poverty.

Litigator Pat Maloney, Sr., who spent his professional life advocating for those who did not have the resources to fight against large corporate structures in court, relates how he was able not only to win verdicts for disadvantaged individuals but to endeavor to change some of the oppressive structures that work against the poor as well. He concludes with a challenge to the next generation of lawyers to make living the option for the poor and caring for the least of our brothers and sisters their highest priority—to obtain justice for the powerless when they are oppressed by the privileged. He wrote this essay in the last weeks of his life, and walking with him in these last days was an inspiring journey that influenced many who had the privilege to be with him.

Throughout all four volumes on the option for the poor, Mary J. Miller has been a tireless collaborator with Gustavo and Daniel. She knows the material inside and out, and her detailed and refined skills have made significant contributions to these publications. She has reminded us again and again how closely tied the option for the poor is with magnanimity. Her dedication, generosity, and intelligence make her essay a fitting conclusion to this volume, and her afterword is, we hope, the first of many published words to come.

The Option for the Poor Beyond Theology is the fruit of a team of people and the support of many different co-workers, colleagues, and friends, particularly those at Notre Dame. We would like to thank in particular Matt Ashley and John Cavadini, current and past chairs, respectively, of the Department of Theology, for their invaluable contributions, and the Kellogg Institute for International Studies for its support of this project. We would also like to thank Gil Cárdenes, Allert Brown-Gort, and Doug Franson for their leadership at the Institute for Latino Studies. Terry Garza, Maribel Rodriguez, Elizabeth Station, Marisa Marquez, and Claudia Ramirez were enormously helpful in handling many of the details related to the conference that resulted in this book. We would also like to thank our great friends and colleagues Virgilio Elizondo and Tim Matovina for their friendship, steadfast support, and insight. And lastly, we would like to thank our confreres in the Dominican Order and the Congregation of Holy Cross who have helped inspire this work and bring it to fruition, and especially Mike and Liz LaFortune, whose generosity and unwavering support helped make this work possible.

NOTES

1. *Human Development Report 2005: International Cooperation at a Crossroads* (New York: United Nations, 2005), 3–4. The World Bank describes three degrees of poverty: extreme or absolute poverty, moderate poverty, and relative poverty. Extreme poverty means living on less than one dollar per day. People in this category do not have enough to survive and lack the basic necessities of life; extreme poverty is "poverty that kills." More than 8 million people worldwide die each year, twenty thousand die each day, because they are too poor to survive. Moderate poverty is defined as living on one to two dollars per day. People in this

category have just barely the basic needs of life. Relative poverty, defined as a household income below the national average, means a living standard below the common middle class. See www.worldbank.org and Jeffrey Sachs, *The End of Poverty* (East Rutherford, N.J.: Penguin Press, 2005), 20–24.

2. More information about these books and accompanying films is available at www.nd.edu/~dgroody.

CHAPTER 1

On Professors and Poor People

A Jurisprudential Memoir

ROBERT E. RODES, JR.

*But let the brother of low degree glory in his high estate, and the
rich, in that he is made low.*

—James 1:9–10

A_s I begin to write this chapter I am sitting in front of a computer in a large, comfortable office, surrounded by large, comfortable
books, and a less comfortable quantity of loose papers. I have been looking at the latest of a series of e-mails regarding people who cannot raise
the security deposits required before the local gas company will turn
their heat back on. They shiver in corners of their bedrooms or burn their
houses down with defective space heaters. The public agency that is sup-
posed to relieve the poor refuses to pay security deposits, and the private
charities that pay deposits are out of money. A bill that might improve

---

This chapter was originally published as an article in the *Journal of Law and Religion* and is reprinted here with permission. Robert E. Rodes, Jr., "On Professors
& Poor People—A Jurisprudential Memoir," *Journal of Law and Religion* 22
(2006–7): 527ff.

matters has passed one house of the legislature and is about to die in committee in the other house. I unexpectedly fell in with a former student
who works in the field of utility regulation. She has promised to send me
more e-mails on the subject and has given me her card. I am about to fill a
briefcase with student papers on whether a lawyer can encourage a client
in the United States illegally to marry her boyfriend in order not to be
deported. When I have done that, I will go home for the weekend to my
large, comfortable house.

It is easy to wonder if I have opted for the poor in any meaningful
way when I am so far from being one of them. But I keep telling my students, as they head for Wall Street law firms, that the preferential option
for the poor is not a career choice. It is a matter of giving priority to the
interests of the poor in whatever situation you encounter them. That is
what God calls all of us to do. Some people He calls to a life of voluntary
poverty. All honor to those who have that vocation and live up to it, but
voluntary poverty is not the condition of the poor. The poor are people
who have things happen to them that they do not want to have happen.
As I grow old and my body starts to creak, I begin to feel some solidarity
with such people, but that is hardly an option. My real option—what I
am really called to do—is to use my material and intellectual resources,
such as they are, for the benefit of poor people.

What it comes down to is that I am a law teacher, and my task is to
prefer the poor when I teach law, or, if you like, to teach my students how
to prefer the poor. I propose in this paper to indicate how I have learned—
if I have learned—to do this. I call the paper a jurisprudential memoir
because the study of what laws ought to do and how to make them do it
is called jurisprudence.

INTELLECTUAL FORMATION

I graduated from Harvard Law School in 1952. My teachers were the last
of the great scholars of the first half of the twentieth century who founded
a practical and realistic American jurisprudence with which they hoped
to save the world, or a good part of it. It was said in those days that the
way to Washington was to go to Harvard and turn left, and most of us
were not inclined to disagree.

The twin pillars of our legal thinking were Oliver Wendell Holmes's "American Legal Realism" and Roscoe Pound's "Sociological Jurisprudence." The first told us what the law was, and the second told us what it was for. Law, said Holmes, is "the prophecies of what the courts will do in fact, and nothing more pretentious."[1] But we were not only to predict what they would do; we were to persuade them to do what they should. Pound set before the whole enterprise "a great task of social engineering,"[2] to make the limited resources of the world meet as many human wants as possible with the least possible friction and waste. Pound's technological metaphors dominated our aspirations, and infected them with a pervasive hubris.

The growth of social legislation beginning in the late nineteenth century and culminating under the presidency of Franklin Roosevelt, represented for us a new understanding of the proper way to put our profession to work. Much of our study of constitutional law consisted of deploring the mossback judges who used to strike these statutes down, and praising their enlightened successors who let them stand. I studied labor law under Archibald Cox, who was to become the nemesis of Richard Nixon. I was one of the first generation of law students to take a course in administrative law, the operation and control of government agencies. Two years later, when I was working for Liberty Mutual Insurance Company administering compensation for injured workers, I found myself in a roomful of the best insurance lawyers in Massachusetts, convened in an emergency meeting to discuss a proposed administrative procedure act for the state. I was the only person in the room who had taken a course in administrative law, and the only person, or so I thought, who had a clue as to what was going on.

Those few of us who were Catholic connected all this beneficent legislation with something called Catholic social teaching, to which we were exposed on a parochial level, and ultimately with natural law, of which we got fleeting glimpses in Lon Fuller's jurisprudence course and in undergraduate courses in philosophy or theology. Part of the teaching involved the concept of social justice, the virtue we practice by doing our best to reform the structures of society so that they will render to people what is due them. A few older scholars hinted that a number of these Catholic teachings had entered into our social legislation through their influence on some of Roosevelt's advisers.[3]

Two years out of law school I left Liberty Mutual and started teaching. One of my first assignments was modern social legislation, out of a casebook by that name.[4] It dealt with the Elizabethan poor law that was in force pretty much unchanged in many states, with other forms of relief, with Social Security, with workmen's (now called workers') compensation, and with wages and hours laws. It gave firm support to the conviction that justice, not charity, was behind these laws, and at least tacit support to the idea that these laws were doing what needed to be done.

The actual poor were largely invisible in those days. I remember reading in a national magazine that a charitable organization that distributed Christmas turkeys to poor families could not find enough poor families to dispose of all its turkeys. At least for me, and I believe for many others, the poor were brought back into view by two people, Bill Stringfellow and Michael Harrington. The first I knew personally, the second I knew from his book.

In the summer of 1959, when I had been teaching for five years, at Notre Dame for three, I came upon an article in the *Harvard Law School Bulletin,* "Christianity, Poverty, and the Practice of the Law," by William Stringfellow. He had come directly from law school to East Harlem, then the most miserable part of New York City, "to live here, to practice law here, to take some part in politics, to be a layman in the Church."[5] He described his milieu in terms that were soon to become familiar, although I found them a revelation at the time:

> Poverty is my very first client in East Harlem—a father whose child has died from being bitten by a rat. . . . Poverty is a widow on welfare whose landlord cuts the heat knowing that the winter will end before the complaint is processed. Poverty is an addict who pawns the jacket off his back to get another fix. . . . Poverty is the payoff to a building inspector not to report violations of the building code. . . . Poverty is the relentless daily attrition of contending with the most primitive issues of human existence: food and cleanliness and clothing and housing and heat and rest. Poverty is an awful vulnerability.[6]

He had no answers to the problems he set forth in five pages of careful description and analysis. He simply said that "the awful vulnerability of the poor is in fact the common vulnerability of every man to death. And from the power of death no man may deliver his brother." The Christian presence in the world of the poor is not "some commitment to generous charity, nor fondness for 'moral and spiritual values.' . . ."

> It is, instead, the knowledge that there is no pain nor privation nor humiliation nor disaster nor scourge nor distress nor destitution nor hunger nor striving nor anxiety nor temptation nor wile nor suffering nor frustration nor poverty which God has not known and borne for men in Jesus Christ. He has borne death itself on behalf of men and in that event He has broken the power of death once and for all.[7]

We brought Stringfellow out to talk to our students in the spring of 1960. He began by telling them that his main distinction was that he was the lowest paid graduate of the Harvard Law School. He described for them the situation in East Harlem and the work that he did. Hand after hand went up at the end of his talk, with students asking how these problems could be solved. He said that the world does not solve its problems; it only rearranges them. He was scornful of the social workers that commuted in from Westchester with a view to making East Harlem like Westchester. But he did not insist on all Christian lawyers joining him in East Harlem. His concern was death, and death is everywhere. What he said that most impressed me was that the role of a Christian is to bring out the witness to Christ that is latent in every situation.

Ultimately, I could not accept Stringfellow's insistence on total alienation from the powers of this world.[8] I kept believing that there is a Christian way to exercise power, and that the role of a Christian lawyer is to persuade those who exercise power to exercise it in that way. I had started on a decades-long study of the legal development of the Church of England as an attempt to retain the medieval church-state synthesis in a pluralist world.[9] I came up with an ecclesiology that accepted at least the theoretical possibility of a public order conformable to God's will. In 1979 I published an article entitled "Pluralist Christendom and the Christian Civil Magistrate."[10] It appeared in the *Capital University Law Review* with various other papers on theology and law including a republication of Stringfellow's piece from the 1959 *Harvard Law School Record*.[11] But my encounter with Stringfellow had permanently raised my consciousness regarding the condition of the poor. When I read Michael

Harrington's *The Other America*[12] in 1962, I learned a lot more about poverty, but none of it came as a surprise to me.

I cannot remember when I first read *The Communist Manifesto*. It was probably when I was in law school. At any rate, it has been part of my intellectual furniture for most of my academic life. It is quite wrong in many respects, but no one who has studied the nineteenth century can fail to take it seriously. Where it went wrong was not in its description of its own time, but in its prediction of the future. It had become obvious by my time that capitalism was not about to destroy itself, as Marx and Engels had predicted it would. Keynes had shown that capitalists did not have to eat each other up in battles over markets because they could create their own markets by not underpaying their workers. But I found the Marxist version of class dialectic persuasive. It shed a good deal of light for me on the legal developments of the nineteenth and early twentieth centuries. I never accepted the idea that law must inevitably serve the interests of the ruling class, but I realized more and more that that was what it would do unless we made it do something better.

My picture of class dialectic was completed by two books, *The Organization of Man*, by William H. Whyte,[13] and *The New Class*, by Milovan Djilas.[14] Djilas, a leading Yugoslav Communist until he wrote this book, argued that the assumption of power by the proletariat as Marx and Engels envisaged it could not come to pass because the proletariat was not adequately organized. Accordingly, a class of surrogates grew up to exercise power on their behalf. With rigorous Marxist methodology, Djilas showed how this class, more or less coextensive with the Communist Party, had acquired power in the Soviet Union and in the Communist states of Eastern Europe, and how they exercised their power when they had it. Djilas believed that the bureaucracies of the capitalist states did not constitute a class as the ruling Communist parties did.[15] There I parted company with him. It seemed to me that the class I belonged to had become powerful in about the same way the Eastern Communists had. Corporate managers as surrogates for the suppliers of capital, labor organizers as surrogates for workers, government officials as surrogates for the general public, and lawyers as surrogates for everybody had more in common with each other than with their respective constituencies. Capital was no longer in control of industry: managers hired their capital as they did their labor, and when they lost their capital, they proceeded under the bankruptcy laws to get more. Whyte's book was a persuasive description of the ethos of this class, and of the way they exercised power. Putting the two books together, I came to the conclusion that just as the transition from feudalism to capitalism came peacefully in England while it required a revolution in France, so the transition from capitalism to managerialism came peacefully in the West while it required a revolution in Russia. This perception gave me useful insights into a number of legal developments during the last half of the twentieth century.

At this point, I had come a long way from sociological jurisprudence. The renewed awareness of continuing poverty undermined confidence in Pound's technological metaphors. If social engineering is what lawyers do, they are not doing it very successfully. At the same time, the class dialectic of Marx and Djilas indicates that social change is being brought about by forces quite other than law.

I came upon Jacques Maritain's *On the Philosophy of History*[16] shortly after it came out in 1957. Maritain presented a complex and sophisticated philosophy, one of whose tenets was what he called "the law of the ambivalence of history":

> [A]t each moment human history offers to us two faces. One of these faces gives grounds to the pessimist, who would like to condemn this period of history. And the other gives grounds to the optimist, who would like to see the same period as merely glorious.[17]

The role of human endeavor—and therefore the role of law—in any period, therefore, is to enhance the good and resist the evil that is inevitably present in any historical situation.

This introduction to the philosophy of history provided a further critique of sociological jurisprudence. Law, unlike other social forces, is under human control. We have this or that law because people in authority choose that we shall have it. In the last analysis, the project of sociological jurisprudence is to use this power of choice to take control of history. The thing cannot be done. We can have considerable success in solving this or that problem, but the overall course of history can be neither predicted nor controlled. As Herbert Butterfield put it in *The Whig Interpretation of History*,[18] a book that made a profound impression on me when I encountered it in my study of English church history, "Perhaps

the greatest of all the lessons of history is this demonstration of the complexity of human change and the unpredictable character of the ultimate
consequences of any given act or decision of men."[19] So it would seem
that the role of our profession in history is neither to follow it and implement it, as the Marxists say, nor to take control of it as the project of
sociological jurisprudence supposes. Rather, it is to stand outside the process, making incremental infusions of justice as the opportunity presents
itself. This formulation has a certain affinity for traditional natural law
doctrine: that too envisages a stance outside history and values to be introduced into the process from without.[20] At this point in my thinking, I
had to cope with Jacques Ellul's radical undermining both of natural law
and of any pursuit of justice by the legal profession. Bill Stringfellow gave
me Ellul's *The Theological Foundation of Law*[21] to read when it first came
out in English in 1960, and I did a review of it for the *Natural Law
Forum*.[22] Ellul argued that natural law is a fact of creation that you have
to take into account when you make laws, just as you have to take the
shape of the body into account when you make clothes, but that as all
creation was corrupted by the Fall, there is no basis for regarding natural
law as either just or good. The purpose of human law is not to implement
natural law, and not to support a good life, but simply to preserve the
world for judgment:

> Law is commissioned to make life possible for man and to organize so-
> ciety in such a way that God may maintain it. . . . Just as rights are granted
> to man for the sake of the covenant, the world is preserved with a view to
> the coming judgment. . . . The world is preserved in order that the Word
> may be proclaimed and that salvation in Jesus Christ be announced.[23]

This doctrine precludes any attempt of law to be salvific, and consider-
ably discourages any attempt to be utilitarian, or even just:

> The demonic temptation of law consists of a vision of society without a
> purpose, or of a purpose other than the judgment of God, realised *hic et
> nunc* in the preaching of the gospel. Again we must point out that when
> law organizes society for the sake of man's happiness, or production, or
> power and glory, or of riches, and not for the sake of the judgment, it
> ceases to preserve the world.[24]

Within his understanding of preserving man for the covenant and the world for judgment, Ellul left room for only a modest aspiration to use the law for what other people would see as social justice: "[T]he social, economic, and political conditions of life, brought about by law, must prevent man from being cornered by death."[25]

In 1975 I put together a sweeping critique of the sociological jurisprudence of my youth in a little paper called "Law, Social Change, and the Ambivalence of History."[26] I drew heavily on Maritain and Butterfield. Reading the piece today, I see Ellul lurking in the background. I do not mention him, but I seem to be groping for a way to transcend the limited role he assigns to law without returning to the discredited and hubristic metaphors of social engineering.

What I came up with was a project for replacing technological metaphors with verbal ones:

> When we make or invoke laws we are using words to make claims on other people, and through people, on history. There are manipulative elements of course, but fundamentally we are not manipulating people, we are addressing them. We are not being "engineers" or using "instruments," we are being spokesmen.[27]

I managed to work this spokesmanship into a pretty high aspiration, but not one that could be pursued with much confidence in the outcome: "To demand justice passionately, resourcefully, and against all odds is the mark of humanity in its pilgrimage through time."[28] I ended up saying that "the lawyer should, after all, be content with the role of advocate," and that in the advocacy of social change, "though he is no stranger to bizarre tribunals and equivocal results, he has the word of the Lord of history that those who hunger and thirst after justice will be filled."[29]

It was not until 1979 that I read Fr. Gutiérrez's *A Theology of Liberation*.[30] I had been working on other things, and had only gradually become aware of the important place liberation theology was beginning to occupy in Catholic social doctrine. But finally I went to a colleague more current on such matters than I and asked him what book on the subject I should read if I were to read only one. Naturally, he gave me Gutiérrez.

Gutiérrez's teachings as I extracted them from his book were these: (1) People's response to God is blocked by unjust economic, social, and political institutions, therefore we owe it to our neighbors to rescue them from these institutions by reforming or dismantling them; (2) God calls us to the work of doing so, and assures us of its value in building the Kingdom; (3) unjust institutions create a class struggle between victims, who have a stake in reforming or dismantling them, and beneficiaries, who have a stake in leaving them intact; (4) human solidarity is achieved not by disregarding class struggle but by siding with the victims; (5) the reform or dismantling of unjust institutions, in addition to liberating the victims, liberates the beneficiaries from living on the flip side of other people's misery.[31] These principles filled gaps in my thought like missing pieces of a jigsaw puzzle. The focus on liberation permits a purposeful deployment of legal skills without buying into the tattered project of sociological jurisprudence. Instead of trying to put together a globally effective structure, we can work at reforming or demolishing institutions that we have in front of us to remedy evils and injustices that we observe. Because liberation is open-ended, we can pursue it with good purpose despite Butterfield's warning that we cannot foresee all the results of what we are doing. Liberation is just, and justice is to be done although the skies fall. By the same token, because the work of liberation is eschatologically validated, we do not have to worry about validating it historically. The ambivalence that Maritain perceives is no problem for us. And where Ellul assigns us the static function of preserving the world for judgment, Gutiérrez allows us to work to bring about God's Kingdom. Even though we cannot accomplish the work, God values it, and will use it in some way:

> Faith proclaims that the brotherhood which is sought through the abolition of the exploitation of man by man is something possible, that efforts to bring it about are not in vain, that God calls us to it and assures us of its complete fulfillment, and that the definitive reality is being built on what is transitory. Faith reveals to us the deep meaning of the history which we fashion with our own hands: it teaches us that every human act which is oriented toward the construction of a more just society has value in terms of communion with God.[32]

Gutiérrez's eschatological emphasis clarified for me a problem I had begun to notice in traditional natural law doctrine—its failure to cope with tragedy. Our nature may teach us how we ought to behave, and our laws may profitably implement the teaching, but the hard work of our profession is done where the teachings are violated and we are left with the pieces to pick up. Nature does not tell us about picking up pieces, but theology does. And what it tells us is that since the original Fall we all have pieces to pick up, and that God does not intend for us to be put back together the way we were. He intends for us to be on our way to a destiny which eye has not seen nor ear heard. That destiny is compatible with our nature but not defined by it. Our job, whether as lawyers or simply as human beings, is not to deliver people to that destination, for we do not know how to do that, but to set them on their feet and take the stumbling blocks out of their path.

Unlike Marx, Gutiérrez relativizes class struggle. By doing so, and by attributing class divisions to unjust institutions, he clarified for me the role of law in the dialectical process. Anyone who studies legal history enough will recognize that laws can often be adopted not because they serve the interests of the ruling class, but because they are deemed just no matter whose interests they serve. Reflecting on the same history in the light of Gutiérrez's observations, I came to see that laws, once adopted, can sometimes support the rise of new classes to take advantage of them rather than maintaining the hegemony of classes already in place. Even if they were enacted for the sake of justice, they can become unjust through the new class structures to which they give rise, and thereby give rise to a class of victims to set off against the class of beneficiaries. Given these perceptions, I could see each dominant class in its turn appropriating in support of its hegemony the values behind the laws that had first empowered it—whether or not it continued to implement those values. I attached to this phenomenon the name *false consciousness*—a term which Marxists use in a somewhat different way.

It was as a remedy for false consciousness that I adopted the liberationists' preferential option for the poor. The actual term did not appear in Gutiérrez's book. In his introduction to the revised edition, he says that its first official use was by the Latin American bishops at Puebla in 1979, although "it was a formula that theologians in Latin America had already begun to use in preceding years."[33] It was used by John Paul II in a number of places, including his major social encyclical *Centesimus Annus*.[34] The American hierarchy used it in their 1986 pastoral letter *Economic Justice for All.*[35] I began using it in about 1985. I equated it with the view Charles Kingsley expressed in a novel I had read a little earlier, *Yeast* (1851):

> I think honestly . . . that we gentlemen all run into the same fallacy. We fancy ourselves the fixed and necessary element in society, to which all others are to accommodate themselves. "Given the rights of the few rich, to find the condition of the many poor." It seems to me that other postulate is quite as fair: "Given the rights of the many poor, to find the condition of the few rich."[36]

Putting together all these different influences, experiences, and reflections, I have come up with what I have, perhaps too sanguinely, labeled a "jurisprudence of liberation."[37] In what follows, I will set forth the principles of that jurisprudence as briefly as I can, and try to show the way they point to the preferential option for the poor, and support its exercise.

LIBERATION JURISPRUDENCE

The first principle is that individuals, communities, and humanity as a whole are called to a journey, a pilgrimage, to a destiny that fulfills human nature, but transcends it in ways we do not understand. That destiny is adumbrated in every historical situation—as the Second Vatican Council puts it, the Kingdom of God is "already present in mystery."[38] We can know the general direction of the journey. We can discern and attempt to cope with obstacles and deviations. But we cannot know the end well enough to adopt a definitive strategy for reaching it. Institutions and systems committed to a known and therefore spurious destiny are simply additional obstacles. For this reason, liberation has a primary place among the objects of law. It relates the enterprise to obstacles that can be observed and understood rather than to goals that can be perceived only in mystery.

Our professional skills can therefore be deployed for purposes to which they are adequate. We can deal with problems as they arise, and when, as often happens, our solutions give rise to new problems, we can deal with them as well. When people fall by the wayside, we can pick them up, dust them off, set them on their feet, and do the same thing again if they fall again a few paces down the road. The historical indeterminacy of the work is made up for by its eschatological fruition. As Gutiérrez says, it has value in terms of communion with God.

When we serve our clients, we do not merely improve their situation in the existing legal landscape; we change the landscape itself. We propose statutes and regulations and sometimes get them enacted. Our advocacy can bring about new developments in the judge-made law. And our transactional lawyering can establish new ways to use the law and show new changes that it requires. In all these works, our ultimate commitment is to justice. As Sir William Blackstone, author of the primary textbook in our legal system, put it when he embarked on the study of his profession:

> Then welcome business, welcome strife,
> Welcome the cares, the thorns of life,
> The visage wan, the pore-blind sight,
> The toil by day, the lamp by night,
> The tedious form, the solemn prate,
> The pert dispute, the dull debate,
> The drowsy bench, the babbling hall,
> For thee, fair *Justice*, welcome all![39]

Our pursuit of justice involves the replacement of unjust laws and institutions. It is a task that will not be completed this side of the eschaton, because the forces of history and the creativity of evil are constantly making just laws and institutions operate unjustly.

When new laws and institutions appear, new classes arise to take advantage of them. The feudal landholding class came to power through legal arrangements calculated to provide local administration and police in countries with no effective infrastructure. The capitalist class came to power through legal arrangements calculated to allow for more creative use of resources as society became more settled and more prosperous. The managerial class came to power through legal arrangements calculated to distribute more fairly the wealth created by capitalists and the people they hired to work for them.

Each of these classes, when its power has been consolidated, has tended to take control of the legal system. While I do not believe a ruling class makes laws merely to protect and perpetuate its own hegemony, it does tend to overvalue its contribution to the common good, and that of the laws and institutions on which its power is founded. It was common for feudal landholders to believe that only their paternal benevolence kept the peasantry from anarchy and ruin, and for capitalists to believe that only the free operation of the market could provide enough goods and services to keep society from collapsing. It is common for managers and professionals today to believe that the interplay of economic, social, and technical forces is too complicated for any but themselves to understand. And each class has tended naturally to make and apply laws in accordance with its beliefs.

It is false consciousness that leads a whole society to believe that the ruling class continues to implement the values that led to the adoption of the laws on which its power is based, and that those values continue to be the ones most in need of being implemented. For Marxists, consciousness is false only when it leads other classes to support the hegemony of the ruling class. Members of the ruling class may have the same consciousness, but for them it is not false. The distinction between truth and falsehood, like everything else in the Marxist system, is class-bound. But as Christians we believe in an objective reality beyond class. Any consciousness that does not conform to that reality is false for everybody.

The preferential option for the poor is the primary remedy for false consciousness. It involves, as the name implies, preferring the interests of the poor to those of other people involved in whatever project is under consideration. It is a claim for the poor and an ascesis for the ruling class. I call it an ascesis because I cannot see that strict justice requires it. If it were possible to judge evenhandedly between rich and poor, I should suppose strict justice would be satisfied. But it is common Sunday school morality that if we set out to do no more than is required of us we will end up doing less. As a practical matter, we of the ruling class can do justice to the poor only by preferring them.

LIVING WITH THE OPTION

If we are to succeed in implementing a preferential option for the poor, there are several points that we have to make clear at the outset. First, as I tell my students, the preferential option for the poor is not a career choice. I stress this point because I am a law teacher, and my students have immediate choices before them. If they take what they call "public interest" jobs—as prosecutors, public defenders, legal aid lawyers, or counsel to government agencies—they will serve the poor a good deal of the time, but the pay is so low that they believe they will not be able to support their families and pay off their student loans. If they go with the major law firms that pay astronomical salaries, they will be financially secure, but they will mostly serve the rich. I tell them that the burdens of the poor are being fashioned in the major law firms faster than they can be relieved by the public interest offices. One way of opting for the poor, therefore, is to bring their claims to the attention of corporate clients, who are often thoughtless rather than malicious in the harm they do, or at least are willing to alleviate the harm if it is not too expensive to do so.

Next, the preferential option for the poor is not a power base. The poor, like the proletarians in Milovan Djilas's analysis, cannot take power for themselves because they lack the organization and expertise required to exercise power in a modern state. But there are many politicians with the requisite credentials ready and willing to exercise power on their behalf, or on behalf of this or that constituency among them. Such politicians are easy prey to false consciousness. Having been elected to serve the poor, they continue to believe that they are doing so, whatever compromises they accept. Worse, having come to power through the victimization of their constituents, they have a stake in that victimization continuing, a stake which may unconsciously color their attitude toward efforts to make things better. It is important for politicians, like other members of the elite, to exercise a preferential option for the poor, but those who serve poor constituencies do not necessarily have a privileged way of doing so. We can serve the poor at least as effectively by confronting and challenging power on their behalf as by exercising it on their behalf.

In the end, it seems that the preferential option for the poor is not so much a doctrine as a habit of heart and mind, a way of looking at situations to which our doctrines may apply. Nor, it seems, is there a discrete body of people who are always and everywhere the poor. The poor are those who in a particular situation lack something that they need for a fully human existence. It may be useful employment in one place, education or health care in another. Or in a particular transaction, the poor are those whose needs are left out of account. In a corporate merger or a plant closing, the poor are the workers who will lose their jobs. In a condominium conversion, the poor are the tenants who cannot afford to buy the converted units. When a new medicine is put on the market, the poor are the sick people who cannot afford to buy it. In the war on drugs, the poor are the Bolivian peasants who try to eke out a modest living growing coca leaves. All these transactions involve lawyers, and as lawyers committed to the preferential option for the poor, we must look steadily at the poor people affected by them, and keep their concerns on the table as we deploy our advocacy and negotiating skills in the affairs of our various clients.

My friend and colleague Tom Shaffer, preeminent among thinkers and writers on the lawyer-client relation, has paid a good deal of attention to the idea that the practicing lawyer is a retailer of justice.[40] The metaphor comes from Arthur Train's fictional lawyer, Ephraim Tutt.[41] If it is a good one—and I think it is—then I suppose academic lawyers such as myself, along with legislators and appellate judges, must be wholesalers. Unlike practicing lawyers, we are responsible for the coherence, integrity, and utility of the whole system as well as for the outcome of individual cases and transactions.

That responsibility offers important additional opportunities for false consciousness. It is easy to believe that we live and prosper under a basically beneficent system, that the misfortunes of those who, unlike ourselves, fail to prosper under it are either the result of their own improvidence or the inevitable consequences of an imperfect world, and that if we tinker more than incrementally with the system unimaginable disasters will ensue. The belief sometimes takes the form of a global methodology—cost-benefit analysis—or of a jurisprudential theory—law and economics. In other cases it simply fuels opposition to a particular reform. If we free the slaves, they will all starve. If we give women the vote, families will be destroyed. If we make employers hire blacks, all their white workers will quit. If we pay workers a living wage, we cannot compete with manufacturers based in Guatemala or Thailand.

Against any manifestation of this argument, the preferential option for the poor prevails by virtue of the maxim *fiat justitia ruat coelum*, let justice be done though the skies fall. The maxim applies to social justice as surely as to other forms of justice. And to achieve social justice we must prefer the poor. They are the ones who are not receiving their due under the system as it stands. They cannot wait for us to weigh in an exact balance the claims of the prosperous classes to go on prospering. Our calling as Christians is to resist known evils even at an unknown cost. We cannot know all the consequences of our actions, and some of the consequences we may well regret. But a world in which we do what we can about the poverty we encounter, and then do our best to cope with the consequences as they arise, is a better world than one in which we pusillanimously allow our neighbors to languish in a poverty that we could alleviate if we would.

It is our faith that our efforts will not ultimately be in vain that spurs us on. The Second Vatican Council tells us:

> [A]fter we have obeyed the Lord, and in His Spirit nurtured on earth the values of human dignity, brotherhood and freedom, and indeed all the good fruits of our nature and enterprise, we will find them again, but freed of stain, burnished and transfigured, when Christ hands over to the Father: "a kingdom eternal and universal, a kingdom of truth and life, of holiness and grace, of justice, love and peace." On this earth that Kingdom is already present in mystery. When the Lord returns it will be brought into full flower.[42]

Jurisprudence cannot assure us of this consummation. Faith can.

NOTES

1. Oliver Wendell Holmes, "The Path of the Law," *Harvard Law Review* 10 (1897): 457, 461.

2. Roscoe Pound, *Social Control through Law* (New Haven, Conn.: Yale University Press, 1942), 64–65.

3. See George Q. Flynn, *American Catholics and the Roosevelt Presidency* (Lexington: University of Kentucky Press, 1968); David J. O'Brien, *American Catholics and Social Reform* (New York: Oxford University Press, 1968).

4. Stefan A. Riesenfeld and Richard C. Maxwell, *Modern Social Legislation* (Brooklyn, N.Y.: Foundation Press, 1950).

5. William Stringfellow, "Christianity, Poverty, and the Practice of Law," *Harvard Law School Bulletin* 10 (1959): 4; reprinted in *Capital University Law Review* 8 (1979): 451.

6. Ibid., 451–52.

7. Ibid., 458.

8. See William Stringfellow, "Christ and the Powers of Death," in *A Keeper of the Word,* ed. B. W. Kellermann (Grand Rapids, Mich.: Eerdmans, 1994), 192–203; Walter Wink, "Stringfellow on the Powers," in *Radical Christian and Exemplary Lawyer,* ed. Andrew W. McThenia, Jr. (Grand Rapids, Mich.: Eerdmans, 1995), 17–30; Andrew W. McThenia, Jr., "An Uneasy Relationship with the Law," in *Radical Christian and Exemplary Lawyer,* 167–80.

9. See my *Ecclesiastical Administration in Medieval England* (Notre Dame, Ind.: University of Notre Dame Press, 1977); *Lay Authority and Reformation in the English Church* (Notre Dame, Ind.: University of Notre Dame Press, 1982); *Law and Modernization in the Church of England* (Notre Dame, Ind.: University of Notre Dame Press, 1991).

10. Robert E. Rodes, Jr., "Pluralist Christendom and the Christian Civil Magistrate," *Capital University Law Review* 8 (1979): 413ff.

11. Stringfellow, "Christianity, Poverty, and the Practice of Law," 4; reprinted *Capital University Law Review* 8 (1979): 451ff.

12. Michael Harrington, *The Other America—Poverty in the United States* (New York: Macmillan, 1962).

13. William H. Whyte, *The Organization of Man* (New York: Simon and Schuster, 1956).

14. Milovan Djilas, *The New Class* (New York: Praeger, 1957).

15. Ibid., 42–44.

16. Jacques Maritain, *On the Philosophy of History* (New York: Scribner, 1957).

17. Ibid., 52.

18. Herbert Butterfield, *The Whig Interpretation of History* (New York: Scribner, 1931).

19. Ibid., 21.

20. Robert E. Rodes, Jr., "Maritain's On the Philosophy of History," *Natural Law Forum* 3 (1958): 210.

21. Jacques Ellul, *The Theological Foundation of Law,* trans. M. Wieser (Garden City, N.Y.: Doubleday, 1960).

22. Robert E. Rodes, Jr., "Review of Jacques Ellul's 'The Theological Foundation of Law,'" *Natural Law Forum* 8 (1963): 188.

23. Ellul, *The Theological Foundation of Law,* 102–3.

24. Ibid., 103.

25. Ibid., 102.

26. Robert E. Rodes, Jr., "Law, Social Change, and the Ambivalence of History," *Philosophy and Civil Law, Proceedings of the American Catholic Philosophical Association* 49 (1975): 164ff.

27. Ibid., 167.

28. Ibid., 169.

29. Ibid., 170.

30. Gustavo Gutiérrez, *A Theology of Liberation,* ed. and trans. Caridad Inda and John Eagleson (Maryknoll, N.Y.: Orbis, 1973).

31. Ibid., 275–76.

32. Ibid., 237–38.

33. Gustavo Gutiérrez, *A Theology of Liberation,* rev. ed., ed. and trans. Caridad Inda and John Eagleson (Maryknoll, N.Y.: Orbis, 1988), xxvi.

34. John Paul II, *Centesimus Annus* (1991), §57. Available at http://www.vatican.va/edocs/ENG0214/_INDEX.HTM.

35. U.S. Council of Catholic Bishops, *Economic Justice for All* (Washington, D.C.: National Council of Catholic Bishops, 1986), §52.

36. Charles Kingsley, *Yeast,* Bideford ed. (New York: Cooperative Publication Society, 1899), 108.

37. My theory is set forth at greater length in Robert E. Rodes, Jr., *Pilgrim Law* (Notre Dame, Ind.: University of Notre Dame Press, 1998).

38. *Gaudium et Spes* (1965), §39. Available at http://www.vatican.va/archive/hist_councils/ii_vatican_council/documents/vat-ii_cons_19651207_gaudium-et-spes_en.html.

39. David Lockmiller, *Sir William Blackstone* (Chapel Hill: University of North Carolina Press, 1938), 193.

40. Thomas L. Shaffer, *American Legal Ethics* (New York: Matthew Bender, 1985), 495.

41. Ibid.

42. *Gaudium et Spes* §39.

CHAPTER 2

The Option for the Poor and Business Ethics

GEORGES ENDERLE

AN ODD COUPLE

The option for the poor and business ethics seem to be an odd couple. If business ethics itself is an oxymoron, as many people have claimed since the 1970s, this connection seemingly is an oxymoron to the power of two. Despite histories of over forty years, little interaction has taken place between the two, and many contradictions seem to have prevented productive communications. The undercurrent of the option for the poor supposedly is anticapitalism and antibusiness. Solidarity with the poor who are oppressed by the capitalistic system and exploited by the profit-seeking companies and businesspeople entails radical criticism of these barriers to liberation. Opting for the poor means primarily sharing wealth and prosperity rather than producing them. The overwhelming power of business and economics in our societies needs to be curbed and downsized rather than given more freedom in the process of globalization.

On the other hand, business ethics seems to focus on the ethical responsibilities of businesspeople and business organizations, as emphasized particularly in the United States, while ignoring the plight of the poor affected by systemic forces. Incremental improvements are on the agenda but not systemic change. From the mainstream perspective of business and economics, the core interests lie in the success of companies and markets, not in social problems and social activism. Success is about making money and creating wealth, not spending other people's money and redistributing prosperity. For many scholars, economics as a field is considered value-free and defined by instrumental rationality, in which a religiously motivated preference for a group of people, the poor, makes no sense.

This sharp contrast, unfortunately, has characterized the relationship between the option for the poor and business ethics to a large extent. But at last the time has come, it seems to me, to bring these distant camps closer to each other and engage them in a productive dialogue. In my view, each side clearly needs the other: the option for the poor might inspire business ethics, and business ethics might enrich the option for the poor. Before discussing these perspectives in detail, I would like to reflect on my journey during the last forty years. In multiple ways it has exposed me to new and unexpected challenges and compelled me to adjust and redirect my work.

MY JOURNEY FROM THE OPTION FOR THE POOR TO BUSINESS ETHICS

During my studies in Christian theology in Lyon (France) and Münster (Germany), I was fortunate to familiarize myself with Gustavo Gutiérrez's first pamphlet, *Théologie de la Libération,* and Johann Baptist Metz's writing, *Political Theology.* Deeply impressed, I felt at the same time the need to see and study the concrete reality of poverty in developing countries. My trip to and stay in India opened to me a completely new world. Upon my return and after serious consideration and the completion of my theological studies, I decided to study economics, motivated by Ignatian spirituality to understand the world and in particular the material side of poverty. I wrote my MA thesis on poverty in the United States and my doctoral dissertation on personal distribution of income and wealth. My interest in economics and my choice to study in Fribourg, instead of my hometown of St. Gall, were clearly influenced by my antibusiness attitude. In the 1970s in student circles and beyond, the capitalistic system, along with the socialist system, was criticized, and radical changes in society were called for.

It was not until my trip to the United States in 1982 that I became acquainted with the emerging field of business ethics and realized the crucial role of corporations and their impact on society. Back at the University of St. Gall, I gradually gained a more differentiated view of the business world, thanks to my contacts with several outstanding managers and entrepreneurs. However, my second PhD (*habilitation*) in business ethics on poverty in Switzerland stirred up a great deal of controversy in the media and among a certain group of entrepreneurs, probably because my study, drawing on Amartya Sen's work, covered a wide range of aspects: from conceptual issues to poverty statistics, the moral right to a decent livelihood for everybody, and the institutional implications.

At that time, I was not able to see any link between the fight against poverty and the role and responsibility of companies and businesspeople. It would be another ten years before I realized that such a link is crucial from the perspective of globalization. Important steps for moving in this direction have been part of my teaching experience with MBA students at the University of Notre Dame and at the China Europe International Business School (CEIBS) in Shanghai, China. Here I have met with many young businessmen and -women who, in pursuing their business careers, are likely to bear heavy responsibilities in the future. What kind of business ethics do they need? What does the option for the poor mean in all this?

Before answering these questions, let me pause for a moment to reflect on the spiritual side of my journey, which, of course, is an unfinished one in many senses. It appears that over the years four factors have motivated and pushed forward my search, which I consider to be a kind of incarnational process. A drive to be more concrete led me to go to India, to study economics and business, to analyze poverty in the United States and Switzerland, to converse with managers and entrepreneurs, and to try to understand business students. A drive to bring together and reconcile two worlds and competencies draws from the Jesuit mission of "service of faith and commitment to justice" (the theme of the 32nd General Congregation of the Society of Jesus in 1975) and underlies my dual educational interests and my two-pronged approach to business ethics.[1] A drive to understand and live up to our responsibilities assigns great importance to values that give equal weight to personal and institutional ethics. A deep concern for the poor is considered to be the test case for the authenticity of the three previously mentioned motivations.

THE REALITIES OF POVERTY AND CORPORATE-DRIVEN GLOBALIZATION

Compared with the situation of the 1970s when the option for the poor was developed and business ethics began to emerge, the world has changed dramatically. Indeed, the reality of poverty has not disappeared. Statistics show that the world population has grown from 3,692 million people in 1970 to 6,895 million in 2010.[2] The total number of poor people living on less than $1.25 a day, a very crude indicator of poverty, has considerably decreased from 1,938 million in 1981 to 1,289 million in 2008. But poverty, measured by the number of people living on less than $2 a day, has decreased only slightly in the same period of time from 2,585 million to 2,471 million; excluding China, it has even increased substantially from 1,613 million to 2,076 million (see table 2.1). More detailed numbers over the period from 1990 through 2009 draw a mixed picture and indicate opposing trends in different world regions (see table 2.2). This empirical evidence suggests that the connection between globalization and poverty is not straightforward, neither in the sense that globalization exacerbates poverty nor in the sense that it alleviates poverty. But it remains true that at present (2008) more than 1.2 billion people live on less than US$1.25 per day, and almost 2.5 billion (or nearly 37 percent of the world population) on less than $2 a day. It is noteworthy that recent studies are available that provide an in-depth look into the complexities of defining and measuring global poverty: *Defining Poverty in the Developing World* (2007), *Absolute Poverty and Global Justice* (2009), and *Debates on the Measurement of Global Poverty* (2010).[3]

Another major factor is the pervasive role of transnational corporations (TNCs) in the process of globalization that is rightly called corporate-driven globalization. A few compelling statistics may illustrate this fact. The first is the number of parent companies and their foreign affiliates, unequally distributed across the world regions (see table 2.3) and producing one quarter ($15.6 trillion) of the world's gross domestic

Table 2.1. People living on less than $1.25 and $2 a day in 2005 PPP*

Proportion of people living on less than $1.25 a day (PPP) (%)

Developing country groups	1981	1987	1993	1999	2005	2008
East Asia and Pacific	77.2	54.1	50.7	35.6	17.1	14.3
China	84.0	54.0	53.7	35.6	16.3	13.1
Eastern Europe and Central Asia	1.9	1.5	2.9	3.8	1.3	0.5
Latin America and the Caribbean	11.9	12.0	11.4	11.9	8.7	6.5
Middle East and North Africa	9.6	7.1	4.8	5.0	3.5	2.7
South Asia	61.1	55.3	51.7	45.1	39.4	36.0
Sub-Saharan Africa	51.5	54.4	59.4	58.0	52.3	47.5
Total	52.2	42.3	40.9	34.1	25.1	22.4
Total excluding China	40.5	38.1	36.6	33.6	27.8	25.2

Number of people living on less than $1.25 a day (PPP) (millions)

Developing country groups	1981	1987	1993	1999	2005	2008
East Asia and Pacific	1096.5	847.6	870.8	655.6	332.1	284.4
China	835.1	585.7	632.7	446.3	211.9	173.0
Eastern Europe and Central Asia	8.2	6.8	13.7	17.8	6.3	2.2
Latin America and the Caribbean	43.3	49.3	52.5	60.1	47.6	36.8
Middle East and North Africa	16.5	14.6	11.5	13.6	10.5	8.6
South Asia	568.4	593.0	631.9	619.5	598.3	570.9
Sub-Saharan Africa	204.9	256.8	330.0	376.8	394.9	386.0
Total	1937.8	1768.2	1910.3	1743.4	1389.6	1289.0
Total excluding China	1102.8	1182.5	1277.6	1297.0	1177.7	1116.0

Proportion of people living on less than $2 a day (PPP) (%)

Developing country groups	1981	1987	1993	1999	2005	2008
East Asia and Pacific	92.4	81.6	75.8	61.7	39.0	33.2
China	97.8	83.7	78.6	61.4	36.9	29.8
Eastern Europe and Central Asia	8.3	6.3	9.2	12.1	4.6	2.2
Latin America and the Caribbean	23.8	22.4	21.7	22.0	16.7	12.4
Middle East and North Africa	30.1	26.1	22.1	22.0	17.4	13.9
South Asia	87.2	84.5	82.7	77.8	73.4	70.9
Sub-Saharan Africa	72.2	74.3	78.1	77.5	74.1	69.2
Total	69.6	64.8	63.1	57.4	46.9	43.0
Total excluding China	59.3	58.2	57.8	56.1	49.9	47.0

Table 2.1. People living on less than $1.25 and $2 a day in 2005 PPP* *(cont.)*

Number of people living on less than $2 a day (PPP) (millions)

Developing country groups	1981	1987	1993	1999	2005	2008
East Asia and Pacific	1312.9	1279.0	1300.7	1137.6	757.5	659.2
China	972.1	907.1	926.3	769.7	481.6	394.6
Eastern Europe and Central Asia	35.7	28.8	43.1	57.0	21.7	10.4
Latin America and the Caribbean	86.8	92.2	99.9	111.4	91.7	70.5
Middle East and North Africa	51.8	53.9	53.5	59.8	52.7	44.4
South Asia	810.6	905.9	1010.4	1068.8	1113.1	1124.6
Sub-Saharan Africa	287.6	350.4	434.0	503.3	559.1	562.3
Total	2585.3	2710.2	2941.5	2937.9	2595.8	2471.4
Total excluding China	1613.2	1803.1	2015.2	2168.2	2114.2	2076.8

*These calculations are done in so-called international dollars or PPP (purchasing power parity) dollars. Instead of simple exchange rates, PPP reflects a more accurate estimate of the standard of living in a country because it accounts better for the average living costs (mainly measured in food costs) in that country. For instance, with 1 USD, one can buy, on average, more food in India than in the United States.

Sources: S. Chen and M. Ravallion, "The Developing World Is Poorer Than We Thought, but Not Less Successful in the Fight Against Poverty," *Quarterly Journal of Economics* 125:4 (2010): 1599; S. Chen and M. Ravallion, "An Update to the World Bank's Estimates of Consumption Poverty in the Developing World," World Bank website, Feb. 29, 2012, pp. 5, 6.

product in 2010.[4] According to the World Investment Report 2004,[5] there exist more than 60,000 parent corporations worldwide with over 900,000 foreign affiliates (defined in terms of a minimum of equity ownership by parent firms). In addition to these affiliates, TNCs have a variety of nonequity arrangements with other firms, such as franchising, licensing, subcontracting, and management contracts, as well as inter-firm arrangements like strategic alliances and partnerships.

Moreover, the international production system, massively enhanced by increasing foreign direct investments, has expanded and deepened substantially over the period from 1990 through 2010 (see table 2.4). In 2010 the inward stock of FDI, a broad measure of the capital component of international production, stood at $19 trillion. Sales by foreign affiliates, a broad measure of the revenues generated by international production, reached an estimated $33 trillion in 2010, while their value-added

Table 2.2. Changes of social and economic indicators, 1990–2009, by world regions

	East Asia + Pacific	Europe + Central Asia	Latin America + Caribbean	Middle East + North Africa	South Asia	Sub-Saharan Africa	High Income Economies	World
Population increase (in Mio.)[1]	344	11	139	127	435	320	142	1491
GNI increase per pers. (in $) PPP[1]	5,056	6,853	5,646	4,600	2,127	994	18,687	5,879
Poor people (1990–2008 in Mio.): at $1.25 a day in 2005 PPP[2]	-642	-7	-16	-6	-46	96	..	-620
Poor people (1990–2008 in Mio.): at $2 a day in 2005 PPP[4]	-675	-22	-28	-9	166	173	..	-393
Life expectancy at birth (years)[1]								
Male	4	2	6	8	6	5	5	4
Female	4	2	5	8	7	4	3	4
Maternal mortality rate (per 100,000 live births) 1990–2008[3]	-111	-35	-54	-122	-320	-220	0	-140
Gross enrollment ratio (% of relevant age group)1991–2009[4]								
Primary								
Male	-12	0	5	0	15	26	-1	4
Female	-3	1	2	11	33	30	-1	12
Secondary								
Male	28	5	30	14	11	15	9	15
Female	41	3	36	23	24	13	8	22

Table 2.2. Changes of social and economic indicators, 1990–2009, by world regions (cont.)

	East Asia + Pacific	Europe + Central Asia	Latin America + Caribbean	Middle East + North Africa	South Asia	Sub-Saharan Africa	High Income Economies	World
External balance of goods and services (% of GDP)[1]	4	4	-2	15	-3	-5	0	0
FDI net inflows ($ millions)[1]	127,074	85,239	70,263	28,786	38,864	32,265	-96,619	1,133,516
Net official development assistance ($ per capita)[1]	0	17	4	-4	4	19	-3	8
External debt (total $ millions)[1]	599,870	1,074,144	457,899	4,176	227,086	23,476	..	..
Domestic credit provided by banking sector (% of GDP)[1]	56	..	11	-31	17	22	61	38
Net migration thousands 2005–2010[5]	-3,781	-1,681	-5,214	-1,089	-2,376	-1,810	..	15,895

Sources:
1. World Bank: World Development Indicators (online).
2. Chen and Ravallion 2010, 1599; Chen and Ravallion 2012, 5, 6.
3. World Bank Report 2012, 385.
4. World Bank Report 2012, 383.
5. World Bank Report 2012, 401.

Table 2.3. Number of parent corporations and foreign affiliates, by area and economy, latest available year

	Parent corporations based in economy	Foreign affiliates located in economy
Developed economies	45,077	102,560
Western Europe	36,133	75,664
European Union	30,709	64,464
Other Western Europe	5,424	11,200
North America	4,674	19,437
Other developed countries	4,270	7,459
Developing economies	14,192	580,638
Africa	1,163	6,849
Latin America, the Caribbean	2,475	46,117
Asia	10,535	527,119
South, East, Southeast Asia	9,614	505,763
(China)	350	424,196
West Asia	919	13,639
Central Asia	2	7,717
Pacific	19	553
Central and Eastern Europe	2,313	243,750
World	61,582	926,948

Source: UNCTAD, *World Investment Report,* 2004, 273–75.

(product) stood at an estimated $6.6 trillion. The table also shows that the total assets of foreign affiliates multiplied by more than 12 times since 1990. In addition, cross-border mergers and acquisitions have increased by 3.4 times.

Beyond these statistics, what else has changed in terms of poverty and global companies since the 1970s? I would like to mention two points. First, the understanding, conceptualization, and measurement of poverty have improved substantially. Amartya Sen's groundbreaking work, masterfully summarized in *Development as Freedom* and *The Idea of Justice,*[6] has revolutionized not only poverty studies but also the foundations of ethics and economics. Greatly influenced by his work, the United Nations Development Program has published, since 1990, the *Human*

Table 2.4. Selected indicators of FDI and international production, 1990–2010 (billions of U.S. dollars)

		Value at current prices			
	1990	*2005–2007 average*	*2008*	*2009*	*2010*
FDI inflows	207	1,472	1,744	1,185	1,244
FDI outflows	241	1,487	1,911	1,171	1,323
FDI inward stock	2,081	14,407	15,295	17,950	19,141
FDI outward stock	2,094	15,705	15,988	19,197	20,408
Cross-border M&As	99	703	707	250	339
Sales of foreign affiliates	5,105	21,293	33,300	30,213	32,960
Value-added (product) of foreign affiliates	1,019	3,570	6,216	6,129	6,636
Total assets of foreign affiliates	4,602	43,324	64,423	53,601	56,998
Exports of foreign affiliates	1,498	5,003	6,599	5,262	6,239
Employment of foreign affiliates (thousands)	21,470	55,001	64,484	66,688	68,218
GDP	22,206	50,338	61,147	57,920	62,909
Gross fixed capital formation	5,109	11,208	13,999	12,735	13,940
Royalties and license fee receipts	29	155	191	187	191
Exports of goods and non-factor services	4,382	15,008	19,794	15,783	18,713

Source: UNCTAD, *World Investment Report,* 2011, 24.

Development Reports, providing a wealth of useful information on development and poverty issues which was unimaginable in the 1970s.

Second, increasingly in the last few years, voices have been raised to urge a reconsideration of the role of companies and particularly TNCs in the fight against world poverty. As George Lodge claims, corporations hold the key to combating global poverty because they can bring business know-how and the profit motive into play,[7] and in a similar vein C. K.

Prahalad and Allen Hammond try to make the business case that serving the world's poor can be done profitably.[8] Moreover, a kind of rapprochement between two traditionally separate, if not antagonistic, camps has begun to evolve: between international organizations and development agencies on the one hand and the corporate world on the other. In 1999 UN Secretary-General Kofi Annan proposed the Global Compact to world business leaders in order to make globalization work for all the world's people,[9] and in 1997 the Global Reporting Initiative began to issue, after broad consultation, global guidelines for economic, social, and environmental responsibilities of companies and is now developing its fourth generation.[10]

Given these realities of poverty and corporate-driven globalization, multiple challenges are posed to the option for the poor and business ethics, in both practical and theoretical terms. I would next like to outline a theological view of business ethics and the option for the poor and then concentrate on some theoretical challenges for them based on my experiences in poverty research and business ethics, with the understanding that this scholarly interest is ultimately for practical reasons.

THEOLOGICAL VIEW OF BUSINESS ETHICS AND THE OPTION FOR THE POOR

According to the testimony of the gospel, the "new creation" does not take place outside the basic conditions of human beings—that is, being bodily creatures shaped by historical circumstances. Rather, the new creation brings new life within our bodily and historical conditions. In this theological horizon of meaning is posed the question of "new life" in general, in business and the economy in particular. Here too, God, the giver of life, has generated, amid the "history of oppression," the "history of life" in which people are able to do justice to their human fellows and to nature entrusted to them. Consequently, business ethics in the broad sense, including the individual and organizational actors and the economic system as well, is understood as diminishing the history of oppression and promoting the history of life.[11] It is called to reflect critically on the factual context that keeps one mired in historical action in business and to promote active conversion (*metanoia*) toward new life in business.

From this perspective, the elimination of poverty becomes a major task of business and economic ethics.[12] The history of oppression by poverty is to be transformed into a history of life in which all human beings can live free of poverty, in developing countries as well as in rich nations. Today this is not only a dream or a moral obligation but also a feasible option. As a recent ad in major newspapers around the world, published by the UNDP Initiative Teams to End Poverty, puts it: "What's more surprising: the fact that we now live in a world where almost a quarter of the population lives in absolute poverty? Or the fact that for the first time ever, we possess the wealth, technology, and knowledge to create a poverty-free world in less than a generation?"[13]

Obviously, the elimination of poverty is also a major task grounded in and resulting from the option for the poor, which can be characterized as follows: "A central dimension of biblical vision, likewise present in the other great religions, is that God has become God of the poor and the outcast and that compassionate solidarity with the poor is the decisive criterion of authentic religion and fidelity to God. This has been seen especially significant and pressing at the end of the twentieth century among the poor majorities of the world."[14] So the theological vision of God as the God of the poor leads to compassionate solidarity with the poor.

It is noteworthy that both the option for the poor and the theological understanding of business ethics include several similar theological and anthropological assumptions. Most importantly in this context, they are carried by an inner movement toward the concrete and the bodily, a process of incarnation and embodiment. It is expressed by a German saying, attributed to Friedrich Christoph Oetinger in the eighteenth century, "Die Leiblichkeit ist das Ende der Wege Gottes." Freely translated, it says, "God's paths do not end before they reach and shape the bodily world." The literal translation states that "the embodiment is the terminal or final destination of God's paths." In other words, life is a process of love that tends to become ever more concrete.

A second assumption of anthropological nature concerns the meaning of the body.[15] It contrasts with the Greek dualistic conception that takes the body as the prison or tomb of the soul (Plato), or as a part that the human being has (Aristotle). Rather, this meaning contains the biblical notion that designates the whole human being in his or her original unity.

The body is not external to the "I" as if it were possessed as a mere instrument. It is something that the human being is. According to Saint Thomas Aquinas, the body is the substantial expression of the soul in which the soul first achieves its concrete reality. The soul cannot fulfill itself without making use of matter. The greater its self-fulfillment, that is to say, the more the human being becomes spirit, the more the soul (the human being) becomes the body. This means that the body is the medium of all communication and that conversely the soul fulfills itself in proportion as human beings live with bodily human fellows in a bodily world. It follows, then, that this conception of the body might have far-reaching consequences for the notion of poverty, economics, and business.

NECESSARY CONDITIONS TO ADDRESS THE CHALLENGES

The realities of poverty and corporate-driven globalization pose enormous challenges. Is it possible and desirable to redefine and redirect corporate-driven globalization in such a way that it combats and eliminates poverty? What can the option for the poor and business ethics contribute to address these challenges?

To begin with, I see two necessary conditions that both the option for the poor and business ethics must fulfill in order to meet those challenges. The first is the sustained engagement in the inner movement toward the concrete and the bodily, which, in my view, has not been pursued consistently enough until now. Unfortunately, many advocates of the option for the poor have remained fairly abstract when it comes to understanding the reality of the poor. They have contented themselves with a purely theological approach or a questionable social science approach, using rather simple conceptual and analytical frameworks, and trying to explain poverty in exclusively systematic terms, be it in mechanistic or Marxist ones. By doing so, they have lost sight of the concrete poor, along with the concrete reality of business and the economy. Similarly, on the side of business ethics, by and large, the problem of poverty has not been a central issue. Moreover, many efforts have been made, particularly in continental Europe, to investigate the conditions of the possibility of business ethics while neglecting to address the concrete challenges that individuals, companies, and whole economies have to face. In sum, without a continued commitment toward the concrete, business ethics cannot fulfill its task of enhancing the ethical quality of decision-making and action at all levels of business.

The second necessary condition concerns the anthropological conception of the unity of body and soul. As long as a dualistic conception prevails, the positive sense of prosperity, business, and economics cannot be appreciated adequately, and the lack of prosperity of the poor is not taken seriously enough. The body, and with it the bodily world, is a mere instrument without value in itself. Not surprisingly, such a view leads to the neglect of or even contempt for the bodily world, which, as a reaction, may turn into a kind of soulless materialism. In other words, only a balanced conception of the body can provide the option for the poor and business ethics with the necessary anthropological condition to address the challenges of poverty and corporate-driven globalization.

CHALLENGES TO THE OPTION FOR THE POOR

In line with the inner movement toward the concrete and with the balanced conception of the body, the option for the poor faces challenges in terms of analysis and in terms of ethics. For a more concrete and deeper understanding of reality, the theology of the option for the poor needs to cooperate with all academic disciplines that can elucidate the complexities of poverty. This holds true not only for pragmatic and pastoral-theological reasons but also for systematic and moral-theological ones. The multidimensional reality of poverty is of high theological relevance. It is therefore surprising that the work of Amartya Sen, which helps enormously to analyze and evaluate poverty and justice issues, has been adopted by advocates of the option for the poor only lately and to a rather limited extent.

Moreover, the option for the poor must necessarily become involved in a deeper understanding of the business and economics that form a large part of globalization and poverty as well. Only with intimate knowledge in this field is it possible to raise a substantive critique and propose feasible alternative approaches. Otherwise, compassionate solidarity with the poor remains a laudable ideal that inspires private charity but does not affect economic policies and structures.

A particularly sore subject appears to be the widespread negative attitude among advocates of the option for the poor toward creating wealth, which, by the way, is not synonymous with making money.[16] Creating wealth is considered to be necessarily exploitative or at least an inferior activity that has merely instrumental value. In contrast, distributing and sharing wealth enjoys a much better reputation, associated with fraternal love and altruism. However, this attitude seems to be questionable indeed, apart from the fact that production and distribution of wealth cannot be disentangled so easily. If the poor are taken seriously as agents, their capacity for creating wealth appears to be of paramount importance.

In many instances, the option for the poor has sailed under the flag of anticapitalism and antibusiness and has called for a radical change of the economic system. Unfortunately, this exclusive focus on systemic issues has carried with it, in fact, a neglect for what companies and individuals can do already to combat poverty and help to change a deficient system. In order to address the challenges of poverty and corporate-driven globalization, a systemic approach of course remains important. But it should be complemented by upgrading the indispensable roles of companies, including small and medium-sized companies as well as transnational corporations,[17] and of individual businesspeople. It seems to me that a higher general appreciation of business is in order, if business is to be more than an ugly servant for meeting material needs. As a matter of course, business would then be held accountable also to higher ethical standards. It goes without saying that such a positive understanding of business that grows from fair criticism would have far-reaching implications for the role and reputation of business education.

Regarding the challenges to the option for the poor in terms of ethics, I would like to submit the following considerations. As a central dimension of biblical vision, the option for the poor per se does not contain, to my knowledge, an elaborated moral theology but does include important moral-theological implications. In reflecting on the option for the poor in Christian theology, it therefore might be advisable to develop a more explicit and comprehensive moral-theological conception of this vision.

Moreover, this conception would have to be translated into and expressed by the medium of philosophical ethics because the gospel brings new life to each time in a particular manner and thus has to engage in critical and constructive communication with the contemporary pluralistic world.[18]

Such a moral-theological development could benefit from the work already done, particularly by Amartya Sen. It would be fascinating to see how his capability approach, with the basic notion of concrete freedoms, and his ethics-related conception of economics can enrich the option for the poor and, at the same time, gain new perspectives from moral theology. Furthermore, this moral-theological conception could inspire the spirituality of businesspeople, the ethical orientation of business education, and the ethics of business organizations.

CHALLENGES TO BUSINESS ETHICS

The realities of poverty and corporate-driven globalization pose equally daunting challenges to business ethics in terms of analysis and ethics as well. For companies it is already difficult to compete with integrity in international business.[19] This is all the more so when they are increasingly expected to serve the world's poor because this seems to contradict their business purpose and own interests. However, if one can demonstrate, as Lodge, Prahalad, Hammond, and others try to do, that doing business with the poor is in the enlightened self-interest of the companies, or that serving the poor can be profitable, companies might be more interested in this kind of strategy.[20] Indeed, many small companies have been successful in working with the poor, a prime example being the Grameen Bank and the microcredit movement.[21] That big transnational corporations are encouraged to do the same is therefore not surprising.

What should we think of this newly propagated role of companies? Does it open a bright perspective for the poor? Or will it turn out to become just another disguised strategy for exploiting the poor? In my view, there is no question that companies of all sizes, including the big corporations, should play a more active role in combating and eliminating poverty. This task is too big to be left to governments and nongovernmental organizations (NGOs). To target the poor directly, rather than vainly placing one's hopes in trickle-down effects of general growth, has proved to be effective in public policies and is likely to be so in corporate strategies too. Serving the poor requires a great deal of entrepreneurial imagination, as well as human and financial resources, and it is not objectionable that the profit motive plays an indispensable role. However, this new strategy is bound to fail if it is based solely on the profit motive and not also on the ethical responsibility of the companies as corporate citizens to serve the poor for intrinsic reasons (because "it is the right thing to do"). Indeed, many business scholars and practitioners, along with business critics, dispute the validity of the second, deontological argument. But I would contend that it is equally important because it expresses the respect for the poor as partners, treating them not only as means to make profit. Only such a dual motivation can provide the foundation for sustainable business with the poor. It is stronger than the mere business case and consequently should be embraced and also clearly stated in public.

In struggling with the challenge of turning corporate-driven globalization toward poverty elimination, the option for the poor can be of great help to business ethics in practical and theoretical terms. Too often the work in business ethics is absorbed by dealing with inner corporate issues and problems in rich countries. The option for the poor can widen the horizon and strengthen the sensitivity to world poverty. It offers a powerful vision that helps to keep the focus on the poor as agents who are to play a crucial role not only in civil society and government but in business as well. Also, it insistently reminds those concerned with individual and organizational issues that many problems need to be fixed at the level of the economic system and in the light of distributive justice. Moreover, with the necessary expertise, the option for the poor can exert a strong impact on the understanding of business and economics and their ethical implications. Last, but not least, business ethics in the global context needs the resources of the world's religions in general and of Christian theology in particular. The option for the poor can provide a fascinating and powerful horizon of meaning, strengthen motivation, and enhance implementation in the work with the poor.

Both the option for the poor and business ethics face enormous challenges that will lead corporate-driven globalization to confront, combat, and eliminate poverty. Why should they not engage in a closer and more collaborative relationship?

NOTES

1. See my publications "Business Ethics" in *The Blackwell Companion to Philosophy,* 2nd ed., ed. N. Bunnin and E. P. Tsui-James (Oxford: Blackwell, 2003), 531–51; "Business Ethics as a Goal-Rights-System," in *Applied Ethics in a Troubled World,* ed. E. Morscher, O. Neumaier, and P. Simons (Dordrecht: Kluwer, 1998), 151–66; *Handlungsorientierte Wirtschaftsethik. Grundlagen und Anwendungen* [Action-oriented business ethics. Foundations and applications] (Bern: Haupt, 1993).

2. World Bank: World Development Indicators, available at http://data bank.worldbank.org/ddp/home.do?Step=2&id=4.

3. F. Stewart, R. Saith, and B. Harriss-White, eds., *Defining Poverty in the Developing World* (New York: Palgrave Macmillan, 2007); E. Mack, M. Schramm, S. Klasen, and T. Pogge, eds., *Absolute Poverty and Global Justice. Empirical Data— Moral Theories—Initiatives* (Burlington, Vt.: Ashgate, 2009); S. Anand, P. Segal, and J. E. Stiglitz, eds., *Debates on the Measurement of Global Poverty* (New York: Oxford University Press, 2010).

4. UNCTAD, World Investment Report 2011, 25.

5. UNCTAD, World Investment Report 2004, 273–75.

6. A. Sen, *Development as Freedom* (New York: Anchor Books, 1999), and *The Idea of Justice* (Cambridge, Mass.: Harvard University Press, 2009).

7. G. C. Lodge, "The Corporate Key," *Foreign Affairs* 81:4 (2002): 13–18.

8. C. K. Prahalad and A. Hammond, "Serving the World's Poor, Profitably," *Harvard Business Review* (Sept. 2002): 48–57.

9. Global Compact, United Nations: www.unglobalcompact.org.

10. Global Reporting Initiative (GRI): www.globalreporting.org.

11. Enderle, "Business Ethics," 531–51.

12. See G. Enderle, "Das Armutsproblem als Paradigma der Wirtschafts-ethik" [The problem of poverty as paradigm of business ethics], in *Neue Summe Theologie,* Band 2, ed. P. Eicher (Freiburg: Herder, 1989), 342–73.

13. *Financial Times,* Oct. 18, 2002; see www.teamstoendpoverty.org and www.netaid.org.

14. R. Muñoz, "Option for the Poor," in *Dictionary of Third World Theologies,* ed. V. Fabella and R. S. Sugirtharajah (Maryknoll, N.Y.: Orbis Books, 2000), 154.

15. K. Rahner and H. Vorgrimler, *Dictionary of Theology,* 2nd ed. (New York: Crossroad, 1981).

16. G. Enderle, "A Rich Concept of Wealth Creation beyond Profit Maximization and Adding Value," *Journal of Business Ethics* 84 Supplement 3(2009): 281–95.

17. G. Enderle, "Global Competition and Corporate Responsibilities of Small and Medium-sized Enterprises," *Business Ethics: A European Review* 13:1 (2004): 51–63.

18. F. Böckle, "Anthropologie und Sachgesetzlichkeit im Dialog zwischen Moraltheologie und Wirtschaftsethik," in *Ethik und Wirtschaftswissenschaften,* ed. G. Enderle (Berlin: Duncker und Humblot, 1985), 55–68.

19. R. T. De George, *Competing with Integrity in International Business* (New York: Oxford University Press, 1993).

20. Lodge, "The Corporate Key," 13–18; Prahalad and Hammond, "Serving the World's Poor, Profitably," 48–57.

21. M. Yunus, *Banker to the Poor. Micro-Lending and the Battle against World Poverty* (New York: Public Affairs, 1999); M. Yunus, "The Micro-Credit Movement: Experiences and Perspectives," in *Improving Globalization,* ed. M. C. Arruda and G. Enderle (Rio de Janeiro: Editora FGV, 2004), 15–33; N. Wimmer, *Green Energy for a Billion Poor: How Grameen Shakti Created a Winning Model for Social Business* (Vaterstetten, Germany: MCRE Verlag, 2011).

CHAPTER 3

The Multidimensionality of Poverty

JAVIER MARÍA IGUÍÑIZ ECHEVERRÍA

The option for the poor seeks to lift those who exist in the conditions of poverty out of their impoverished state. It is therefore necessary to understand who the poor are and why they are poor. Poverty confronts us with a difficult topic. As a category, it is hard to define. In some sense we can say that "the generic term 'poverty' hides more than it reveals."[1] As a concept, it is also used more and more.[2] One way of looking at this topic is looking at its multidimensionality.[3] In this essay I will present five aspects of multidimensionality,[4] most of them departing more or less completely from unidimensional economic perspectives.[5]

INSIDE THE ECONOMY

The first of the multidimensionalities that I will present remains inside the realm of economics but breaks the unidimensionality present in the most common measure of poverty: income. Poverty, like economics, is multidimensional.[6] One of the most important intraeconomic distinctions we can make is between absolute and relative poverty. But these two dimensions can be defined and measured in terms of income or assets.[7]

The privileged indicator of a country's economic growth is measured by the gross domestic product (GDP) per capita. But the magnitude of growth of the GDP has its limitations. As Vinod Thomas has noted:

"The quality, dispersion, composition, and sustainability of that growth are just as important."[8] By looking at the multifaceted dimensions of poverty, we can seek to understand better those aspects of growth that influence poverty. But such differentiations do not help us get closer to that nature of poverty since I am referring basically to the properties of one variable: income. As Amartya Sen has said, some criticisms to the economicism are, indeed, expressions of unhappiness with monism.[9]

One justification for this intraeconomic multidimensionality is that the economy appears as the best tool to improve all dimensions of life. Alice O'Connor reminds us that growth has been considered the best tool to solve racial discrimination at work, for instance. There is no better policy against such discrimination than the scarcity of laborers in the market.[10] It is also easier to analyze the connection between poverty "in the midst of plenty"[11] since both poverty and wealth are measured with the same metric. But one of the greater strengths of income is that its level and growth are statistically correlated to the level and evolution of many other indicators of poverty. In spite of these, and other similar reasons, the main dynamism today is on the side of broadening approaches to the poverty problem.

ECONOMIC AND NONECONOMIC DIMENSIONS OF POVERTY

The second manner in which the dimensions of poverty are expanded includes two different and alternative movements: the first one incorporates diverse dimensions but deals mainly with income levels; and the second is more radical since it deals exclusively with the ends of poverty, but it adds some noneconomic dimensions as well and puts these dimensions on the same footing as income. Income defines poverty, while the noneconomic dimensions offer new aspects that are equal in importance to income and give rise to this multidimensional view of poverty.[12] Much of our analysis here is based on the view of poverty as it is understood in the United States. After all, "contemporary poverty research is very much an American invention with a degree of specialization and an institutional apparatus unmatched in other parts of the world."[13]

One powerful current of thought today is that "economic effects arise out of noneconomic factors."[14] For instance, and more precisely, "to understand the determinants of poverty in all its dimensions, it helps to think in terms of people's assets, the returns to (or productivity of) these assets, and the volatility of returns."[15] In this case, each dimension becomes instrumental and, in that sense, "capital." Everything becomes or should become capital including social relations, physical appearance, age, gender, race, virtues, and other qualities. So, at a more general level, many forms of capital emerge: social, human, and also cultural.[16]

This type of multidimensionality emerged during the 1960s in the United States, and was a way of avoiding questions about structural change in the economy, and also of concentrating attention on the peculiarities of specific groups of poor. "Conditions no longer call for deep-seated and widespread social change. Rather, the discussion now is on helping the poor. Expropriation of property is no longer seriously considered as a remedy. In its place is the press for limited social reform that takes into consideration the social and economic characteristics of the poor while preserving the essential character of existing social and economic institutions."[17]

The starting point was the "War on Poverty." The key analytical distinction was between two types of poverty: "Poverty related to specific people, families, and groups is different from mass chronic poverty. Most societies suffer from a mixture of both, but one usually predominates."[18] The consequence of this distinction is theoretical and practical. "The accumulative forces that tend to perpetuate mass poverty are different from those related to the poverty of specific people and groups. The measures to deal with poverty in one case are quite different from those in the other. In treating poverty, therefore, society must make the distinction and determine which kind of poverty predominates and deserves priority attention."[19]

The second step in the argument for this type of multidimensionality was the definition of the predominant poverty in the United States. Two elements seem to influence the selection of the kind of poverty relevant to the War on Poverty in America. The first is that, being a country of successive waves of immigrants who escaped poverty leads to the impression that "historically, we have had no fixed class of poor people."[20] The second is that in the context of a prolonged expansion, it was not difficult to consider any remaining poverty to be residual. "In the United States of the 1960s, poverty may be most clearly understood as the problem of certain specific people, whose personal, social, and demographic characteristics must in some way be altered lest they be condemned to remain poor."[21] The information used to justify this case-by-case poverty was the same used in the following decades in the poor countries, including race, gender of the head of the family, age of the family head, urban-rural distinction, and level of education.[22] This way of characterizing the poor became the standard method of the multilateral agencies and researchers for analyzing poverty and designing policies. Household surveys replaced, as the privileged tool, the study of the changing structure of industry, the analysis of technological change, and the absorption of labor by firms, and other side topics. The problem of employment became a problem of employability. This approach was widely applied to the underdeveloped countries in the following years. In this way, what was considered useful for analyzing and attacking the poverty remaining after the structural problems had been solved, at least conjecturally, became the tool to fight against poverty in countries where such "mass chronic poverty" was by far the dominant feature.

In the case of mass poverty, the problem should be addressed with demand policies and public works in order to create employment. After the economy has done its work, and unemployment and poverty have become marginal, policy measures from the supply side would be enough. But once the burden of the problem was on the side of the poor themselves, the attack on poverty resulted in policies that did not need to address the structural aspects and could concentrate in the market-empowering of the people. In other words, remaining poverty was the result of lack of personal capital—that is, information, training, family structure, attitudes toward work, and several other things.[23]

An important consequence of this approach was that the poverty problem became that of the limits of the undercapitalized poor themselves.[24] In other words, "individual theories attribute the primary cause of poverty to individual failings or, more neutrally, to individual differences—the central argument being that the poor are different from the nonpoor in some significant way."[25] At this point of our argument it will not be a surprise to find that "individual differences in income and wealth among people are to be expected in any society, because of differences in natural abilities, age, physical, and emotional health, motivation and self-reliance, the effects of various prejudices, residence in depressed communities, and just plain luck."[26]

In the same text the authors of this chapter of the book continue with a characterization relevant to our main point. "In some cases, however, a whole society suffers from a massive and chronic condition caused by insufficient or underdeveloped natural resources, the lack of an industrial base, factors related to heritage and tradition, and political and social weakness. Although mass chronic poverty and poverty linked to specific human beings and groups can blend and overlap, contrasts between the two types are great enough to serve constructively in guiding policy and preventing mistakes."[27] The key point is, then, that the natural, economic, cultural, and political variables constitute a structural impediment to reducing poverty where this is massive and chronic. Also the policies aimed at individuals and groups will not do the job in those cases.

Within that framework, individual differences between poor and nonpoor were disaggregated, and those differences became dimensions of the poverty problem, mainly as factors causing income poverty. Several of those factors or the lack of them have been redefined more recently as capitals. It was the individual's responsibility to increase any of the diverse individual capitals that were marketable. Later on, these capitals would be classified in a more general form as social, natural, political, or cultural. In this way, multidimensional perspective is applied to the factors influencing poverty, but this is still defined in unidimensional terms as income poverty.

SHARING THE DEFINITIONAL STATUS WITH NONECONOMIC VARIABLES

The next most influential multidimensional approach to the definition and measurement of poverty today is probably that combining income and other noneconomic components. The World Bank assumes and adopts in the *World Development Report 2000/2001* "the now traditional view of poverty"[28] that includes material deprivation and some minimum education and health. This view on the part of the World Bank is expressed in the following way by Kanbur and Squire: "The definition of poverty, beginning with a focus on command over market-purchased goods (income), has expanded to embrace other dimensions of living standards such as longevity, literacy, and health. As we have learned more about and from the poor, the concept has developed further to reflect a concern with vulnerability and risk, and with powerlessness and lack of voice."[29] In the incorporation of these last elements the interesting and in many cases terrible testimonies of the very poor seem to have been quite influential.[30]

This approach is, indeed, quite old. For instance, in the 1960s, Denis Goulet indicated that "relativity [of economic indicators] is further compounded . . . by the general acceptance of non-economic 'social' indicators of development: gains in literacy, schooling, health conditions and services, provision of housing, and the like."[31] This "general acceptance" during the 1960s did not survive the more mainstream economic view of development and its reduction to growth during the following years.[32]

Avoiding Economics (Income) in the Definition

A third route is to consider income as a factor influencing poverty understood as some human deprivation. Two are among the most interesting and well-known paths. The first is the design and use of the Human Development Index, the second the design of the Human Poverty Index. Both are inspired mainly by Sen's "capabilities approach" but also by the "basic needs" perspective.[33] First, we will present one of the practical reasons behind the suspicion that income is not a good enough indicator when more direct aspects of poverty are available.

Focalization and Income

Income is not a direct enough expression of poverty, although it is a very important explanatory factor. One reason to look for more direct measures of poverty is, however, practical. Focalized attacks on poverty may miss the target when they are guided by the income measurement. The poverty line is not good enough to localize those requiring particularly intensive support. Ruggeri shows that in the case of Peru, the indicator per capita consumption, which is conceptually closer to the poverty situation than income, is not good enough to reach stunted children (chronic malnutrition), those who self-report morbidity, or those who fail to reach functional literacy (four years of schooling). For instance, "one in five stunted children is in a non-consumption poor household and more than 60% of the poor children do not suffer from long term malnutrition. Clearly, child malnutrition is a phenomenon whose determinants go beyond monetary poverty."[34]

> Income is not sufficient as an indicator to reach the poor with policy. The association between low educational achievement for 12–15 year olds and monetary poverty is strong and significant. Even so, a fifth of the children in this age group who have not yet achieved functional literacy are to be found in non-poor households. At the same time, however, 68% of the poor children in this age bracket have had at least 4 years of primary education, which shows that monetary poverty in itself is not sufficient to reduce the chances of a child reaching this minimal level of education within a reasonable amount of time.[35]

This suggests that in many cases it is better to use more direct expressions of poverty than income.

From Income to "Income"

The interaction among diverse factors is important to explain poverty, but this does not mean that those factors have the same conceptual status. For instance, income and education interact in different ways, but clearly income is less of a final objective than education. The Human Development Index (HDI) is a composite measure of development presented every year by the United Nations Development Program (UNDP) which includes life expectancy and education, but also a measure of human development obtained through the expenditure of income.[36] This is the meaning of the deflated measure of income. The quantitative aspect of the transformation of income in human development is very simple, but it may hide the qualitative element involved.[37] The greater the level of income of a country, the smaller the impact of an absolute increment in income on human development.

The conceptual tool behind this transformation is not the well-known "decreasing marginal utility" of utilitarian economics; rather, as

Griffin reminds us, we are dealing with the decreasing ability of material wealth to increase human capabilities.[38] Once the transformation is made, income has the same status and final good as education and life expectancy, and the three of them can be used to elaborate the HDI. In this way, and in a more radical way, "a vision centered in commodities is transformed in one centered in persons."[39]

Dispensing with Income

The Human Development Report 1997 presents a Human Poverty Index (HPI) where poverty, understood as poverty of life and opportunities, is clearly viewed multidimensionally, but more importantly its objective is to improve the evaluation of development from a "deprivational perspective," or, as to rephrase, from the "perspective of the poor." The point is that income, especially private income, is not sensitive enough to the progress and regress of the poor.

The HPI includes, as does the HDI, life expectancy and basic education. By leaving these factors aside we can concentrate on the third component of the HPI, which in turn has three elements: the proportion of people with access to health services, the proportion with access to safe water, and the percentage of malnourished children under five years old. In this way, income, mainly private, is not a factor.[40] There are several reasons to move one step ahead in this direction. First, the poverty line is inadequate for evaluating the quality of life in different cultures and lifestyles.[41] It is also important to remember that the poverty line does not help to detect malnutrition among the poor in rich countries. A policy reason is also behind this change away from income; several components of the HPI can be improved with public funds before the families themselves increase their private income. Extreme poverty eradication does not have to await the increase in family incomes.

FREEDOM AS AN END AND AS AN EVALUATIVE CRITERION

The changes in perspective on poverty just summarized have been mainly inspired by the "capabilities approach" to development. However, the most important contribution by Sen and other development thinkers is not the widening of the concept to introduce multiple dimensions, but its deepening. "Poverty must be seen as the deprivation of basic capabilities rather than merely as lowness of incomes, which is the standard criterion of identification of poverty."[42] The main reason is that "poverty can be sensibly identified in terms of capability deprivation; the approach concentrates on deprivations that are intrinsically important (unlike low income, which is only instrumentally significant)."[43] There is hierarchy involved in this distinction.[44]

But the depth is also related to the deepness of the poverty priorized. Poverty implies the violation of basic or elemental freedoms, "like being able to avoid such deprivations as starvation, under nourishment, escapable morbidity and premature mortality, as well as the freedoms that are associated with being literate and numerate, enjoying political participation and uncensored speech and so on."[45]

These basic freedoms include those related to the basic needs of consumption. The "basic needs approach" that insists on the eradication of extreme poverty converged from its very beginning with Sen's research. In fact, Stewart also presents the relationship between the goods consumed and their result in terms of full life achievements as critical in her view of what should be considered the focal end point of the analysis. A "meta-production function" would take such a deepening perspective into account.[46] She criticizes planning because "no attempt is made to identify how income gets translated into welfare."[47] "But the basic needs approach does take an independent definition—health and education—and consequently requires the extra step of identifying the metaproduction function."[48] This extra step is similar to what Sen insists upon when asking what happens to the human being after getting the things he or she obtains in the market.

The multidimensional approach is also there. A full life that "of course include[s] elements—material, social, cultural, and political"—is excessive as an objective of policy, and it is necessary to select some of them. In a policy-oriented approach, two objectives that represent a very minimal vision of such a life are health and certain levels of education. Both "are necessary conditions for the achievement of other aspects of a full life in poor societies."[49]

The Great Freedoms and the Modern Dimensions

Common language often uses terms like *economic* or *political* to deal with some spheres of life and rules of behavior, often to refer to causes.[50] The fourth road to multidimensionality of poverty is based on what can be considered the modern freedoms. Walzer presents synthetically a paradox: "Liberal theorists preached and practiced the art of separation, they drew lines, marked off different realms, and created the sociopolitical map with which we are still familiar. . . . Liberalism is a world of walls, and each creates a new liberty."[51]

Modernity organized the multidimensional life in its own way. We are interested in this strategy because deprivations can also be viewed as separated accordingly. In fact, the most commonly viewed aspect of poverty became the economic aspect, which we are departing from in this classificatory essay. But we can also find political poverty[52] and, increasingly, cultural and other poverties. [53]

The Self-Regulated Systems and Their Interactions

We are interested in dealing with this modern classification approach because it easily brings into the discussion about poverty its structural aspect. These different spheres can be seen as "worlds" of rules and self-regulating processes that reproduce their internal order, and with them, their own polarities and deprivations. Poverty is not merely an individual's feature; it is also a structured social state of affairs. Terms like *mechanism, system, cultures,* and *values,* among others allude most of the time to the self-organized components of our lives, but also to the difficulties involved in the eradication of the worst aspects of such orders. One of the most infamous is the persistence of poverty in the midst of wealth.[54]

Since the beginning of capitalism, the self-regulated nature of the economic sphere has impressed the intellectuals, and partly explains the emergence of terms like *general equilibrium, reproduction, stability, convergence,* and others. From the Physiocrats and Smith to Polanyi,[55] more recently, and to Krugman[56] the continuity of the economic order has been a key element of the social analysis. Clearly, questions about the structural restrictions on the individual's actions can hide small possibilities of initiative. But a current risk is the opposite. Policy against poverty is being reduced to an infinite sum of small focalized projects with uncertain results. A new balance is needed.

Types of Rights and Freedoms

The division of spheres of life into self-regulated worlds includes the classification of rights and, of course, the right to be free. This freedom can also be viewed as multidimensional. In this respect, there is a debate about the convenience of closing the dimensions involved and using them to evaluate progress in those aspects of freedom generally agreed upon or more universal.

Concretely, Sen resists the pressures to go into a classification of basic and irreducible components of freedom. The concrete elements of freedom seen as a goal, as an end, are no doubt diverse among cultures, and among individuals,[57] and Sen seems to be trying to include them as they appear in the public discussion, the widest possible spectrum of cultural and personal views of its meaning. If we understand his perspective, different kinds of freedom, public debates, concerted policies, and other elements, that are mainly found in democratic regimes, are necessary conditions, but the goals themselves, the styles of life undertaken, are kept open and unspecified except when basic aspects, matters of life and death, and a minimum of human interaction and communication, are considered.

When Sen deals with the causes of poverty or with the factors of development—that is, from an instrumental perspective—he is more specific and considers three spheres: economic, political, and social.[58] Cultural freedom could be added.[59] Poverty is economic when referring, although not exclusively, to low income, lack of food, and also restrictions on participation in trade or in the labor market.[60] Political poverty refers to freedom of expression or to participation in the electoral process, among other things.[61] Social poverty refers to lack of access to education or to health and other services provided by the public sector.[62] In general, we can say that Sen's use of these terms does not have the dense theoretical connotation we have tried to outline above. It is more a classificatory convenience than an attempt to dig into the structural causes of the existence or reproduction of poverty. As Denis Goulet has said, "Specialized definitions of development need not be totally incompatible with more comprehensive terms such as maturation and contemporaneity. 'Economic,' 'social,' and 'political' development are simply methodological constructs adopted within specific disciplines to study aspects of a change process which they 'abstract' from a total reality which comprises, beyond facts, meanings and symbols."[63]

Another discussion in this widening and thickening of the meaning of poverty would have to concern whether freedom and its expansion is the only goal of development and the only space in which poverty should be assessed. For instance, Goulet suggests that freedom should be accompanied by sustenance and by esteem.[64] In any case, this discussion should start analytically with a precise definition of the term *freedom*. The enriched meaning of this word cannot incorporate everything valuable inside,[65] but the critique of its narrowness from the more classical liberal perspective is an important contribution to a more realistic view of development and poverty.[66]

TOWARD MORE SPECIFIC MORAL-PHILOSOPHICAL MULTIDIMENSIONAL VIEWS OF DEVELOPMENT

Development is more and more commonly viewed as human flourishing, the achievement of a good life. This puts us in the realm of philosophical thought. Human development, as distinguished from economic development, has to incorporate wider and deeper aspects of life than the economic ones.

A valuable life as an objective is in itself a motivating force to act in some specific ways. Values become, then, an important element in establishing what is pushing individuals and collectives to act. We have included them implicitly when dealing with capitals like the social and, even more, the cultural. Values are seen as capital.

The importance assigned to values is not new. Goulet noted long ago that "'development' is above all a question of values."[67] His criticism of the instrumental use of values is even more useful today: "Conventional social science research on values is deficient because it is incapable of treating values other than instrumentally. It views the values of a populace either as aids or as obstacles to achieving development, itself is uncritically assumed to be good. The result is that values are subordinated to the goals of development. Yet it is this very equation that has to be inverted, for development itself is but an instrumental good."[68]

From there to multidimensionality there was not even one step. As the author insists in the same paragraph:

> What is conventionally termed development—dynamic economic performance, modern institutions, the availability of abundant goods and services—is simply one possibility among many, of development in a broader, more critical sense. Authentic development aims at the full realization of human capabilities: men and women become makers of their own histories, personal and societal. They free themselves from every servitude imposed by nature or by oppressive systems, they achieve mastery over nature and their own wants, they create new webs of solidarity based not on domination but on reciprocity among themselves, they achieve a rich symbiosis between contemplation and transforming action, between efficiency and free expression. This total concept of development can perhaps best be expressed as the "human ascent"—the ascent of all men in their integral humanity, including the economic, biological, psychological, social, cultural, ideological, spiritual, mystical, and transcendental dimensions.[69]

Today, there are many efforts in the same direction. Sabina Alkire has offered a comprehensive overview of many of them.[70] As she says, each multidimensionality effort responds to different questions and philosophical approximations. For instance, Nussbaum refers to the political principles needed for a better world, Max-Neff responds to a new vision of human needs, Narayan and her team refer to declared perceptions by the poor themselves. Other studies include those by Schwartz on universal values, Cummins on quality of life, Ramsay on universal psychological needs, and Doyal and Gough on basic human needs, among many others.[71]

A good illustration of the kind of effort involved is that of Alkire, based on Finnis et al., to answer the requirements of philosophical foundation and, at the same time, of specification coming out of Sen's proposal. The proposal classifies values in the sense of reasons to act in seven categories or dimensions: (1) life itself (maintenance and transmission—health and safety); (2) knowledge and aesthetic experience (engagement of the capacities to know and to feel); (3) excellence in work and play (transforming the world of nature); (4) friendship (various forms of harmony); (5) self-integration (inner peace); (6) self-expression, or practical reasonableness (consistency between one's self and its expression); (7) religion (harmony with a more-than-human source of meaning and value).[72]

FROM THE SOCIAL SCIENCES TO OTHER DISCIPLINES AND DIMENSIONS

To conclude, we should say that the treatment of poverty is older and more developed in the social sciences than in other disciplines. It is not surprising that the dialogue between the option for the poor in theology and other disciplines had to start with the social sciences.[73] This essay has been organized in dialogue with the economic and mainly monistic view of poverty.

Indeed, philosophical approaches to poverty are not so well established. If the encyclopedias reflect what is already commonly accepted as a topic in the field, then it seems that the field does not yet consider poverty important. It may not be a surprise that *The Encyclopedia of Philosophy* includes only the entries "poverty of philosophy," referring to Marx, and "poverty of historicism," referring to Popper, but in more recent volumes, like Mario Bunge's *Dictionary of Philosophy,* and the *Dictionary of World Philosophy,* there is no specific entry.[74] It is even more surprising given the difficulties in the field of ethics.[75] In psychology it is emerging as a topic,[76] and, as we noted above, it is easier to expect its presence in sociology and social sciences in general.[77] Indeed, each discipline colors the meaning of the topic analyzed. That is why "the new forms of poverty can be fully understood only in the context of theories of social change."[78] It is normal then that "contemporary ideas about poverty are . . . partly produced by the agenda and methods of the social sciences."[79] Economics has incorporated the topic in its own way.[80]

NOTES

1. David Miller, "Introduction," in *Pluralism, Justice and Equality*, ed. David Miller and Michael Walzer (Oxford: Oxford University Press, 1995), 123. A scientific approach cannot go very far in history if, as Miller annotated in 1965, "an examination of poverty studies over the past 15 years shows that each study establishes its own definition of poverty and all apologize for the inadequacy of the definitions that are used." Herman P. Miller, "Major Elements of a Research Program for the Study of Poverty," in *The Concept of Poverty* (Washington, D.C.: Chamber of Commerce of the United States, 1965).

2. In this essay I understand poverty as expressed by Filler: "Between subsistence and the opportunity for growth," at least if we understand by this growth as a multidimensional process. Survival and fulfillment may be the relevant extremes, and in the next pages we will move all the way along this route in dialogue with the most common economic perspective. Louis Filler, "Poverty," in *A Dictionary of American Social Reform* (New York: Philosophical Library, 1963).

3. Why a multidimensional analysis? We will see in the next section one of the historical justifications given to such approaches in the United States during the1960s. Here we will not evaluate its virtues and risks; it will be enough to answer that question with the help of Alkire: "One fundamental reason for a serious account of dimensions is to give a secure epistemological and empirical footing to the multidimensional objective of human development." Furthermore, "a second fundamental reason is practical and relates to the need for effective methodologies for communities to evaluate tradeoffs." It is also important to "identify unintended impacts" of policies or processes and to avoid confusion among different perspectives on development. Sabina Alkire, "Dimensions of Human Development," *World Development* 30:2 (2002): 181–205.

4. The essay is organized more or less according to the degree of departure. It is not, then, a history of the meaning of the concept, nor a view of the also extremely important synthetic approaches to poverty. We should note that in spite of the benefits of a multidimensional approach to poverty, we should not discard the advantage of simplicity. A consequence of multidimensionality is that causal relations become more difficult to establish. Various components of poverty and various factors behind each one of them make the analysis particularly complex. Furthermore, these proposals for constructing a multidimensional approach to development and poverty are not easy to operationalize. Simple views of poverty have the advantage of focusing attention on some of its features, those

that are most relevant at some moment in history, in some place in the world, and very importantly, with some specific objective in mind. The long list of dimensions and their different combinations reduces the risk of unconscious unilateralism but introduces its own difficulties.

5. We will understand *dimension* in a very general way, as in the dictionary: "any of the component aspects of a particular situation." Alkire, "Dimensions of Human Development." A more precise analysis would have to "identify and formulate questions appropriate to each particular situation, preserve the essential nature of each problem, and to present the full methodology required for its analysis," and include "variations not only between specimens of different types but also between specimens of the same type." J. Aitchison, *The Statistical Analysis of Compositional Data* (London: Chapman and Hall, 1986), 1–2. A deeper analysis of the meaning of dimension should be undertaken. Here we should be careful to distinguish as well as possible the difference in dimensions. Dimensions make difference more complex, but unidimensional approaches do not impede differences.

6. Henry Bartoli, *Rethinking Development: Putting an End to Poverty* (Paris: UNESCO-Economica, 2000).

7. Thomas M. Shapiro and Edward N. Wolff, *Assets for the Poor: The Benefits of Spreading Asset Ownership* (New York: Russell Sage Foundation, 2001).

8. Vinod Thomas, *The Quality of Growth: Lessons for Equity and Sustainability* (New Delhi: National Council of Applied Economic Research, 2000), 150.

9. Amartya Sen, *Development as Freedom* (New York: Anchor Books, 1999).

10. Alice O'Connor, *Poverty Knowledge* (Princeton: Princeton University Press, 2001). That is why, perhaps, employment has always had an importance of its own as a variable. As Stewart signaled: "The first big movement towards making growth possible took the form of employment as the objective of development." Frances Stewart, *Basic Needs in Developing Countries* (Baltimore: Johns Hopkins University Press, 1985), 9.

11. Filler, "Poverty," 612.

12. A more refined discussion about this concept-building strategy should incorporate Marcuse's criticisms of the empiricist treatment of concepts. Herbert Marcuse, *One Dimensional Man* (Boston: Beacon Press, 1964), 12–17.

13. O'Connor, *Poverty Knowledge*, 3.

14. Ben Fine, *Social Capital versus Social Theory: Political Economy and Social Science at the Turn of the Millennium* (New York: Routledge, 2001).

15. World Bank, *World Development Report 2000/2001: Attacking Poverty* (New York: Oxford University Press, 2001).

16. Michael Fairbanks, "Changing the Mind of a Nation: Elements in a Process for Creating Prosperity," in *Culture Matters: How Values Shape Human*

Progress, ed. Lawrence E. Harrison and Samuel P. Huntington (New York: Basic Books, 2000).

17. Task Force on Economic Growth and Opportunity, *The Concept of Poverty.*

18. Ibid., 6.

19. Ibid., 7.

20. Ibid., 5. Except, we should say, for African Americans and the American Indians.

21. Oscar Ornati, "Affluence and the Risk of Poverty," *Social Research* 31:3 (Autumn 1964): 337. In the introductory summary it is indicated that "available data show clearly that poverty in America is a problem of individuals, families, and groups with 'poverty-linked' characteristics that make it difficult or impossible for them to fit into the economy." Task Force on Economic Growth and Opportunity, *The Concept of Poverty,* 5. Poverty in America is, therefore, considered a problem of the poor—a supply-side problem, and not the "massive and chronic condition of the American economy and society as a whole" that should merit a demand-side policy.

22. Task Force on Economic Growth and Opportunity, *The Concept of Poverty,* 6. Antecedents of a similar distinction can be found in I. M. Rubinow, "Poverty," in *Encyclopedia of the Social Sciences,* vol. 11, ed. Edwin R. A. Seligman (New York: Macmillan, 1937).

23. The current mood seems to be different, dominating a strong pessimism about the economic possibilities for attacking poverty. The multidimensional perspective could be viewed also as an evasion from economics. "In the first half of the twentieth century, poverty was seen as a pervasive condition affecting large numbers of working-class people. In the post–World War II period, it came to be seen as a problem of excluded minorities. More recently, views about the poor have been colored by the perception that attempts to solve the problem of poverty have failed." David Cheal, *New Poverty: Families in Postmodern Society* (Westport, Conn.: Greenwood Press, 1996), xvi. For other expressions of this distrust in the economy see Shapiro and Wolff, *Assets for the Poor,* 1; Hernando De Soto, *El misterio del capital* (Lima: El Comercio, 2000), 251; Lawrence E. Harrison, "Why Culture Matters," in *Culture Matters: How Values Shape Human Progress,* xvii; Jeffrey Sachs, "Notes on a New Sociology of Economic Development," in *Culture Matters: How Values Shape Human Progress,* 29; and Bernard M. S. Van Praag and Michael R. Baye, "The Poverty Concept When Prices Are Income Dependent," *Journal of Econometrics* 43 (1990): 153.

24. O'Connor, *Poverty Knowledge,* 231.

25. V. Villemez, "Poverty," in *Encyclopedia of Sociology,* ed. E. F. Borgatta (New York: Macmillan, 2000).

26. Task Force on Economic Growth and Opportunity, *The Concept of Poverty*, 6. Certainly, Galbraith was no part of what he called a "groupal" or "insularist" view of poverty in the United States. In spite of the defects that can be found in such division of "poverties," the contrast is still useful for the analysis of poverty in any country. John K. Galbraith, *Economics and the Public Purpose* (New York: New American Library, 1958).

27. Task Force on Economic Growth and Opportunity, *The Concept of Poverty*, 6–7.

28. World Bank, *World Development Report 2000/2001: Attacking Poverty* (New York: Oxford University Press, 2001), 15. Available at http://www.wds .worldbank.org/external/default/WDSContentServer/IW3P/IB/2001/09/18/00 0094946_01083004025527/Rendered/PDF/multi0page.pdf.

29. Ravi Kanbur and Lyn Squire, "The Evolution of Thinking about Poverty: Exploring the Interactions," in *Frontiers of Development Economics: The Future in Perspective,* ed. G. M. Meier and Joseph E. Stiglitz (New York: Oxford University Press, 2001), 183–84.

30. Deepa Narayan, *Voices of the Poor: Can Anyone Hear Us?* (New York: Oxford University Press, 2000). Indeed, the number of dimensions can be infinite. If we apply these dimensions that we could call "measurement dimensions," like level, variation, vulnerability, risk, powerlessness, and others, to each of the deeper dimensions of poverty, like longevity, literacy, health, and others, we would have a quite extensive matrix.

31. Denis Goulet, *The Cruel Choice: A New Concept in the Theory of Development* (Cambridge, Mass.: Atheneum, 1971).

32. A similar proposal was presented in 1874 by Nishi Amane, a Japanese thinker who summarized happiness by what he called three secondary principles: *mame, chie* y *tomi*—that is, health, knowledge, and wealth. Takashi Koizumi, "Morals and Society in Japanese Philosophy," in *Companion Encyclopedia of Asian Philosophy,* ed. Brian Carr and Indira Mahalingam (London: Routledge, 1997), 797.

33. See Sen, *Development as Freedom.*

34. Caterina Ruggeri, "The Many Dimensions of Deprivation in Peru: Theoretical Debates and Empirical Evidence," working paper 29 (Queen Elizabeth House, Oxford University, 1999). "It is interesting to compare these results with those obtained by using the extreme definition of poverty which is based on the ability to buy only a minimally adequate food basket (table 4). While the number of cases consistently ranked increases to 67%, the percentage of children whose stunting goes unnoticed if using a monetary measure rises to half of the stunted children."

35. Ibid.

36. United Nations, *Human Development Report* (Oxford: Oxford University Press, 1999).

37. S. Anand and A. K. Sen, *Contribución a la Nota Técnica del Informe de Desarrollo Humano* (New York: United Nations Development Progam, 1999).

38. Keith Griffin, "Human Development: Origins, Evolution and Impact," *Ponencia presentada al Congreso Análisis de 10 años de desarrollo humano* (Bilbao: HEGOA Instituto para el estudio del desarrollo y de la economía internacional, 1999).

39. Ibid., 3.

40. United Nations Development Programme, *Human Development Report 1997* (Oxford: Oxford University Press, 1997).

41. Sen, *Development as Freedom*, 88.

42. The criticism by Sen of the "opulent" view of life, that based in "having" as opposed to "being" and "doing," can be easily related to that of Marcuse: "It was not freedom because man, and not only the slave, not only the laborer, remained chained to a world of things which controlled his existence instead of being controlled by him." Herbert Marcuse, "The Containment of Social Change in Industrial Society," in *Towards a Critical Theory of Society: Collected Papers of Herbert Marcuse,* ed. Douglas Kellner (New York: Routledge, 2001), 2: 87.

43. Sen, *Development as Freedom*, 87.

44. Ibid. However, "the perspective of capability does not involve any denial of the sensible view that low income is clearly one of the major causes of poverty, since the lack of income can be a principal reason for a person's capability deprivation."

45. Ibid., 36.

46. Stewart, *Basic Needs in Developing Countries*.

47. Ibid., 5.

48. Ibid.

49. Ibid., 4.

50. We are not going to deal with economic (Gary Becker, *The Economic Approach to Human Behavior* [Chicago: University of Chicago Press, 1978]) or political (Robert A. Dahl, *Modern Political Analysis,* 4th ed. [Englewood Cliffs, N.J.: Prentice-Hall, 1984]) rationalities applied to family, friendship, or other spheres of life.

51. Michael Walzer, "Liberalism and the Art of Separation," *Political Theory* 12 (1984): 315. The greater the number of walls, the greater the freedom. Keeping the enemy outside seems to be the game. We could say that these freedoms are conquered at the price of narrowing them.

52. See, for instance, Pedro Demo, *Pobreza política. Polémicas de nosso tempo,* 5th ed. (Campinas–SP Brasil: Editora Autores Asociados, 1996).

53. Deprivation is "failure to obtain goods, services, rights and activities which, in any given society, form the basis of normal social and economic behavior." Gerry Rodgers, ed., *The Poverty Agenda and the ILO: Issues for Research and Action* (Geneva: International Institute for Labour Studies, 1995), 7.

54. Sen, *Development as Freedom*; World Bank, *World Development Report 2000/2001: Attacking Poverty,* 3.

55. Karl Polanyi, *The Great Transformation* (Boston: Beacon Press, 1957).

56. Paul Krugman, *The Self-Organizing Economy* (Oxford: Blackwell, 1996).

57. Sen, *Development as Freedom,* 15–16.

58. Ibid., 10, 31, 38–39. Although "individual freedom is quintessentially a social product" and therefore so is poverty, this author uses the term *social* in a more restricted sense.

59. Amartya Sen, *The Future and Our Freedoms* (Castellón, Spain: University of Castellón, 2001). The debate on the cultural aspect is in itself very important. For instance, "the first and main point is that our culture at present gives us ample ways to reflect on ourselves as individuals, but not as cultural creatures. Where we would expect to find accounts of the person exercising the fullness of moral and political choice, we find a blank cipher. Utility theory shows the person as a choosing machine, but the choices are treated piecemeal. Their implications for a moral standpoint are overlooked, and heavier weight is put on the right of a person to stay alive than to live according to choice." Mary Douglas and Steven Ney, *Missing Persons: A Critique of the Social Sciences* (Berkeley: University of California Press and The Russell Sage Foundation, 1998), 183–84.

60. Sen, *Development as Freedom,* 11, 25–30, 94, 112–16. The accent on the freedom of exchange is important since it is instrumentally important for growth, but even more important as a constitutive element of freedom independent of the results of the exchange in terms of income. Sen, *The Future and Our Freedoms,* 10.

61. Sen, *Development as Freedom,* 11, 35, 38.

62. This can be phrased in economic terms. For instance, T. H. Marshall defined them as "a universal right to a real income which is not proportionate to the market value of the claimant. It is an entitlement." Ralf Dahrendorf, "Citizenship and Social Class," in *Citizenship Today: The Contemporary Relevance of T. H. Marshall,* ed. Martin Bulmer and Anthony M. Rees (London: UCL Press, 1996), 39.

63. Goulet, *The Cruel Choice,* 334.

64. Denis Goulet, *Etica del desarrollo. Guía Teórica y Práctica* (Madrid: IEPALA-AECI, 1999). Other authors are also thinking along the same lines. For instance: "There are two shortcomings in his treatment of development as freedom. First we noted an over-extension of the emphasis on freedom at the cost of other values, to the extent that all capabilities that women and men could acquire are now to be understood as freedoms. However, some important values, such as those associated with friendship, respect, and care, cannot be adequately understood in terms of individual freedom. Second, we found the concept of freedom to be under elaborated, since it lacks sufficient distinction between autonomous

agencies on the one hand and the variety of values which may be promoted through such agency on the other hand; and also between capability as a set of opportunities, and capabilities as skills and capacities that can be nurtured." Irene Van Staveren and Des Gasper, "Development as Freedom—Contributions and Shortcomings of Amartya Sen's Development Philosophy for Feminist Economics," working papers series no. 365 (The Hague: Institute of Social Studies, 2002), 19.

65. Neither can the term *poverty*. Fusch advised long ago some "caution against the notion that poverty is the cause of all man's ills." Victor Fusch, "Toward a Theory of Poverty," in *The Concept of Poverty,* 72.

66. For instance, a distinction along this line of preoccupation suggests that poverty should have a narrower meaning than most of the ones explored in this essay: "Multiple deprivations are a broader notion than poverty." Rodgers, *The Poverty Agenda and the ILO,* 7.

67. Denis Goulet, "An Ethical Model for the Study of Values," *Harvard Educational Review* 41:2 (May 1971): 205. "I define a 'value' as any object or representation which can be perceived by a subject as habitually worthy of desire."

68. Ibid., 206.

69. Ibid., 206–7. In a similar vein we can benefit from the expressions of Tawney: "A society is free in so far, and only in so far, as, within the limits set by nature, knowledge, and resources, its institutions and policies are such as to enable all its members to grow to their full stature, to do their duty as they see it, and—since liberty should not be too austere—to have their fling when they feel like it." R. H. Tawney, *Equality,* 4th ed. (London: Capricon, 1952), 268.

70. Alkire, "Dimensions of Human Development."

71. See Narayan, *Voices of the Poor: Can Anyone Hear Us?*

72. Alkire, "Dimensions of Human Development."

73. Gustavo Gutiérrez, "Teología y ciencias sociales," *Páginas* 63 (Sept. 1984).

74. P. Edwards, ed., *The Encyclopedia of Philosophy* (New York: Macmillan, 1963); Mario Bunge, *Dictionary of Philosophy* (Amherst, N.Y.: Prometheus Books, 1999); and P. A. Iannone, ed., *Dictionary of World Philosophy* (New York: Routledge, 2001).

75. For instance, L. C. Becker and C. B. Becker, eds., *Encyclopedia of Ethics,* 2nd ed. (London: Routledge, 2001). One of the few exceptions is Georges Enderle, "Pobreza," in *Dicionário de ética economica,* ed. G. Enderle, K. Homann, M. Honecker, W. Kerber, and H. Steinman (Brasil: Editora da Universidade do Vale do Rio dos Sinos, 1997), 472. Traducción de: *Lexicon der wirtschafts ethik* (Freiburg: Herder, 1993). At the end of that entry it is specified that "summarizing, due to its high relevance and complexity, the problem of poverty should be directly understood as a paradigm of economic ethics."

76. In the *Encyclopedia of Human Behavior* (ed. V. S. Ramachadran [New York: Academic Press, 1994]) there is no such entry. In others, the term is introduced in relation to problems of expression typical of schizophrenia. The possibilities are, however, interesting. For instance, it is a pity that peniaphobia, fear of poverty, is not developed further. A notable exception is *Encyclopedia of Psychology* (Oxford: Oxford University Press, 2000), in the entry by the American Association of Psychologists where "poverty in infancy" is included, and extensively, "poverty in adults." The emotional aspect should not be discarded so easily. After all, "the more we study poverty the more we find that it is not just an economic problem. It is an emotional, cultural, and political problem as well. Herman P. Miller, "Major Elements of a Research Program for the Study of Poverty" in *The Concept of Poverty*, 115.

77. One example is in *The International Encyclopedia of the Social Sciences* (New York: Macmillan, 1968), where one finds the strong contribution of Eric J. Hobsbawm. More recently, another serious example is *The Encyclopedia of Sociology*.

78. Cheal, *New Poverty: Families in Postmodern Society*.

79. Ibid., 17.

80. In almost all economics dictionaries and encyclopedias there exists an entry under "poverty."

CHAPTER 4

Are the Poor Happier?

Perspectives from Business Management

MATT BLOOM

I often have the privilege of sharing the science of happiness, through presentations and speeches, with a variety of audiences. I have found that a topic that holds great interest for people is the relationship between wealth or income and happiness. When scientists began to study happiness, money was one of the first topics they explored. A long series of scientific investigations has produced one of the most consistent results in the study of happiness: that wealthy or high income earners are, at most, only somewhat happier than the average person. That is, these studies indicate that having a great deal of money does not seem to provide one with the capacity or resources to "buy" much additional happiness. Most people seem delighted to hear that this is the case. There appears to be a pervasive desire to know that money cannot buy happiness and thereby to be assured that the super rich do not get more happiness on top of all the other perks wealth seems to bring to them. It is particularly surprising to see this delight among audiences in the United States given that we are, by most indicators, the wealthiest country in the world. We still want to know that there is more to happiness than money and all the purportedly "good" things that money can buy.

I think there is an intuition deeply buried in this response about what is essential for the happiness of individuals and societies: that if some people live very well with too much money while others suffer with too little, then no one can be truly happy. This intuition is very consistent with the emerging science of happiness which provides compelling evidence that the monetary inequalities the poor experience do cause them to suffer significant unhappiness. This intuition, like the science of happiness, is also very consistent with the profound wisdom contained in the preferential option for the poor which emphasizes the fundamental interdependence of all people. The science of happiness is one more confirmation that the way a society treats its poor and marginalized has implications for the well-being of all its members.

But this response is also severely muddled by misunderstandings. When I ask people to explain why happiness is not very strongly connected to money, one answer is offered far more often than any other. "The poor are not encumbered by the trappings of wealth," the logic goes, "and so they are free to pay attention to the more important things in life, those things that *truly* bring us more happiness." This is a romanticized notion of being poor, and though it is very deeply held, it simply is not true. While the wealthy or those with large salaries are only a little bit happier than most of us, they are certainly much happier than the truly poor, and so are we. Studies of happiness have been conducted in almost every country in the world, and they have consistently shown that people living below the poverty level of their country are much, much less happy than those whose income or wealth places them above the poverty line. In other words, the poor are much less happy than the wealthy, the super rich, *and* much less happy than the average income earner. Research also confirms that people in poorer countries are, on average, less happy than those in richer countries.[1]

Many factors are important for our happiness, but on the issues of money the science is clear: the poor are not happier, and in fact they are significantly less happy. At least some of the reasons underlying this relationship are straightforward and clear: the poor cannot buy the necessities of life, things such as food, clothing, and shelter, and because their basic life needs are not met, they are less happy. Maslow's famous hierarchy of needs[2] captures this succinctly, and at least in terms of this first, most basic level of needs he appears to be right. A study by Di Tella and McCullough is illustrative. They analyzed data from the Eurobarometer Survey Series, a twenty-eight-year study of 16 European countries, and the 2005 World Gallup Poll of 132 countries. These researchers found that substantial and sustained increases in well-being were experienced by raising incomes of individuals in poorer countries, but not in wealthy countries.[3] They interpret these data to suggest that increasing income to cover "basic needs" results in sustained increases in well-being. Research confirms Maslow's proposition that it is hard to be very happy when you are worrying about feeding, clothing, or sheltering yourself and your loved ones.

A vast array of studies shows that poverty is related to more than just lower levels of happiness: the poor are subject to much worse physical and mental health, including a significantly higher incidence of heart, lung, and vascular disease; greater likelihood of developing obesity and diabetes; and much higher rates of depression, anxiety, neuroses, and other psychological ailments.[4] Consequently, the poor are both less happy and less healthy, which is the recipe for a vicious, downward spiral of increasing unhappiness. Of course, there are always outliers in any group, and we can certainly find very poor individuals who are at the top of the happiness charts, but these individuals are rare among the poor. Again, the science is clear that if all else is equal, being poor will have very detrimental effects on one's happiness. Money is, therefore, a necessary determinant of happiness, but as I will explore below, it is not sufficient for high levels of happiness.[5]

What about the relationship between money and happiness for those of us above the poverty line? Objectively, more money holds plenty of promise for increasing our happiness as well. The finer things in life are called that for a reason: they can bring us pleasure, they can foster enjoyment, and they can enhance our well-being. We should not constrain our thinking here to such things as luxury cars, opulent jewelry, or meals at five-star restaurants. Money can provide many more prosaic resources that can be happiness-producing. Things like a vacation with family and friends, a day at the ballpark, the ability to purchase a good book, or the often sublime pleasure of going to a restaurant so that one does not have to cook another meal can enhance our lives and bring us true happiness. More money brings us more opportunities for these kinds of life-enriching experiences. Nearly fifty years ago, Cantril interviewed over twenty thousand people in thirteen countries and found that, almost universally, everyone believed that more money would make them happier.[6] Cantril found that, regardless of their current wealth or their nation of origin, people desired greater material prosperity because they thought it would bring them greater happiness.

The preponderance of research suggests that more income brings more happiness, but it seems to be associated only with some forms of happiness.[7] In general, more money seems to help us to evaluate our lives as being more satisfying, but it does not help us feel any happier on a daily basis. In a global study, Diener, Ng, Harter, and Arora found that income was most strongly associated with people's life satisfaction, which is the degree to which people are satisfied with their lives compared with what they wanted or expected to get out of life. Those with higher incomes were more inclined to view their lives as satisfying and as having met their expectations. These researchers also found, however, that income was not very strongly related to daily moods and emotions, another important measure of happiness. Specifically, higher income was not related to more good moods and fewer bad ones.[8] Similarly, Kahneman and colleagues found that above-average income earners were more satisfied with their lives, but appeared to be more tense and to spend less time in enjoyable activities than below-average income earners.[9] Research suggests that for those above the poverty line, holding everything else equally, more money creates greater life satisfaction, but not greater daily happiness. A research project that aggregated results from many studies conducted around the world also supports this notion. Howell and Howell found that various indicators of economic prosperity, including income and wealth, had much stronger relationships with happiness in developing nations than in developed nations.[10] In other words, money matters less for happiness as we become wealthier and better paid.

The story of money and happiness is, however, much more complicated. Studies consistently show that the *absolute* amount of money we have matters less than our *relative* income or wealth.[11] Put differently, it is how much money we make compared with others around us that seems to matter more than our total income. Most of us have this nearly irresistible tendency to compare our income and wealth with that of other people, and when we compare, we somehow usually view ourselves as among the "have-nots." Most people report that their income or wealth does not compare very favorably with that of other people, and as a consequence they see their situation as unfair, untenable, and unhappy.

Studies also consistently show that the distribution of income has a very significant impact on the health and happiness of people within a country. For example, Boyce and colleagues found that, as it pertains to happiness, the effect of an individual's rank in an income distribution swamped the effect of absolute income.[12] In other words, relative income was all that seemed to matter, and the lower a person's rank, the lower was their happiness. In addition, more unequal distributions make most people less happy, even rich people, with the super wealthy being the only possible exception. Oishi and colleagues found that Americans were, on average, happiest during years in which national income inequality was lowest. Their study suggests that people tended to respond to greater inequality by trusting other people less and perceiving American society in general as being more unfair. In this study, it was only the highest income earners who seemed to be unaffected by relative income.[13]

To make matters worse, we make these comparisons with almost every group to which we belong, so it is not just how wealthy we are compared with others in our country, but also how our incomes compare with the incomes of our neighbors, members of our social groups, and perhaps most importantly, other employees of the company where we work. The odd paradox is that the "poorest" investment banker at a Wall Street firm is likely to be less happy than those who rank at the top of the firm's pay scale, even though this "poor" financier is likely to be handsomely paid. Neurological research indicates that our brains respond very strongly to perceived "under-reward"; the reward centers of our brains light up in a fire of protest when we think we are getting less than we should.[14] Interestingly, companies with very unequal pay rates seem to have poorer performance as well, so this "relative money effect" seems to do more than just make people unhappy.[15]

A series of studies conducted in Great Britain is illustrative of this research.[16] The Whitehall Studies have investigated the physical and psychological well-being of British civil service workers for over forty years. Among the many important insights yielded by these studies has been the "social gradient" effect. These studies have shown that there is a consistent, measurable decrement in well-being associated with each successively lower step a civil service employee occupies on the pay ladder. Those employees on the second-highest rung have lower well-being than those on the top rung, and those on the third rung have lower well-being than those on the second, and so on, all the way down the ladder. These effects cannot be explained by factors such as access to health care (all British civil service workers receive the same health care), living conditions, or health behaviors such as smoking, obesity, and diet. Whitehall researchers have concluded that it is factors such as work stress, characteristics of jobs, and relationships at work that account for a great deal of this difference, but it is likely that other factors are also at play.

The largest body of research on the relationships between inequality and well-being comes from studies of socioeconomic status (SES). SES captures an individual's economic and social position within a particular social group. It is a measure of one's status relative to others, and it recognizes that status is a psychological variable capturing one's value or worth relative to other people in some social group. This psychological dimension is captured by synonyms such as social prestige, social position, and social rank. SES is usually measured using several variables including income, education, and occupational prestige. In other words, income is one way in which societies and individuals evaluate the relative social status or social value of other people. Higher income earners are, for example, generally perceived to be more intelligent, motivated, talented, and responsible.

A great deal of research indicates very strong relationships between SES and happiness. Low SES is associated with lower levels on a variety of measures of physical and psychological well-being. For example, research indicates that successively lower levels of SES are monotonically related to poorer health.[17] The poorer one is, the sicker one will likely be. Studies show that SES is positively related to allostatic load, which is a primary measure of the wear and tear on the body due to the level of chronic life stress an individual experiences.[18] High allostatic load is a precursor to a variety of health challenges including poor cardiovascular and circulatory health. Once again, factors such as access to good health care, safe living conditions, high-quality education, and the like explain only some of these outcomes so other psychological factors are also at work.

Adler and Snibbe conducted a recent review of research on the social gradient and provide solid evidence that psychosocial factors, in addition to living conditions, underlie this relationship.[19] Several scholars have explored these factors. Gallo and Matthews found that lower SES is related to higher levels of chronic psychological conditions such as hopelessness, anxiety, and hostility toward others, and they found that these factors are then related to a variety of health problems such as circulatory disease, cardiovascular health, depression, and suicide.[20] Neckerman and Torche reviewed a large body of research that indicates historic socioeconomic status influences future social mobility, which is the amount of opportunity individuals have to move upward in income, earnings, or social class.[21] In effect, low SES seems to "trap" people by *severely* limiting their social mobility, which in turn perpetuates the cycle of poverty. Ghaed and Gallo found that subjective social status, a person's self-perceived social status, was related to cardiovascular health in women.[22] This suggests that perceiving oneself to be of lower social class, not just SES itself, matters. Hawkley, Lavelle, Berntson, and Cacioppo found that part of the SES-allostatic load relationship is due to the way in which SES leads to higher levels of hostility, loneliness, and depression.[23] Other research suggests that low SES is more directly related to reduced happiness. Gallo, Bogart, Vranceanu, and Matthew found that lower SES individuals experience more life stress and greater social strain, and had few positive experiences and more negative emotions in their daily lives.[24]

All of this research suggests that the effects of being poor are compounded the lower a person is on the wealth and income ladder of his or her country and community. It is bad enough that being poor means one cannot buy good food, safe shelter, and quality health care; poverty also comes with psychosocial harm that increases its damaging effects on happiness. To be sure, social status is a complex phenomenon, and more research is needed to understand its nuanced effects,[25] but given that inequality in wealth and income is growing in many countries, including the United States and many other developed nations,[26] the detrimental impact of poverty on individuals' happiness could be increasing. Research also indicates that inequality might be bad for everyone, even the rich. Wilkinson and Pickett review a wide range of research that suggests that everyone in a country, including the very rich, suffers from more unequal distributions of income and wealth.[27] They argue that greater inequality leads to greater mental illness, more obesity, more murders, higher rates of imprisonment, more teen births, and decreased levels of trust across social classes. These become societal ills, which then influence the happiness of all a society's members.

Another route through which poverty influences long-term well-being might be through the jobs in which people are employed. Although data on this are very limited, there is some evidence that suggests poverty affects the kinds of jobs that people are able to obtain, which in turn might influence well-being over the long run. In a series of studies, Kohn and Schooler found that lower SES individuals can only obtain poorer quality jobs, which then lead to reduced self-esteem, lower self-confidence, and increased work-related anxiety.[28] Link, Lennon, and Dohrenwend found that socioeconomic status predicted whether individuals were able to obtain jobs that had positive aspects such as the ability to self-direct, control, and plan one's work.[29] Like Kohn and Schooler, they found that lower SES individuals were limited to poorer quality jobs, which in turn made them more prone to experience psychological depression. Being stuck in a low-paying job bodes very poorly for one's future happiness.

A variety of other research[30] suggests what I think may be one of the most important reasons underlying the relative money effect. In many societies, and certainly in most work organizations, money is the most salient and important indicator of one's value to the group. Those who make the most money are usually assumed to be the most valuable to the organization, and so the less one makes, the less valued, important, and significant one feels. At some point, this has implications for our sense of basic dignity and worth. When we are at the bottom of the pay ladder, we also feel that we are at the bottom of the human dignity ladder. As a consequence, one of our most fundamental needs is not fulfilled, and our well-being is profoundly impacted as a result. The more contexts in which we find ourselves among the lowest on the money or income ladder, the more this effect is compounded. The poor are at or near the bottom of every money-based ladder in a society including the income, wealth, and pay ladders. To be sure, societies are making a profound and costly mistake by implicating income and wealth so heavily in their valuations of people and life. Even so, it is the poor who suffer disproportionately from this mistake.

There are many cautionary notes in happiness research about the relationship between money and happiness once basic needs are met. For example, what we expect from and do with money matters a lot in how money influences our happiness.[31] Spending money on other people[32] or on great experiences instead of nice things[33] promotes happiness. We tend to adapt to the things money can buy, so their happiness-inducing effects often wear off over time.[34] And making the possession of money and material goods a central life pursuit is detrimental to happiness.[35] Wanting more than we can buy appears to be a sure path to misery and unhappiness,[36] but for most of us it is very hard to keep ourselves from wanting more. Simply having enough money may impair our ability truly to *savor* the good things in life, which may mean that buying nice things makes us *less* happy.[37] And the mere thought of money can make us think and act to advance only our own self-interests rather than helping others.[38]

Many of the world's wisdom and faith traditions provide profound insights into this relationship between money and happiness, and the Christian tradition, particularly in the notion of the preferential option for the poor, is certainly no exception. When I ask people what the Bible says about the connection between money and evil, most assume that the Bible warns that money is the root of all evil, but that is not the case. The author of 1 Timothy 6:10 warns that the *love* of money is the root of all kinds of evil, and science affirms this aphorism. It is not wealth or income per se that matters, but rather it is the way we think about and use our money that seems to matter most. Both these admonitions and research warn us that to be happy we should avoid comparing what we have with what other people possess,[39] or if we have to compare, we should look to those who have much less and thereby see all the more clearly how much we really do have. We also discover that it is not money or possessions that make us happy, but relationships and all the good things relationships bring into our lives. It is in this sense that the science of happiness is very consistent with the preferential option for the poor. Both remind us of the need to prioritize people over possessions, profit, and power.

The most important lesson from research on money and happiness is that the relationships between the two are very complex. As research indicates, poverty makes us less healthy and less happy, it seems to doom us to low-paying and stressful jobs, and if that were not enough, poverty seems to set us on a downward trajectory resulting in worsening conditions that are difficult to overcome. But more money is not an unalloyed good, so as incomes and wealth rise, we need to be very careful in how we think about and use money. We also need to remember that the science of happiness clearly indicates that other factors matter as much as or more than money. These include loving families and good friends, fun activities and events, meaningful work, deeply held life values we can consistently enact, opportunities to grow, learn, and develop our talents, religion and spirituality, and a sense of purpose in life.[40]

There are many examples of how these essentials of happiness manifest themselves in the lives of people. For example, nearly one hundred billionaires have decided to give the majority of their wealth to philanthropy. In the letter explaining his decision to give 99 percent of his fortune to charity, Warren Buffett notes that if he were to spend his fortune on himself or his family, "neither our happiness nor our well-being would be enhanced," and he emphasizes that "the asset I most value, aside from health, is interesting, diverse, and long-standing friends."[41] Jane Dutton, a wonderful scholar of organizations and work, tells of Luke, a custodian at a hospital, who views caring for the patients and their families as the most important part of his work and his most precious reward.[42] Luke has found happiness in his work despite his low wage. I have seen many profound examples of this in my own research. There are the dozens of humanitarian workers I have interviewed who, despite low pay and demanding work in some of life's most difficult circumstances, find profound joy and enduring happiness in working to alleviate the suffering of others. Likewise, there are highly paid physicians who find the most satisfaction from their work when they volunteer at a local health care clinic. Perhaps most salient for me is the case of the woman who cleaned my office during my first few years at Notre Dame. She would leave me notes of encouragement and kindness, and whenever I saw her, she was smiling and happy. Among her secrets to happiness were leading the local community garden, spending time with her grandchildren, and Friday night card games with lifelong friends.

Even so, research is clear that the poor suffer greatly, and this alone should be impetus for wide-scale social change. We need to stop romanticizing poverty as somehow setting people free to pursue things that really matter. Research strongly suggests that this idea is a fiction, and a potentially damaging one if we allow it to keep us from addressing poverty. Furthermore, science is clear that sufficient wealth and income should make the pursuit of the better things in life even easier, not harder, for us and for others. When we have more for ourselves, we also have more to share, so there is the potential for greater happiness for more people. The science of happiness confirms the importance of the preferential option for the poor: sharing wealth means we are also sharing happiness.

NOTES

1. R. Ingelhart and C. Welzel, *Modernization, Cultural Change, and Democracy: The Human Development Sequence* (New York: Cambridge University Press, 2005); E. Diener, M. Diener, and D. Diener, "Factors Predicting the Subjective Well-being of Nations," *Journal of Personality and Social Psychology* 69:5 (1995): 851–64; E. Diener and S. Oishi, "Money and Happiness: Income and Subjective Well-being Across Nations," in *Culture and Subjective Well-Being*, ed. E. Diener and E. M. Suh (Cambridge, Mass.: MIT Press, 2000), 185–218; Richard Layard, *Happiness: Lessons from a New Science* (New York: Penguin Press, 2005); R. Lucas and U. Schimmack, "Income and Well-being: How Big Is the Gap between the Rich and the Poor?," *Journal of Research in Personality* 43:1 (2009): 75–78; D. W. Sacks, B. Stevenson, and J. Wolfers, "Subjective Well-being, Income, Economic Development, and Growth" (working paper 16441, National Bureau of Economic Research, 2010), http://www.nber.org/papers /w16441.

2. A. H. Maslow, "A Theory of Human Motivation," *Psychological Review* 50 (1943): 370–96.

3. R. Di Tella and R. McCulloch, "Happiness Adaptation to Income and to Status in an Individual Panel," *Journal of Economic Behavior and Organization* 76:3 (2010): 834–52.

4. C. Lund, M. De Silva, M. Plagerson, S. Cooper, D. Chisholm, J. Das, M. Knapp, and V. Patel, "Poverty and Mental Disorders: Breaking the Cycle in Low-income and Middle-income Countries," *Lancet* 378 (2011): 1502–14; OECD, "Poverty and Health" (Organization for Economic Cooperation and Development and World Health Organization, 2003), whqlibdoc.who.int /publications/2003/9241562366.pdf; R. Wilkinson and M. Marmot, "Social Determinants of Health: The Solid Facts" (World Health Organization, 2003).

5. P. Kesebir and E. Diener, "In Pursuit of Happiness: Empirical Answers to Philosophical Questions," *Perspectives on Psychological Science* 3 (2008): 117–26.

6. H. Cantril, *The Pattern of Human Concern* (New Brunswick, N.J.: Rutgers University Press, 1965).

7. E. Diener and Oishi, "Money and Happiness"; D. Kahneman, A. Krueger, D. Schkade, N. Schwarz, and A. Stone, "Would You Be Happier If You Were Richer? A Focusing Illusion," *Science* 312:5782 (2006): 1908–10.

8. E. Diener, W. Ng, J. Harter, and R. Arora, "Wealth and Happiness Across the World: Material Prosperity Predicts Life Evaluation, Whereas Psychosocial

Prosperity Predicts Positive Feeling," *Journal of Personality and Social Psychology* 99:1 (2010): 52–61.

9. Kahneman et al., "Would You Be Happier If You Were Richer?"

10. R. Howell and C. Howell, "The Relation of Economic Status to Subjective Well-being in Developing Countries: A Meta-analysis," *Psychological Bulletin* 134:4 (2008): 536–60.

11. C. J. Boyce, G. D. A. Brown, and S. C. Moore, "Money and Happiness: Rank of Income, Not Income, Affects Life Satisfaction," *Psychological Science* 21 (2010): 471–75; K. Dynan and E. Ravina, "Increasing Income Inequality, External Habits, and Self-reported Happiness," *American Economic Review* 97:2 (2007): 226–31; M. Hagerty, "Social Comparisons of Income in One's Community: Evidence from National Surveys of Income and Happiness," *Journal of Personality and Social Psychology* 78:4 (2000): 764–71: Howell and Howell, "The Relation of Economic Status to Subjective Well-being in Developing Countries," 536–60; S. Oishi, S. Kesebir, and E. Diener, "Income Inequality and Happiness," *Psychological Science* 22:9 (2011): 1095–1100.

12. Boyce et al., "Money and Happiness."

13. S. Oishi, S. Kesebir, and E. Diener, "Income Inequality and Happiness."

14. E. Tricomi, A. Rangel, C. F. Camerer, and J. P. O'Doherty, "Neural Evidence for Inequality-Averse Social Preferences," *Nature* 463 (2010): 1089–92.

15. M. Bloom, "100 Years of Compensation," in *Handbook of Organizational Behavior*, ed. Cary L. Copper and Julian Barling (Thousand Oaks, Calif.: Sage Publications, 2008), 300–317.

16. J. E. Ferrie, ed., *Work, Stress, and Health: The Whitehall II Study* (London: Council of Civil Service Unions, 2004); B. J. Marmot, M. Oldfield, and J. Smith, "The SES-Health Gradient on Both Sides of the Atlantic," in *Developments in the Economics of Ageing*, ed. D. Wise (Chicago: University of Chicago Press, 2008).

17. N. E. Adler, W. T. Boyce, M. Chesney, S. Cohen, S. Folkman, R. Kahn, and S. L. Syme, "Socioeconomic Status and Health: The Challenge of the Gradient," *American Psychologist* 49 (1994): 15–24; E. Adler, M. Marmot, B. McEwen, and S. Stewart, *Socioeconomic Status and Health in Industrialized Nations: Social, Psychological, and Biological Pathways* (New York: New York Academy of Sciences, 1999).

18. L. D. Kubzansky, I. Kawachi, and D. Sparrow, "Socioeconomic Status, Hostility, and Risk Factor Clustering in the Normative Aging Study: Any Help from the Concept of Allostatic Load?," *Annals of Behavioral Medicine* 21 (1999): 330–38.

19. N. Adler and A. Snibbe, "The Role of Psychosocial Processes in Explaining the Gradient between Socioeconomic Status and Health," *Current Directions in Psychological Science* 12 (2003): 119–23.

20. L. C. Gallo and K. A. Matthews, "Understanding the Association between Socioeconomic Status and Physical Health: Do Negative Emotions Play a Role?," *Psychological Bulletin* 129 (2003): 10–51.

21. K. Neckerman and F. Torche, "Inequality: Causes and Consequences," *Annual Review of Sociology* 33:1 (2007): 335–57.

22. S. Ghaed and L. Gallo, "Subjective Social Status, Objective Socioeconomic Status, and Cardiovascular Risk in Women," *Health Psychology* 26:6 (2007): 668–74.

23. L. Hawkley, L. Lavelle, G. Berntson and J. Cacioppo, "Mediators of the Relationship between Socioeconomic Status and Allostatic Load in the Chicago Health, Aging, and Social Relations Study (CHASRS)," *Psychophysiology* 48:8 (2011): 1134–45.

24. L. C. Gallo, L. M. Bogart, A. Vranceanu, and K. A. Matthew, "Socioeconomic Status, Resources, Psychological Experiences, and Emotional Responses: A Test of the Reserve Capacity Model," *Journal of Personality and Social Psychology* 88 (2005): 386–99.

25. P. A. Braverman, C. Cubbin, S. Egerter, S. Chideya, K. S. Marchi, M. Metzler, and S. Posner, "Socioeconomic Status and Health Research: One Size Does Not Fit All," *Journal of the American Medical Association* 294:22 (2005): 2879–88.

26. J. K. Galbraith and M. Berner, eds., *Inequality and Industrial Change: A Global View* (New York: Cambridge University Press, 2001); L. Keister and S. Moller, "Wealth Inequality in the United States," *Annual Review of Sociology* 26 (2000): 63–81.

27. R. Wilkinson and K. Pickett, *The Spirit Level: Why More Equal Societies Almost Always Do Better* (London: Allen Lane, 2009).

28. M. Kohn and C. Schooler, "Job Conditions and Personality: A Longitudinal Assessment of Their Reciprocal Effects," *American Journal of Sociology* 87:6 (1982): 1257–86; M. Kohn and C. Schooler, *Work and Personality: An Inquiry into the Impact of Social Stratification* (Norwood, N.J.: Ablex Publishing, 1983).

29. B. G. Link, M. C. Lennon, and B. P. Dohrenwend, "Socioeconomic Status and Depression: The Role of Occupations Involving Direction, Control, and Planning," *American Journal of Sociology* 98:6 (1993): 1351–87.

30. S. T. Fiske, *Envy Up, Scorn Down: How Status Divides Us* (New York: Russell Sage Foundation, 2011); S. T. Fiske and H. R. Markus, *Facing Social Class: How Societal Rank Influences Interaction* (New York: Russell Sage Foundation, 2012).

31. W. Johnson and R. Krueger, "How Money Buys Happiness: Genetic and Environmental Processes Linking Finances and Life Satisfaction," *Journal of Personality and Social Psychology* 90:4 (2006): 680–91; S. E. G. Lea and P. Webley, "Money as a Tool, Money as a Drug: The Biological Psychology of a Strong Incentive," *Behavioral and Brain Sciences* 29 (2006): 161–209.

32. E. Dunn, L. Aknin, and M. Norton, "Spending Money on Others Promotes Happiness," *Science* 319:5870 (2008): 1687–88.

33. L. Van Boven and T. Gilovich, "To Do or to Have? That Is the Question," *Journal of Personality and Social Psychology* 85:6 (2003): 1193.

34. S. Frederick and G. Loewenstein, "Hedonic Adaptation," in *Well-being: The Foundations of Hedonic Psychology*, ed. D. Kahneman, E. Diener, and N. Schwarz (New York: Russell Sage Foundation, 1999), 302–29; Kahneman et al., "Would You Be Happier If You Were Richer?"

35. J. E. Burroughs and A. Rindfleisch, "Materialism and Well-being: A Conflicting Values Perspective, *Journal of Consumer Research* 29 (2002): 348–70; T. Kashdan and W. Breen, "Materialism and Diminished Well-being: Experiential Avoidance as a Mediating Mechanism," *Journal of Social and Clinical Psychology* 26:5 (2007): 521–39.

36. E. C. Solberg, E. Diener, R. E. Lucas, and S. Oishi, "Wanting, Having, and Satisfaction: Examining the Role of Desire Discrepancies in Satisfaction with Income," *Journal of Personality and Social Psychology* 83 (2002): 725–34.

37. J. Quiodbach, E. W. Dunn, K. V. Petrides, and M. Mikolajcsak, "Money Giveth, Money Taketh Away: The Dual Effect of Wealth on Happiness," *Psychological Science* 21 (2010): 759–63.

38. K. D. Vohs, N. L. Meade, and M. Goode, "Merely Activating the Concept of Money Changes Personal and Interpersonal Behavior," *Current Directions in Psychological Science* 17 (2008): 208–12.

39. Several verses before the biblical caution is 1 Timothy 6:6, which states, "But godliness with contentment is great gain"—another good answer to the question of what the Bible has to say about money and happiness.

40. R. A. Emmons and R. F. Paloutsizan, "The Psychology of Religion," *Annual Review of Psychology* 54 (2003): 377–402; Kahneman, E. Diener, and Schwarz, *Well-being: The Foundations of Hedonic Psychology*; C. L. M. Keyes, D. Schmotikin, and C. D. Ryff, "Optimizing Well-being: The Empirical Encounter of Two Traditions," *Journal of Personality and Social Psychology* 86 (2002): 1007–22; S. Lyubomirsky, L. King, and E. Diener, "The Benefits of Frequent Positive Affect: Does Happiness Lead to Success?," *Psychological Bulletin* 136 (2005): 803–55; R. M. Ryan and E. L. Deci, "On Happiness and Human Potentials: A Review of Research on Hedonic and Eudaimonic Well-being," *Annual Review of Psychology* 52 (2001): 141–66.

41. Warren Buffett, "The Giving Pledge," available at http://givingpledge.org/#warren_buffett.

42. J. E. Dutton, G. Debebe, and A. Wrzesniewski, *A Social Valuing Perspective on Relationship Sensemaking* (Ann Arbor: University of Michigan Press, 2002).

CHAPTER 5

The Option for the Poor and the Indigenous Peoples of Chile

PATRICIO A. AYLWIN AND
JOSÉ O. AYLWIN

In what way has the option for the poor directed our action in favor of the indigenous peoples of Chile as president of the republic on one hand and as advocate and defender of the indigenous peoples' rights on the other?

Upon reflection, we dare to think that the main factor that has inspired us to take a certain stance is what we could call our common "vocation for justice." That is what moved us not only in our youth to study law and to be lawyers, but also later in life has directed our steps: the search for the common good and for social justice through political action on the side of the father, and the struggle for human rights on the side of the son. In these endeavors both of us faced, in diverse ways, the disconcerting reality of the indigenous peoples who live in the nation of Chile and form the national community: Aymaras, Quechuas, Atacameños, and Collas in the north; Rapa Nui on the Isla de Pascua; Mapuches in the center and south of the country; and Yámanas and Kawéskar in the extreme south. Although the unofficial statistics say that the indigenous population is close to a million out of the total of 15 million who constitute the population of Chile, the census of 2002 affirmed that the number reached 700,000 persons, among whom more than 87 percent are Mapuche.

BACKGROUND FOR UNDERSTANDING THE REALITY OF THE INDIGENOUS PEOPLE

As we know, numerous peoples lived in the South American continent before the arrival of the Europeans. The majority of these first peoples, diverse in their cultures, possessed a territory within which they freely ruled their destinies on the basis of their own juridical systems and forms of social and political organization. The arrival of the Europeans, who thought that the indigenous people were savages or inferior, as people without god or law, put an end to their condition as sovereign countries. Since then, these peoples have been the object of political, juridical, economic, and cultural subordination, first to colonial governments and later to national states.

Influenced by the liberal ideas present in the creation of many Latin American states in the nineteenth century, the republican governments declared judicial equality of the indigenous people along with the rest of the population, and also rendered their land to the law of common rights. As a consequence of this development, as well as the economic expansion, a lot of indigenous towns, especially in agricultural areas, were deprived of their land and placed in concessions (*resguardos,* Colombia), reductions (*reducciones,* Chile) or reserves (*reservas,* Argentina).

As a result of such processes, the estimated 50 million indigenous people in Latin America—almost 10 percent of the total population of the region—usually live today in the poorest sectors of the country to which they belong. The progressive loss of their ancestral lands, the bankruptcy of their traditional community economies, and the displacement and migration from the country to urban centers that these phenomena have caused—these are some of the factors explaining the level of poverty among the indigenous. The discrimination the indigenous people suffer in such centers by the nonindigenous sectors, and the difficulties that they encounter trying to obtain a job, also aggravate the poverty of the indigenous people.

The marginalization of indigenous people is evident not only in the economic situation but also in the political arena. Generally, indigenous people are excluded from the places where decisions are made, even though those decisions affect them. They are left at the mercy of the decisions that other sectors of the population—usually the nonindigenous elite—make for them. Regrettably, Chile is not an exception in this case. First colonial politics and later the republican state deprived the indigenous peoples of an important part of their lands, denied the richness of their cultures, and tried to build a homogenous nationality in which there was no option for the indigenous peoples but to assimilate. Consequently, they were forced gradually to the lowest ranks of the social scale.

A recent study on the human development of the Mapuche population in the country found that 32.9 percent of them are poor, in contrast to the 20.1 percent among the nonindigenous population. The Mapuche attain 7.2 years of schooling, in contrast to 9.6 for those who are not indigenous. The literacy rate (both reading and writing) among the Mapuche is as high as 88.6 percent, while among those who are not indigenous it is 95.3 percent. The income per person for indigenous people was $64.975 (about US$100), in contrast with $134.077 (more than US$200) for nonindigenous people.[1]

It is not by accident then that the Special Rapporteur of the United Nations for the rights of indigenous peoples, Rodolfo Stavenhagen, proved in the mission report that he presented to Chile in 2003 that there is a "close correlation between poverty and indigenous identity in the country."[2] Discrimination toward the indigenous world clearly resides in the political arena, where indigenous participation is practically nonexistent in decision making at the national level, as in the National Congress and the judiciary.

STEPS BY THE FIRST DEMOCRATIC GOVERNMENT AFTER THE DICTATORSHIP

During the second half of the 1980s, and coinciding with the downfall of the military government, the most representative organizations of the Mapuches, Aymaras, and Rapa Nui banded together and filed several lawsuits for the protection of their threatened rights, in particular their right to the land, and demanded the establishment of a new relationship with the state. Among their central demands were, particularly, the acknowledgment of the ethnic and cultural diversity that up to that time had been denied in the country; the participation of their representatives in the application of indigenous policies by the state; the legal protection of their lands and waters; and the granting of fiscal lands or private lands acquired by the state in order to end the process by which the members of their communities were kept as uneducated peasants and lower-class workers. What was needed was to allow for the expansion of their lands and support for the economic and cultural development of their people and communities.

Aware of the need to assume Chilean society's debt to the indigenous peoples, and with the purpose of reaching a new stage in the relations between the Chilean state and the indigenous peoples, we supported in 1989 the statement of a commitment to their most representative organizations which was known as the Acuerdo del Nuevo Imperial,[3] or Agreement of the New Empire. In that agreement, the signers expressed a willingness to work together in order to achieve the constitutional recognition of the indigenous peoples and of their fundamental economic, social, and cultural rights.

In fulfillment of that agreement, the government, which later achieved the triumph of the Reconciliation of Parties for Democracy (Concertación de Partidos por la Democracia, Aylwin 1990–94), created the Special Commission for the Indigenous Peoples (Comisión Especial de Pueblos Indígenas, CEPI), which was made up of representatives of the different indigenous peoples in the country. This entity elaborated, by means of a process that included the active participation of indigenous communities throughout the country, a previous project of legal and constitutional reform. Based on this work carried out by CEPI, the government proposed, for the consideration of the National Congress, a legal project to acknowledge the indigenous peoples and their rights, and another project for the reform of the political constitution with the same purpose. To this was added a project for ratifying settlement number 169 of the International Organization of Work (Organización Internacional del Trabajo, OIT) on the indigenous peoples in independent countries (1989).

Unfortunately, the last two initiatives did not find, among the opposing conservative sectors represented in the National Congress, the openness that the indigenous organizations had hoped for. The only proposal that was approved by Parliament was law number 19.253, of October 1993, advancing the protection, promotion, and development of the indigenous peoples. The initiative for the constitutional recognition of the indigenous peoples, as well as ratification of agreement number 169 of the OIT (1989) dealing with their rights, did not have the support of the opposing parliaments, and even now has not been approved.

The law 19.253—for the protection, promotion, and development of the indigenous peoples—which is fully in force, was considered in its moment a historic marker that put an end to the legislation supporting integration that up until then had ruled in Chile. Under this law, the indigenous peoples, their ethnic background,[4] and their communities are recognized, as well as the duty of the state and of society to respect, protect, and promote their development and that of their cultures. Additionally, the indigenous lands are protected by mechanisms established for their expansion through a fund for indigenous lands. The development of the indigenous peoples is promoted through the establishment of a fund for that purpose. Indigenous cultures and languages are recognized through the creation of intercultural bilingual educational programs for indigenous students. Finally, indigenous participation is promoted in the definition and implementation of policies relating to the indigenous world by the creation of the National Corporation for the Development of the Indigenous Peoples (Corporación Nacional de Desarrollo Indígena, or CONADI), a bipartisan integrated organization of the government and the indigenous peoples which is in charge of implementing public policy on this matter.

THE PUBLIC POLICY DEVELOPED UNDER THE INDIGENOUS LAW

On the basis of the law approved at the end of the first democratic government after the dictatorship, an important effort has been developed by the state with the cooperation of indigenous organizations, for the purpose of rendering effective the rights recognized in it for the indigenous peoples, and establishing a more just relationship and solidarity among them, the state, and the rest of the civic society. In this way CONADI inspired a policy that in many aspects benefited the indigenous peoples and their communities. A highlight among their activities would be the actions dealing with the lands, which, up to 2002, allowed the acquisition, clearing, and/or regularization of more than six hundred thousand acres for the benefit of more than ten thousand indigenous families.[5] Another important action was the activities created for indigenous development and culture, which have been made stronger in the last years since the Origins Program (Programa Orígenes) began to function.[6]

Nevertheless, there were limitations to this policy—insufficient resources were marked by the state for its implementation, and the number of indigenous urban sectors included in it (which today are in the majority) were too few. Above all, however, insufficient attention was given to the indigenous reaction before projects from public and private investments were implemented in indigenous areas, among them projects for highways and hydroelectric power. This generated conflict between the state and the indigenous peoples toward the end of 1990s. This conflict was manifested in several ways, such as the occupation of roads and pieces of land that had been reclaimed. The indigenous communities, particularly the Mapuche, were very active in showing their disapproval of such investment projects, and in recovering ancestral lands usurped by nonindigenous people.

The conflict was expressed also in actions on the part of the state resulting in the detention and prosecution of a significant number of indigenous persons involved in the occupation of roads and land. Beyond the need to maintain public order, which is the duty of all authority, the action by the state has been questioned by the indigenous peoples, as well as more recently by the Special Rapporteur of the United Nations for the Rights of the Indigenous Peoples. So through this action by the state, the conflict, which in its origin was essentially political, became judicialized.

THE COMMISSION FOR HISTORICAL TRUTH AND
A NEW AGREEMENT

In this context the government of President Lagos decided in 2001 to create the Commission for Historical Truth and a New Agreement (La Comisión de Verdad Histórica y Nuevo Trato).[7] It was about a greater challenge, in which we feel it is our duty to participate, due to our conviction that the Chilean state and society must make the maximum effort to establish new forms of relationships that will be more just and in solidarity with the indigenous peoples, based on the acknowledgment of mistakes in the past and on reciprocal respect.

Following the presidential order, the commission conducted a historical analysis of the relationship between the original peoples, the state, and Chilean society; the next step was to carry out a series of recommendations directed to the "advancement towards a new agreement of the Chilean society and its re-encounter with the indigenous peoples." After almost three years of activity, not without complexities and misunderstandings on the part of some sectors, the commission laid out its final report in October 2003.

At its core, the report from the Commission for Historical Truth and a New Agreement gives a review of the history of our indigenous peoples and of their relationship with the Chilean state. Following a synthesis of modern reality, it offers a group of proposals and recommendations to facilitate the possibility of a new agreement between the state and the indigenous peoples.

In the historical part, the report acknowledges that the indigenous peoples are the "first peoples" to inhabit the territory that Chile occupies today, that their history is extensive and dates back thousands of years. It attests that the "European invasion" of its ancestral territories, although a civilizing and religious project (the Conquest), was carried out by means of military actions of great violence, and introduced sicknesses against which the indigenous peoples did not have any defenses. It affirms that in this colonial order, the indigenous peoples almost always occupied a place of subordination. The report describes the liberal concepts that directed, from the beginning, the republic's action toward these people and their components. It identifies the policies imposed by the state between 1881 and 1931 which led to the military occupation of Araucanía and the appropriation of the Mapuche territory, to the incorporation of Rapa Nui into the Chilean territory, and to the expansion of herds through the policy of concessions toward the territories of the Austral peoples, describing them as "liquidationist" policies or "forced assimilation" policies. And finally, the report identifies the period between 1931 and 1971 as one of "frustrated integration."

The report maintains that the principal objective of the government policies toward the indigenous peoples in this period could have been characterized less by the development of actions leading to physical extermination, but more by promoting the indigenous peoples' integration into Chilean society. According to the commission's report, it was a frustrated objective because, at that time, the indigenous voices began to be heard in defense of their identity and rights.

A paragraph from the report summarizes the commission's view of the past relationship of the state with the indigenous peoples:

> Both processes—that of negating the identity and existence of the indigenous peoples in favor of the formation of a single national identity, and that of appropriation of their territory in favor of the consolidation of the national territory—even though they were successful in their objective of serving the formation of the Chilean State/Nation, they had consequences that last even to the present—in some cases disastrous ones—for the indigenous peoples, as it can be abundantly proved by the data that the commission has examined and is evident in this report: territorial reduction, social fragmentation, loss of patrimony, loss of enforcement of their own normative systems, loss of their languages for policies forcing the use of Spanish, and even the death and disappearance of entire indigenous peoples as the Aónikenk and Selk'nam, who were the object of a true genocide since, together with the extinction of their culture, they also annihilated the persons that formed those peoples.[8]

On the basis of these antecedents the commission proposes that the state ratify the agreement given to the indigenous peoples up to now and that a new agreement be inspired by "the respect, equity, mutual acknowledgment, justice, and dignity of all its members."

If the new agreement is conceived in this way—according to the commission—it will demand institutional improvements that would allow the healing of damages done to the indigenous peoples, the improvement of the national juridical order with the purpose of establishing a basis on which a new relationship could be founded, and the establishment of efficient mechanisms for the full achievement of the goals.

In accordance with these principles, the commission recommends improving the political constitution of the state in such a way that it declares "the existence of the indigenous peoples, which form part of the nation of Chile, and acknowledges that they have their own culture and identity." It further acknowledges "that the indigenous peoples of Chile are descendants of the pre-colonial societies which developed in the territory on which the present state of Chile holds its sovereignty, to which they are linked by historical continuity." Moreover, the improved constitution "establishes the duty of the state to guarantee the preservation of the diversity of the cultural ethnicity of the nation and, consequently, the preservation and exercise of the culture and identity of the indigenous peoples, with full respect for the autonomy of its members; and that in accord with said declaration, it acknowledges and guarantees the exercise of a set of collective rights in favor of the indigenous peoples."[9]

Among the collective rights that the commission recommends be constitutionally protected, the report points out the following: political rights, which include, among others, the election of representatives of the indigenous peoples for the Senate and the House; the participation of the indigenous peoples and their integration in government and business structures at the community and regional level; the acknowledgment of the institutions and organizational units proper to each one of the indigenous peoples; and the participation of the indigenous peoples in the discussion, formulation, implementation, and evaluation of laws, policies, and programs that affect their cultures, institutions, territories, and resources.

In regard to territorial rights, the commission acknowledges and demarcates indigenous territories and the rights of indigenous towns to participate in the governance of such spaces. Also in this matter it acknowledges the right of protection of the lands belonging to the indigenous peoples, the demarcation, entitlement, and protection of those lands on which the ancestral indigenous ownership can be proved, and the establishment of mechanisms for reclaiming lands. Additionally, the report acknowledges a set of rights for the indigenous peoples over the natural resources that are found in their lands and territories, which include the right to ownership, use, administration, and benefits. Together with these rights, the report proposes the right of preference for obtaining concessions from the state for the exploitation of natural resources that are found in indigenous territories and lands; rights of protection for the ecosystems, panoramic beauties, and other patrimonial resources needed for their economic and cultural development; and rights for the use, management, and preservation of natural resources found in rural areas protected by the state.

In relation to public and private investment projects in indigenous territories and lands, the report proposes acknowledging the right to be consulted, the right to participate in the social and economic benefits of productive activities on indigenous lands and territories, and the right to compensation for damages caused. In reference to cultural rights, it proposes acknowledging the collective right of the indigenous peoples to take part in the education of their members; the promotion of intercultural education in the regions of indigenous population; the economic, social, cultural, and religious rights and practices of the indigenous peoples, as well as of their customary rights as indigenous peoples.

The report also includes a set of specific proposals in relation to each indigenous people in particular, including a statute about autonomy for Isla de Pascua in favor of the Rapa Nui, and the creation of a corporation for reparations to respond to the claims over lands coming from titles granted by the state to the Mapuche people, suggesting different mechanisms, such as conciliation and expropriation, to try to resolve such claims. Finally, the report proposes the approval and ratification, according to what is needed, of international instruments on the subject of indigenous rights.[10]

Beyond its reception by different political sectors of Chilean society, some of which questioned the report harshly, claiming its proposed policies would favor the formation of ghettos and could threaten the unified state, the report constitutes, in our opinion, a historical document. By reading it, one is able to learn another history, that of the conquered, which up until now has not been told by Chilean history. Beginning with such history, the report points out ethical, juridical-political, and economic-social guidelines by which in the future—let us hope the near future—the most harmonious fellowship can be established with the indigenous peoples in the country, no longer based on imposition and on denial of their past, but on the acknowledgment and respect of their ethnic and cultural diversity in the present time.

SOCIAL TEACHINGS OF THE CHURCH AND THE INDIGENOUS PEOPLES

The social teachings of the Catholic Church give us important guidance as we consider the challenges that the indigenous peoples place before today's Latin American societies. As we know, the discussion within the church of the treatment by the colonizers of the indigenous people is very old. Already in the sixteenth century, Bartolomé de Las Casas vehemently questioned the institutions forced on the indigenous peoples in America—like the *encomienda*—as well as the abuses committed against them by Hispanic authorities in the newly formed colonies. Las Casas argued that the papal bulls justifying the European presence in the New World had as a central objective the conversion of the original population to Christianity. He affirmed, nevertheless, that they did not grant to Spain coercive powers to carry out this task, questioning the use of war against the indigenous peoples, as well as the servitude to which they were subjected. Las Casas argued that natural rights should be given to the whole of humanity, including the indigenous peoples. In agreement with this view, he proposed that the indigenous population of America share the same rights as other populations, and for the same reason neither their lands nor their freedom could be snatched away.

Almost five centuries later, the church forcefully gathers the essence of the words of Las Casas, defending the cultural identity and the rights of the indigenous peoples when these are not recognized by others. Thus John Paul II, addressing the indigenous peoples of Canada, affirmed, "The Church proclaims equal dignity of all peoples and defends their right to maintain their own cultural identity with their different traditions. The Church extols the equal human dignity of all peoples and defends their right to uphold their own cultural character with its distinct traditions and customs."[11] During his visit to Chile in the 1980s, the pope addressed the Mapuche people in Araucanía, affirming with great prophetic strength, "In defending your identity, you are not only exercising a right, but you are fulfilling a duty: the obligation to transmit your culture to the generations to come, in this way enriching the whole Chilean Nation, with your well-known values: the love of the land, the unquenchable love for freedom, and the unity of your families."[12]

Since the Second Vatican Council the church in Latin America has developed a ministry to the indigenous peoples based on the option for the poor which was adopted at the general conferences of the bishops at Medellín (1968) and at Puebla (1979). By means of such pastoral ministry, the church has demonstrated the complex social reality of the indigenous peoples, and at the same time has valued their cultural richness.

A highlight of this ministry was the celebration of the fifth centenary of the arrival of the Spaniards in America. On that occasion, the General Assembly of the Latin American bishops which took place in Santo Domingo in 1992, after asking pardon for "the sin, the injustice, and the violence" committed during those five hundred years of Christian presence in the continent, proposed the development of an "inculturated evangelization" as a new model for pastoral ministry in the continent. According to the bishops, such evangelization should be developed in dialogue with the culture of each people, strengthening their values and denouncing the powers of sin and the injustices that threaten them.[13]

This perspective has also directed the action of the Chilean church in its work with the indigenous peoples. In this way, the church accompanied the indigenous organizations, in the context of the military dictatorship, in defense of the rights that had been violated. Later it supported the process that led to the approval of new indigenous legislation in 1993. In 2000 the Catholic bishops asked pardon for the damage caused to the Mapuche people. In a pastoral letter in 2002, they tried to understand the conflicts that involve the Mapuche people in the south of the country. The essence of the church's message in this pastoral letter is clear:

> We want to join ourselves, with creativity, to this new dynamic that is born from the acknowledgment of the ethnic and cultural plurality of our country. With humility, we have acknowledged, when doing the "purification of the memory" to which his Holiness John Paul II invited us, that in the past many Christians collaborated by their practice or by their silence in the implantation of policies of assimilation or marginalization of the original peoples. Today, following those of our brothers and sisters who assumed the cause of defending the indigenous peoples, we want to contribute creatively to the dignification of the original peoples, and we commit ourselves, from the values of the Kingdom which we announce, to the building up of a more just and fraternal society.[14]

This perspective has enlightened our action in this task. From diverse generations and experiences, and including those from contingent perspectives, sometimes opposing ones, we have agreed that Latin American societies, and more particularly the Chilean society and state, should put an end to the marginalization and discrimination of which, for a long time, the indigenous peoples have been the object due to their ethnicity and cultures. We also agree that the states should not only recognize juridically their diversity and recognize themselves as spaces that are ethnically and culturally plural, but also that they should establish concrete mechanisms and enforce policies that would allow the indigenous peoples to assume greater degrees of control over their own lives, participating in the decisions of the state that affect them and adopting their own decisions within their communities and territorial spaces.

The question is one of elemental justice, which regrettably, is not always welcomed by some members of Latin American societies who, because of egoism or fear, insist in imposing schemas that result in the political, economic, and social denial and exclusion of the indigenous peoples and of those who form part of it. The task of building up just societies in Latin America happens in a significant way because of the acknowledgment and valuing of our indigenous roots, which after five centuries of European presence, continue to live not only in the population that recognizes itself as the original one, but also among those who have *mestiza* blood.

As long as we do not acknowledge each other in our cultural identity and difference, we will continue to be stratified and exclusionary societies as we have been throughout the course of history. The doctrine on human rights and the social teachings of the Catholic Church, so clearly expressed by the Latin American bishops in recent decades, give very important guidelines that will direct the action of future generations as they respond to this issue, which, in our opinion, will surely be one of the greatest challenges in the twenty-first century.

We hope that future generations will make these teachings their own and will be able to deepen the changes that we have begun to introduce in Latin America and in Chile in recent years, in favor of a more just interethnic and intercultural fellowship, and in solidarity among the different sectors that make up their societies, among them the indigenous peoples.

NOTES

We gratefully acknowledge the assistance of Sr. Rosa Maria Icaza in translating this essay from the Spanish.

1. Program of the United Nations for Development (Programa de Naciones Unidas para el Desarrollo) (PNUD), University of the Border and MIDEPLAN, *Indice de Desarrollo Humano en la Población Mapuche de la Región de la Araucanía,* PNUD, Topics on Sustainable Development no. 8, 2003.

2. Rodolfo Stavenhagen (Special Reporter ONU), "Informe del Relator Especial sobre la situación de los derechos humanos y libertades fundamentales de los indígenas, Misión a Chile," Economic Social Council of the UN l, E/CN.4/2004/80 Add. 3, Nov. 17, 2003, para. 16.

3. Such an agreement was signed by Patricio Aylwin, in the name of Concertación de Partidos por la Democracia, and by representatives of various Mapuche, Aymara and Rapa Nui organizations.

4. Sadly, the Congress rejected the term *pueblo* considered in the project of the law.

5. Literally 250,000 hectares. 1 hectare = 2.47105381 acres; and 250,000 hectares is 617,750 acres.

6. A program that totals, with money from the United States, $130,000, of which $80,000 is given by the BID.

7. The commission was presided over by Patricio Aylwin and was made up of well-known representatives of Chilean society and of various indigenous peoples in Chile.

8. Commission for Historical Truth and New Agreement, *Report of the Commission for Truth and New Agreement with the Indigenous Peoples* (Santiago: La Nación, 2003), Cuerpo III, 126. Available at http://www.gobierno.cl/verdad historica/indice.html.

9. Ibid., 127.

10. Ibid., 127–38.

11. The full text of Pope John Paul II's 1987 speech to the indigenous peoples of Canada can be found at http://www.vatican.va/holy_father/john _paul_ii/speeches/1987/september/documents/hf_jp-ii_spe_19870920_indigeni -fort-simpson_en.html.

12. The full text of Pope John Paul II's 1987 speech to the Mapuche people in Chile can be found at http://www.mapuche-nation.org/english/html/news /n-110.htm.

13. In National Commission for Pastoral Ministry with Indigenous Peoples of the Bishops' Conference in Chile, *Al Servicio de un Nuevo Trato con el Pueblo Mapuche,* Nov. 2002. Available at http://documentos.iglesia.cl/conf/doc_pdf.php ?mod=documentos_sini&id=44.

14. See http://documentos.iglesia.cl/conf/doc_pdf.php?mod=documentos _sini&id=44, p. 2.

CHAPTER 6

Option for the Poor and Option for the Earth

Toward a Sustainable Solidarity

STEPHEN BEDE SCHARPER

On December 3, 1984, at five past midnight, tons of noxious gas from Union Carbide's pesticide plant spewed into the city of Bhopal, India, forming a deadly, enveloping fog. Thousands of women, children, men, parents, and grandparents died agonizing deaths that night—close to 3,800 persons, according to Union Carbide. Approximately 160,000 Bhopal citizens were treated within twenty-four hours in the local hospital, gasping for air, their eyes burning, their throats singed with poison gas, all in wrenching pain. Over 8,000 residents, according to local doctors, perished within the next week. In addition, thousands of domesticated animals, migratory birds, and countless wildlife also perished. It remains the worst industrial accident in history.[1]

If this were the end of the story, it would be sufficient tragedy for a lifetime. Yet the horror continues. Twenty years later, the people of Bhopal are still dying from the effects of the Union Carbide disaster, drinking the contaminated water, eating fish from Bhopal's picturesque but now toxic lakes, and remaining exposed to deadly chemicals that have yet to be cleaned up. Deformed and stillborn children are commonplace in Bhopal, and visitors note few households without someone acutely ill or dying. Some estimate the fatality toll now lies between 16,000 and

30,000, with more than 500,000 inhabitants "injured for life" by the toxic release.[2] Recent medical studies even suggest long-term genetic effects from the gas leaks. Both the Indian government and Dow Chemical, who later bought Union Carbide, consider the matter closed, having achieved a $470 million cash settlement in May 1989.

Welcomed to Bhopal in 1968, the Union Carbide pesticide plant was part of the "green revolution," an initiative to help India and other developing nations achieve agricultural independence through industrial agricultural scientific advances. Framed within a developmentalist approach to economic progress, as marked by U.S. President John F. Kennedy's Alliance for Progress and the United Nations Decade for Development, such programs were heralded as vehicles for initiative, self-reliance, and economic prosperity for underdeveloped nations of the south. Yet, as in Bhopal, so many of these strategies have led to deepening poverty and ecological destruction.

Bhopal is but one notorious example of the deepening suffering that certain development agendas have rendered in nations of the south, where promises of prosperity often yield economic and ecological despair for many generations to come. Bhopal is thus a fitting starting point for a consideration of the nexus among poverty, social justice, and environmental despoliation.

Liberation theology, using the social sciences and attempting to read the Bible through the prisms of the poor, brought an important critique to this developmentalist agenda. By adopting a preferential option for the poor, liberation theologians were able to identify both the economic bias toward the affluent and the failed promises of prosperity ensuing from developmentalist designs. In this essay, I will explore how the option for the poor represents: (a) a perduring challenge to environmental studies, particularly the notion of sustainable development; (b) a foundational critique of the notion of modernity; and (c) a guiding cairn on the path of integrating issues of social justice and ecological sustainability. The preferential option for the poor, as enunciated by Latin American liberation theologians and later elaborated in ecclesial, theological, and philosophical praxis and reflection, is a foundational concept. In other words, it is a core, rather than peripheral, precept for religious reflection, and can also be one, I believe, for environmental studies. As one who toils in both the areas of religious studies and of environmental studies, I wish here to propose that the option for the poor is perhaps one of the most fertile and perduring grounds in which both religious and environmental studies might sink and extend their roots.

OPTION FOR THE POOR: WHAT IS IT?

In order to opt for the poor, one must be nonpoor. In other words, one must be in a privileged position to choose a stance of solidarity; after all, one cannot opt for what one already is. In this sense, the option for the poor, as originally understood, is an opportunity for engaged compassion of the economically and socially privileged with the economically and socially marginalized. Irish theologian Donal Dorr explains the concept this way: "An 'option for the poor,' in the sense in which it is intended here, means a series of choices, personal or communal, made by individuals, by communities, or even by corporate entities such as a religious congregation. . . . It is a choice to disentangle themselves from servicing the interest of those at the 'top' of society and to begin instead to come in to solidarity with those at or near the bottom."[3] Not surprisingly, one of the most succinct definitions of the preferential option for the poor is provided by Peruvian theologian and pastor Gustavo Gutiérrez, "the founding father," if you will, of the theology of liberation. Gutiérrez breaks down the phrase to component parts: poverty and option.

Poverty, he notes, while consisting of social, economic, and political deprivation, ultimately signifies "death, unfair death, the premature death of the poor; physical death."[4] He writes: "In the last analysis, the poverty that is lived in Latin America means a situation of premature and unjust death, from hunger and illness or from the repressive methods used by those who are defending their privileges. Besides physical death there is cultural death from 'the devaluation of races and cultures and from the refusal to recognize the full dignity of women.'"[5] Gutiérrez notes that anthropologists like to say that culture is life: "if a culture is despised, then that life is despised."[6] Moreover, cultural death often marches arm in arm with physical death. "That is why," Gutiérrez continues, "Christian communities in Latin America often speak of the God of Life and reject unjust physical and cultural death as well as other manifestations of selfishness and sin."[7]

What is meant by "the poor?" Gutiérrez notes that the poor are the insignificant, those with no ecclesial or societal heft. He writes the poor person is "the one who must wait a week at the door of the hospital to see a doctor. A poor person is one without social or economic weight, who is robbed by unjust laws; someone who has no way of speaking up or acting to change the situation. Someone who belongs to a despised race and feels culturally marginalized is *in-significant*. In sum, the poor are found in the statistics, but they do not appear there with their own names. We do not know the names of the poor; they are anonymous and remain so. They are insignificant in society but not before God."[8] Gutiérrez provides a compelling eyewitness account of the insignificance of the poor. Participating in the funeral of Archbishop Oscar Romero in San Salvador in 1980, Gutiérrez notes that about forty persons were killed as shots and explosions shattered the celebration in the cathedral plaza.

In his groundbreaking study *A Theology of Liberation: History, Politics, and Salvation,* Gutiérrez developed a compelling notion of liberation with three interrelated, interdependent dimensions: (1) the hope of poor and oppressed persons to achieve economic, social, cultural, and political liberation; (2) the historical reality of poor persons taking the reins of their own destinies and experiencing their agency as historical subjects; and (3) the emancipation, through Jesus Christ, from the bondage of sin.[9]

For Gutiérrez, liberation is a result of what was, in the 1960s, a new political consciousness in Latin America. "Liberation," he noted, "means shaking off the yoke of economic, social, political, and cultural domination to which we have been submitted."[10] In delineating the features of this domination, Gutiérrez and other liberation theologians sought reading assistance from social scientists, especially those who both articulated and critiqued developmentalist economic theory. Noting how international development projects represented a profound and powerful social, economic, cultural, psychological, and even ontological and spiritual agenda, Gutiérrez critiqued key tenets of developmentalist theory, as espoused by such prominent developmentalist theorists as Walt W. Rostow, Alex Inkeles, David McClelland, and Talcott Parsons. He noted how such theorists claimed that societies progressed from preliterate to modern market economies in stages,[11] and that people of underdeveloped nations had to be involved in projects of political maturation to become modern persons, whose traits included a developed sense of punctuality, a more serious interest in efficiency, and a propensity to view the world as calculable.[12] Some claimed that self-reliance and an achievement orientation were essential characteristics of the modern person, arguing that if certain underdeveloped nations could be infused with the need for achievement, entrepreneurial zip would begin to spur economic development.[13] Others, espousing an evolutionary approach like Rostow, suggested that the economics of the first world represented the apogee of the evolutionary process, and underdeveloped nations must be helped on their road to develop *just like* the developed nations.[14]

In all the above designs, the development process was seen as universally applicable, regardless of social, cultural, religious, or ecological context. The developmentalist approach suggested that if a state were merely to create a set of conditions, follow a carefully proscribed developmentalist agenda (and just "add water"), a nation could almost automatically achieve development.

Yet the historical reality failed to follow the theoretical script. As became strikingly evident by the end of the 1960s, the harvest of this agenda was increasingly grim. Ten years of developmentalist projects, green revolution agriculture, and industrialization had yielded not the bright promise of prosperity, but trade imbalances, escalating debt, higher infant mortality, lower life expectancy, and a yawning gap between rich and poor.[15] In short, the developmentalist dream was becoming a nightmare. Moreover, the environmental front fared little better than the socioeconomic one: increasing deforestation, urban industrial pollution, and soil and water contamination from chemical-based agriculture were but a few of development's legacies in nations of the south. Significantly, the developmentalist theoreticians had not only failed to take into account local social, political, economic, and cultural contexts in the regions they sought to improve, they also neglected on the whole to consider their ecological contexts, and viewed nature largely as a neutral backdrop on which to paint their master plans of modernization, providing limitless resources and receptacles for waste.

Building on the core-periphery model of Andre Gunder Frank,[16] who argued that underdevelopment in Latin America was a direct consequence of world capitalist development, with the core exploiting the periphery, liberation theologians and philosophers increasingly viewed development and underdevelopment as Siamese twins rather than distant relatives. In other words, you cannot have one without the other. Nations do not evolve out of this system into the bracing dawn of abundance and economic independence, but rather are locked into a world system, as social theorist Immanuel Wallerstein would argue, of exploitative, dependent economic relationships.[17]

Development leads to dependence, a situation in which the plurality of Latin Americans found themselves by the mid-1960s. Development, for Gutiérrez, finds its true meaning only in the more universal, profound, and radical perspective of *liberation,* which emphasizes the conflictual aspect of economic, social, and political processes.[18] Gutiérrez, in rejecting developmentalism, which had been offered as a balm for the impoverished of Latin America, sought a different term, one that would capture the hopes and aspirations of persons at the bottom and speak to the conflictual nature of society. He chose the term *liberation* in part as an antidote to development.

Rather than an abstract and ahistorical agenda imposed from above, the notion of liberation, generated by those locked in dependence, takes into account society's political, social, and economic struggles, and represents more accurately, Gutiérrez argues, the aspirations of those on the underside of history.

Gutiérrez, however, also had a strong theological rationale for adopting the notion of liberation. Just as he rejected developmentalist economics, so too did he renounce developmentalist theology. Referring to the "theology" of development, Gutiérrez observes that the mode of theological reflection remains unchanged: "The error of development . . . is not a questioning of a type of intelligence of faith; it is not theological reflection in the context of the liberation process; it is not critical reflection from and on the historical praxis of liberation, from and on faith as liberation praxis. To theologize thus will require a change of perspective."[19] For Gutiérrez, the change in perceptive is encapsulated in the term *liberation.*

Moreover, the poverty identified by Latin American liberationist thought in the 1960s continues into the present under the banner of globalization, as exiled Argentinean liberation philosopher Enrique Dussel contends:

Above all, the *reality* out of which such a [liberation] philosophy emerged is today more pressing than ever before in its continuous and maddening spiral of underdevelopment: the misery, the poverty, the exploitation of the oppressed of the global periphery (in Latin America, Africa, or Asia), of the dominated classes, of the marginalized, of the "poor" in the "center," and the African-Americans, Hispanics, Turks, and others, to whom we would have to add women as sexual objects, the "useless" aged gathered in misery or in asylums, the exploited and drugged up youth, the silenced popular and national cultures and all the "wretched of the earth," as Franz Fanon put it, who wait and struggle for their liberation.[20]

In opting for the poor, a liberationist perspective asks *why* people are poor—a key and unsettling query that helped prompt Gutiérrez and others to look at social scientific systems of development and underdevelopment. The poor are not poor because it is God's will, it was argued, but because of structural injustices. They are not underdeveloped persons; rather, they are fully developed persons who are exploited by unjust economic, social, and spiritual oppression. For Gutiérrez, while sin is always a personal and free act, it is also the rupture of friendship between God and humanity and between ourselves and others. It thus has a profoundly social dimension in the liberationist gaze, for such personal sin leads to unjust social, political, and economic structures. Hence, building on the social gospel theology of Walter Rauschenbusch and others, liberation theologians spoke in terms of "social" or "structural" sin,[21] concepts affirmed and explored in subsequent magisterial documents.

When applied to the realm of environmental studies, such queries prompt one to ask, why is there such devastating soil erosion, air pollution, ozone depletion, acid rain, toxic waste sites, and species extinction? Is it simply God's will that humans are destroying the earth, the natural consequence of human progress, or does it pertain to social and political sin, owing to certain economic, political, and cultural systems? The option for the poor compels environmentalists to connect the processes that dehumanize persons to those that denude landscapes. Is there a connection between clear-cut societies in Darfur and clear-cut forests in British Columbia? Moreover, an option for the poor asks the question, why are aboriginal cultures being destroyed in the Amazon along with the rainforest ecosystem in which they dwell? Is there a connection between opting for the poor and opting for the earth?[22]

OPTION FOR THE POOR: A CHALLENGE TO SUSTAINABLE DEVELOPMENT

As intimated, one area where the option for the poor has particular significance surrounds the notion of "sustainable development." This term was a key feature of the "global agenda for change," addressed to the United Nations General Assembly by the World Commission on Environment and Development in 1987. Headed by Gro Harlem Bruntland, Norway's first woman prime minister, the commission, surveying ecological and socioeconomic devastation around the world, articulated the idea of sustainable development, defined as "meeting the needs of the present without compromising the ability of future generations to meet their own needs."[23]

In many ways the notion of sustainable development is an advance over previous forms of economic progress. It takes into account the need to plan for and think about future generations, and begins to equate social and economic progress with the state of the world's ecosystems. The Bruntland report argued that the "ability to anticipate and prevent environmental damage will require that the ecological dimension of policy be considered at the same time as the economic, trade, energy, agricultural, and other dimensions."[24] For those exposed to articulations of the option for the poor, however, the notion of sustainable development is lined with dire warning labels.[25]

The idea of sustainable development, despite its advances, appears to avoid the political and economic critiques of development, such as dependency theory, which characterize much of the liberationist critique from nations of the south. If, as Andre Gunder Frank maintains, one does not have development without underdevelopment, than arguably one does not have sustainable development without "unsustainable underdevelopment." The fact that the nations of the north have not even achieved sustainable development, yet are now trying to help prescribe sustainable plans for nations of the south, breeds more than a little skepticism in the nonindustrialized world. Add to this that the United States, the world's largest emitter of greenhouse gases, refused, under the administration of George W. Bush, to sign the Kyoto Protocol limiting greenhouse gas emissions, and such skepticism deepens.

The option for the poor suggests that the poor and marginalized of the world not only be taken into account as new economic and ecological stratagems are devised, but that they be prioritized. Without this prioritization, environmental strategy that produces new forms of marginalization for the poor and for endangered and impoverished ecosystems may result.

The Social Affairs Commission of the Canadian Conference of Catholic Bishops expressed this point forcefully in its controversial 1983 statement on Canada's economic recession:

> The need and rights of the poor, the marginalized and the oppressed are given special attention in God's Plan for Creation (WA, n. 4). Throughout his ministry Jesus repeatedly identified with the plight of the poor and the outcasts of society (e.g., Phil 2:6–8; Lk 6:20–21). He also took a critical attitude towards the accumulation of wealth and power that comes through the exploitation of others (e.g., Lk 16:13–15; 12:16–21; Mk 4:19). This has become known as "the preferential option for the poor" in the scriptures. In a given economic order, the needs of the poor take priority over the wants of the rich. . . . This does not mean simply handouts for the poor. It calls instead for an equitable redistribution of wealth and power among peoples and regions.[26]

Moreover, the bishops aver that the poor and marginalized must be included in any decision-making process as well as in economic (or environmental) strategies that will affect their lives or attempt to improve their condition: "As subjects of creation, all peoples have rights to self-determination, to define their own future and to participate effectively in decisions affecting their lives. . . . This is essential if working people, the poor and the marginalized are going to exercise their rights to be subjects of their own history. . . . In effect, the participation of the marginalized takes precedence over an order that excludes them."[27]

ADOPTING AN OPTION FOR THE POOR IN
ENVIRONMENTAL INITIATIVES

This option for the poor can also be used to enhance and critique seem-ingly optimistic environmental campaigns, such as habitat and wildlife conservation projects. Unless poor persons are consulted and prioritized in such policy deliberations, one will have misguided environmental initi-atives, such as Project Tiger, according to Indian environmental scholar Ramachandra Guha. Guha argues such a project is reflective of a U.S. deep ecological perspective that privileges "biocentrism" or "wilderness preservation" over "anthropocentrism" or socioeconomic concerns. While wilderness preservation might be contextually appropriate for U.S. so-ciety given its distinctive demographics and settlement history, it is inap-propriate for India, he claims, with its longstanding human settlement and dense population in which agrarian communities have achieved a "finely balanced" relationship with their natural environments. He argues that Project Tiger, a series of conservation parks hailed internationally as a success, was made possible only by displacing existing villages and their inhabitants. Prompted by former hunters from India's declining feu-dal elite, in concert with the World Wildlife Fund and the International Union for the Conservation of Nature and Natural Resources, the project sought to transplant a U.S.-style park system onto the Indian landscape. Claiming that the resulting parks are geared toward affluent tourists, Guha asserts that the needs of the local population were not taken into account. Consequently, more pressing environmental problems facing India's poor, such as water erosion, fuel, air, and water pollution, have been ignored. Such an import of an American wilderness ethic, Guha maintains, ultimately masks the two most pressing ecological dilemmas facing the world: overconsumption by industrialized nations of the north and urban elites within nations of the south; and growing militarization, manifested both in regional conflicts and in the threat of nuclear annihi-lation.[28]

Just as Gutiérrez and other liberation theologians sounded a tocsin of concern over the developmentalist agenda, so too do Guha and other environmentalists of the south issue a warning against recent sustainable developmentalist stratagems. In both cases, the top-down approach of the empowered nations avoids an appreciation of, or a consultation with, the lived experience and social, economic, cultural, and political context of the marginalized, which in many cases constitute the majority of their intended beneficiaries. In addition, in both cases, the poor involved in the stratagems are not only excluded, but also sometimes further disenfranchised.

Just as the three aspects of liberation—economic, historical, and spiritual—have to be taken together in addressing the needs of impoverished persons, so too do economics, politics, and ecology in dealing with impoverished ecosystems. In a sense, they form a seamless fabric out of which the tapestry of sustainability must be sewn. And unless the stitching of that garment includes the hands and hopes of the marginalized poor, the ultimate fruit of that labor may well be used to diminish the poor further, and the ecosystems within which they dwell. In this sense, the Greek notion of *oikos* (household), from which derive the words "economy" and "ecology," has relevance; no household is sustainable in which the children die of starvation or malnourishment, the pets perish from poisons, and the plants die from neglect or wanton destruction.

OPTION FOR THE POOR AND A CRITIQUE OF MODERNITY: THE EMERGENCE OF A SOCIAL ECOLOGY

The option for the poor, combined with a contextualized concern for destroyed ecosystems, has led liberation theologians such as Leonardo Boff and Ivone Gebara of Brazil to adopt a social ecology, as distinct from a wilderness ecology, in a manner similar to that of Ramachandra Guha. Such an ecology sees a correlation between the "cry of the poor" and the "cry of the earth," and pays special attention to marginalized peoples, such as the aboriginal groups in the Amazon, whose traditional lifeways are razed along with the rainforest in pursuing the commercial interests of ranching, mining, and timber, as well as other enterprises. For Boff, the ecological crisis points to a fundamental crisis of the modern world, erected upon an exploitative economic pattern of development and underdevelopment, whose ultimate harvest is death: "We have never seen death on such a scale today caused by unemployment, low wages, disease, and violence. Dozens of still surviving indigenous peoples are rapidly disappearing. In this way, we shall lose forever forms of humanity of which we have great need."[29] As Boff has pointed out, the preferential option for the poor and oppressed in liberation theology leads to a broader critique of the modern project, the modern self, and our role as humans.

Enrique Dussel has been at the forefront of the critique to which Boff refers and succinctly articulates the liberationist critique of modernity:

> We were conscious of being the "other face" of modernity. Modernity was born in 1492. . . . The centrality of Europe eurocentrism originated when Europe was able to dominate the Arab world, which had been the center of the known world up to the 15th century. The "I," which begins with the "I conquer" of Hernan Cortes or Pizarro, which in fact precedes the Cartesian *ego cogito* by about a century, produces Indian genocide, African slavery, and Asian colonial wars. The majority of today's humanity (the South) is the outer face of modernity; it is neither pre- nor anti- nor post-modern, nor can this South "end" or "realize" such a modernity.[30]

Dussel argues that the notion of the modern self did not begin with René Descartes' celebrated insight "I think therefore I am," but rather with the New World conquistadors' apprehension "I conquer, therefore I am." In vanquishing the great Incan and Aztec empires, the European, Dussel argues, discovered himself and herself as modern, rather than primitive, and therefore superior. In this sense, conquest of the other was inherent to the notion of modernity.

Highlighting an insight of Gutiérrez, Dussel notes that, whereas the European political theologians deal with the oppressed but modern human subject, the liberation theologians deal with the oppressed "non-person" of the south.[31] Dussel, after describing what a liberationist vantage critiques, outlines what it envisions: "We propose a philosophy of liberation of the Other that is beyond the horizon of the economic-political-hegemonic world (fratricide), of the eurocentric communication community (filicide), of the phallic eroticism which castrates women (uxoricide) and last but not least, the subject which uses nature as an exploitable mediation for the valorization of the value of capital (ecocide)."[32] Here Dussel stretches his liberationist philosophy to include the biosphere, and links it with other forms of death. In this, his ecology is one that is simultaneously social, economic, political, and ontological, suggesting that the fault lines of the environmental crisis run along those of social, economic, political, gendered, and cultural oppression.

Liberation theologians such as Dussel, Boff, and Gebara are attempting to construct an "alternative and integral modernity."[33] They are fashioning a social ecology that delineates a social justice framework, adopts a preferential option for the poor, and seeks a holistic integration of these approaches within an appreciation of the earth's ecosystems.

CONSTRUCTIVE ECOLOGICAL RESPONSES TO THE OPTION FOR THE POOR

The theological sparks within Jewish and Christian circles engendered by the ecological crisis, whose flames were fanned by the accusatory 1967 *Science* article "The Historical Roots of Our Ecologic Crisis," by Lynn White, Jr., have moved the debate from a few disparate campfires in the early 1960s to countless large, bright, and well-fueled theological and pastoral bonfires today. The notion of stewardship, for example, has been given considerable attention in theological and magisterial reflection, and Creation-centered spirituality has been influential not only within religious congregations but in public policy debates as well. The National Religious Partnership for the Environment, for example, formed in the early 1990s at the prodding of prominent members of the scientific community, continues to bring Jewish and Christian communities in the United States together to address ecological concerns. The work of Mary Evelyn Tucker and John Grim, founders of the Forum on Religion and Ecology, has resulted in ten volumes on world religions and ecology published through Harvard University, as well as an ecology and justice series that they, along with Leonardo Boff, have spearheaded for Orbis Books. Moreover, the Justice, Peace, and Integrity of Creation Initiative of the World Council of Churches in the 1970s put these three concerns together at an institutional level within the Christian context, and this integration continues with the WCC efforts in addressing climate change under the direction of David Hallman. In Canada, the Faith and the Common Good project, spearheaded by Ted Reeve and Bill Phipps, as well as the Canadian Forum on Religion and Ecology, chaired by Heather

Eaton and James Miller, are also attempting to advance theological reflection and pastoral activity around environmental concerns.[34]

Although these initiatives are diverse and growing, they do not on the whole adopt explicitly a preferential option for the poor. Such an option can be discerned, however, in a variety of ecological initiatives around the world, both faith based and secular, a few of which are worthy of mention here.[35]

The social ecology advocated by Guha and Boff, as well as Indian environmentalist Vandana Shiva, is reflected in the hundreds of social/ environmental groups that have been formed in the last two decades throughout nations of the south, with over five hundred emerging in Latin America alone, most of which are located in cities, and all of which adopt a social ecology that sees poverty as a primary environmental issue.[36]

Ecological Debt

Many of these groups have recently coalesced around the notion of "ecological debt," a dynamic synthesizing of an option for the poor with environmental destruction through the lens of international debt. Citing the historical conquest and colonization of their lands, the appropriation and patenting of their various seeds and ancestral knowledge, the continuing ecological destruction of their nations to fuel foreign debt payments, ecological debt groups note that the nations of the north owe an ecological debt to nations of the south which has not been acknowledged, let alone repaid.

As Aurora Donoso, of Acción Ecológica, in Ecuador, writes, this ecological debt encompasses the "biopiracy" of indigenous seeds and indeed human genetic material, as well as a fostering of consumerism and militarization. Because of the comprehensive nature of this term, as well as the passion that underlies its articulation, Donoso's definition of ecological debt is worth quoting:

> When ancestral knowledge and seeds have been appropriated and utilised.
> When science is used to produce hybrid or genetically modified seeds, breaking reproductive cycles for the benefit of transnational corporations which patent life, and attack the food sovereignty of the peoples. . . .

When toxic waste is produced and deposited in Third World countries, especially in the poorest areas.

When the illegitimate, inhuman, and immoral external debt, which has already been paid, is used to enslave people to the service of capital and to sustaining this flow of natural goods, cheap labour, and financial resources from South to North. . . .

When the desecration of life has reached such a point that the industrialised countries have even stolen the genes of the most isolated indigenous communities for the human genome project. . . .

All these forms of appropriation, destruction, and alteration of life, carried out principally by the industrialised countries of the North, are what we call the ecological debt, which those countries owe to the countries of the Third World and the planet.[37]

U'wa Defense Working Group

While ecological concerns raised by the ecological debt groups are often based on Christian and liberal democratic, social justice values, indigenous traditions are also expressed in such struggles. The U'wa, an indigenous community of approximately five thousand people, is a case in point. The U'wa, who live in the sensitive and endangered cloud forest ecosystem of northeast Colombia have been struggling, in recent years, to protect their territory and culture from the development plans of both the Colombian government and Occidental Petroleum, a U.S.-based corporation that obtained an oil-drilling license in 1992 for U'wa land.[38] In the U'wa cosmology, oil is the blood of Mother Earth; to extract it, therefore, is matricide.[39] An U'wa statement was delivered in 1998: "We will in no way sell our Mother Earth, to do so would be to give up our work of collaborating with the spirits to protect the heart of the world, which sustains and gives life to the rest of the universe, it would be to go against our own origins and those of all existence."[40] Having witnessed the unsavory results of oil drilling in other territories (deforestation, oil spills, pollution, loss of culture, and military violence), the U'wa perceive the drilling project as a form of cultural and environmental death. Since 1999 the U'wa have resisted the drilling through civil disobedience, spiritual fasting, and permanent assembly of traditional leaders. Such peaceful protests, however, have been met with violence. In February and June of

2001, nonviolent U'wa demonstrations at the drilling site were violently raided by Colombian police, who killed several children and injured scores of adults. Since their resistance to the drilling commenced, the U'wa have inspired a solidarity movement in almost two dozen countries worldwide.[41]

The Chipko Movement

While not centered on external debt or oil drilling, the Chipko movement, beginning in 1973, also critiques certain aspects of development. Building on the Hindu tradition of *satyagraha,* or nonviolent "soulforce," the Chipko movement in the Indian Himalayas strives "to protect local forests and the people that dwell in them from contract logging, abusive resin-tapping, and other destructive land-use practices or development projects through nonviolent resistance efforts."[42] Employing the practice of hugging trees in order to save them from loggers, Chipko activists exhibit a reverence for nature and use such religious practices as the recitation of Hindu writings and ritual performance during protests.[43] A grassroots movement primarily of impoverished rural women, Chipko puts the rights of subsistence harvesting from the forest against the larger corporate and governmental development interests, and in this represents a movement of and for poor persons and their traditional relationship with the forest.

Ecology Monks

A small group of Buddhist monks in Thailand, known informally as "ecology monks" (*phra nak anuraksa*) discern a nexus between the provenance of suffering (ignorance, greed, and hatred) and ecological despoliation.[44] Deeming environmental activism to be part of their duties as Buddhist monastics, they have adapted traditional rituals and ceremonies to "conscienticize" about the value of nature and its current destruction and galvanize Buddhists to join conservation initiatives. Tree ordination rituals (*buat ton mai*), in which trees are blessed and swathed in saffron robes to denote their sacred status, are reflective of a broader initiative to nourish a conservation ethic springing from Buddhist principles.[45] Monks such as Phrakhru Pitak Nanthakun, Phrakhru

Manas Natheepitak, and Phrakhru Prajak Kuttajitto have coordinated a broad array of grassroots conservation projects, including tree ordinations and planting ceremonies, the establishment of wildlife preserves and sacred community gardens, "long-life" rituals for ecologically jeopardized areas, and sustainable community development and sustainable farming.[46] Ecology monks, like members of the U'wa and Chipko groups, have taken stands against deforestation and pipeline construction, and have also protested environmentally harmful shrimp farming, dam construction, and cash-crop agriculture. Phrakhru Pitak, for example, has set up a nongovernmental organization, Hag Muang Nan Group (Love Nan Group), to oversee the environmental efforts of local village groups, government workers, and other NGOs in his home province of Nan.[47] "As respected leaders of Thai society, monks have a crucial role to play in transforming environmentally destructive attitudes and policies. Similarly, the centrality of the temple in Thai village life makes the conservation efforts of rural monks especially effective; thanks to ecologically minded abbots, forest monasteries in Thailand harbor some of the last remaining natural forests."[48]

Green Nuns

Throughout North America and in various countries throughout the world, a number of religious orders are engaging in "ecoministries." Roman Catholic women's religious congregations in particular have for the last three decades made creative attempts to integrate environmental concerns into the heart of their ministries. These groups have rewritten their chapters and reworked their lands to include community-supported agriculture, energy-efficient and nonpolluting technologies such as solar heating; have turned manicured lawns into wild lands; and preserved seeds and restored polluted or degraded landscapes. Just as women's orders were among the first Catholic communities to embrace institutionally and integrate the teachings of Vatican II (1962–65), so too have they been among the first to incorporate environmental concerns systematically and institutionally in their ministries. Known as "green nuns," these women have consistently adopted both a preferential option for the poor and an interest in the wonders and mystery of Creation, particularly inspired by the important new cosmology of "geologian" Thomas Berry and mathematical cosmologist Brian Swimme.[49] Often, these ministries involve poor and inner-city youth in community-supported agriculture projects and donate the first fruits of their harvest to community food banks.

As the green nuns attest, the option for the poor not only animated Christian justice, peace, and solidarity groups within the churches during the 1970s and 1980s, it also arguably led to the church institutional infrastructure through which environmental concerns are now being expressed, as evinced by the WCC's efforts, as well as the linking of ecological work to justice and peace ministries. The option for the poor, in other words, helped form the institutional hook on which the churches would begin to hang ecological concerns. And, through sharing the same ecclesial foothold, tenuous as it may be in certain cases, the mutual interests and interrelation of these two critical initiatives—social justice and ecology—are being explored and expanded.

CONCLUSION

After reviewing some of the contours of the preferential option for the poor and its relevance for environmental activism and reflection, a variety of conclusions can be drawn. Among these:

1. The impoverishment of the human is embedded in, not parallel to, ecological destruction; in other words, both are expressions of the same processes. Poverty, in this sense, is grounded in unequal ecologies.
2. The poor, as nonpersons, are not only eclipsed in a metaphysical, philosophical sense (modernity), but are also often excluded environmentally in conversations and projects about ecological sustainability.
3. Environmental devastation emerges out of (and contributes to) the unequal conditions of power that characterize the world; moreover, such power differentials are not random but rather are historical and structural.
4. Cosmological and religious shifts to a new appreciation of and regard for the earth have to be integrated within a social analysis of how the global-political economy continues to generate ecologically grounded poverty. Ecological cosmologies are thus challenged to embrace political and economic structures, recognizing their origins in cultural ideas and practices.

As the Bhopal tragedy reveals, and the work of environmental groups in nations of the south illustrates, schemes for development are often more disastrous than fruitful. In viewing Bhopal from the perspective of the poor, certain hidden realities are rendered visible: an abundance of cheap labor, the dubious location of a factory near concentrated and indigent populations as well as a critical watershed, and a political system with weak environmental and labor standards—in short, a population and an ecosystem vulnerable in almost all categories. In Bhopal, economic poverty and loss of jobs that affect the residents' livelihood do not only ruin lives; residents now experience their "livinghood" jeopardized as their entire ecosystem is tainted. Even if the citizens of Bhopal now were to get additional jobs or higher wages, their environment is perhaps permanently contaminated. As Bhopal grimly manifests, the option for the poor is not just about economics and politics, it is fundamentally about the environment as well. In Bhopal, marginalization henceforth occurs along economic, political, and ecological trajectories.

In helping articulate a critique of the developmentalist agenda, the option for the poor provides an important, sobering antidote to the promises of economic and political prosperity emanating from northern nations, as well as a caveat specifically to sustainable development stratagems. The option for the poor also raises a perturbing and still largely undigested critique of the modern project itself, out of which most of our academic and environmental studies programs and initiatives spring. This stance forces privileged environmentalists to look at their own ideological and economic biases, and to take seriously the participation of endangered human communities, such as Amazonian tribal peoples, as well as endangered species, in their proposals. This option has also given rise, as suggested, to several challenging and dynamic movements that are trying to integrate issues of poverty and marginalization within an ecological framework, in hopes that the underside of future well-intentioned social and ecological projects might be discerned before their potential is fully expressed.

NOTES

The author wishes to thank Gustavo Gutierrez and Daniel Groody not only for the invitation to contribute to this volume, but also for the cogent commitments to a more just and life-giving world which underlie their work. I also wish to thank my wife, Hilary Cunningham, for her astute insights, editorial support, and her own inspiring witness to a more gracious environment.

1. For a gripping account of the Bhopal tragedy, see Dominique Lapierre and Javier Moro, *Five Past Midnight in Bhopal*, trans. Kathryn Spink (London: Scribner, 2002). See also Martin Regg Cohn, "Death Stalks Bhopal 20 Years Later: 15,300 Killed in Wake of Disaster," *Toronto Star*, Nov. 27, 2004, 1, 22; and Lindalee Tracey, Peter Raymount, and Harold Crooks, prods. and dirs., *Bhopal: The Search for Justice* (Toronto: National Film Board of Canada, Nov. 2004).

2. Lapierre and Moro, *Five Past Midnight in Bhopal*, 202–3.

3. Donal Dorr, *Option for the Poor: A Hundred Years of Catholic Social Teaching*, rev. ed. (Maryknoll, N.Y.: Orbis Books, 1992), 4. Dorr further describes the import of such solidarity, which implies "commitment to working and living within structures and agencies that promote the interests of the less favored sectors of society. These would include those who are economically poor, the groups that are politically marginalized or oppressed, people discriminated against on sexual grounds, peoples that have been culturally silenced or oppressed, and those who have been religiously disinherited or deprived."

4. Gustavo Gutiérrez, from a talk given at University of Montreal, English translation published in *Promotio justitiae* 57, (1994): 14; referenced in *Gustavo Gutiérrez: Essential Writings*, ed. James B. Nickoloff (Maryknoll: Orbis, 1996), 144.

5. Gustavo Gutiérrez, "The Meaning and Scope of Medellín," in *The Density of the Present: Selected Writings* (Maryknoll, N.Y.: Orbis Books, 1999), 98.

6. Gutiérrez, "Option for the Poor: Assessment and Implications," in *Gustavo Gutiérrez: Essential Writings*, 141.

7. Ibid.

8. Ibid.

9. Gustavo Gutiérrez, *A Theology of Liberation: History, Politics and Salvation* (Maryknoll, N.Y.: Orbis Books, 1973), 36–37.

10. Gustavo Gutiérrez, "Contestation in Latin America," in *Contestation in the Church*, ed. T. Jimenez (New York: Herder and Herder, 1971), 43.

11. Walt W. Rostow, *The Stages of Economic Growth: A Non-Communist Manifesto* (London: Oxford University Press, 1962).

12. Alex Inkeles, "The Modernization of Man," in *Modernization: The Dynamics of Growth*, ed. Myron Weiner (New York: Basic Books, 1966), 138–50.

13. David C. McClelland, "The Impulse to Modernize," in *Modernization*, ed. Weiner, 34–35.

14. Talcott Parsons, *Societies: Evolutionary and Cultural Perspectives* (Englewood Cliffs, N.J.: Prentice-Hall, 1966).

15. June Nash, "Ethnographic Aspects of the World Capitalist System," *Annual Review of Anthropology* 10 (1981): 407.

16. See Andre Gunder Frank, *Capitalism and Underdevelopment in Latin America* (New York: Monthly Review Press, 1967), and *Latin America: Underdevelopment or Revolution?* (New York: Monthly Review Press, 1969).

17. Immanuel Wallerstein, *The Modern World System* (New York: Academic, 1975).

18. Gutiérrez, *A Theology of Liberation,* 36.

19. Gustavo Gutiérrez, "Faith as Freedom: Solidarity with the Alienated and Confidence in the Future," *Horizons* 2:1 (Spring 1995): 30–31.

20. Enrique Dussel, *The Underside of Modernity: Apel, Ricoeur, Rorty, Taylor and the Philosophy of Liberation,* trans. and ed. Eduardo Mendieta (Atlantic Highlands, N.J.: Humanities Press, 1996), 2-3. For further critiques of globalization from a liberationist vantage, see Jon Sobrino and Felix Wilfred, eds., *Globalization and Its Victims,* Concilium 5 (2001) (London: SCM Press).

21. Gustavo Gutiérrez, *The Truth Shall Make You Free: Confrontations* (Maryknoll, N.Y.: Orbis Books, 1990), 136–37.

22. For a perturbing account of the destruction of the Amazon rainforest of Brazil and its aboriginal occupants, see Adrian Cowell, dir. and prod., *Decade of Destruction* (Oley, Pa.: Bullfrog Films, 1990).

23. The World Commission on Environment and Development, *Our Common Future* (New York: Oxford University Press, 1987), 43. I am indebted to Ingrid Leman Stefanovic for her fecund critique of sustainable development from a phenomenological perspective.

24. Ibid., 39.

25. The notion of sustainable development has also been critiqued for its basis in "calculative," positivistic thinking rather than more "originative," holistic modes of inquiry, leading to a less than substantive rethinking of the human-earth relationship called for in our present ecological moment. See Ingrid Leman Stefanovic, "Evolving Sustainability: A Rethinking of Ontological Foundations, *Trumpeter Journal of Ecosophy* 8:4 (Fall 1991): 194–200. See also Stefanovic, *Safeguarding Our Common Future: Rethinking Sustainable Development* (Albany: State University of New York Press, 2000).

26. The Episcopal Commission for Social Affairs, Canadian Conference of Catholic Bishops, "Ethical Reflections on the Economic Crisis" (Dec. 22, 1982), reprinted in *Do Justice! The Social Teaching of the Canadian Catholic Bishops,* ed. E. F. Sheridan, S. J. Sherborrke (Montreal and Toronto: Editions Paulines and the Jesuit Centre for Social Faith and Justice, 1987), para. 15, p. 417.

27. Ibid., para. 17, p. 418.

28. Ramachandra Guha, "Radical American Environmentalism and Wilderness Preservation: A Third World Critique, *Environmental Ethics* 11:1 (Spring 1989): 296–305.

29. Leonardo Boff, *Ecology and Liberation: A New Paradigm* (Maryknoll, N.Y.: Orbis Books, 1995), 102. See also Leonardo Boff and Virgil Elizondo, eds.,

Ecology and Poverty: Cry of the Earth, Cry of the Poor. Concilium 5 (Maryknoll, N.Y., and London: SCM Press and Orbis Books, 1995).

30. Dussel, *The Underside of Modernity,* 20.

31. These points are more fully developed in Enrique Dussel, *The Invention of the Americas: Eclipse of the "Other" and the Myth of Modernity* (New York: Continuum, 1995).

32. Dussel, *The Underside of Modernity,* 21.

33. For a fuller discussion of Boff and Gebara, see my *Redeeming the Time* (New York: Continuum, 1997), 165–83. See also Ivone Gebara, *Longing for Running Water: Ecofeminism and Liberation* (Minneapolis: Fortress Press, 1999); Ivone Gebara and Marie C. Bingemer, *Mary, Mother of God, Mother of the Poor* (Maryknoll, N.Y.: Orbis Books, 1999); Ivone Gebara, "Cosmic Theology: Ecofeminism and Panentheism," in *Readings in Ecology and Feminist Theology,* ed. Mary Heather MacKinnon and Moni McIntyre (Kansas City: Sheed & Ward, 1995), 208–13; and Ivone Gebara, "The Trinity and Human Experience," in *Women Healing Earth: Third World Women on Ecology, Feminism, and Religion,* ed. Rosemary Radford Ruether (Maryknoll, N.Y.: Orbis Books, 1996), 13–23. A helpful overview of ecofeminist reflection in a global context can be found in Heather Eaton and Lois Ann Lorentzen, eds., *Ecofeminism and Globalization: Exploring Culture, Context, and Religion* (Lanham, Md.: Rowman and Littlefield, 2003).

34. A delineation of some of these developments can be found in Stephen Scharper, "The Ecological Crisis," in *The Twentieth Century: A Theological Overview,* ed. Gregory Baum (Maryknoll, N.Y.: Orbis Books, 1999), 224–26. See also Peter W. Baken, Joan Gibb Engel, and J. Ronald Engel, *Ecology, Justice, and Christian Faith: A Critical Guide to the Literature* (Westport, Conn.: Greenwood Press, 1995).

35. One tangible expression of these movements is the World Social Forums in Port Allegre, Brazil (2001, 2002, 2003), and Mumbai, India (2004), which bring together thousands of environmental, social, political, cultural, and religious groups from around the world, especially impoverished nations. As theologian Lee Cormie observes, despite the wide diversity of these gatherings, there are nonetheless significant points of important convergence around ethical and ecological concerns. Lee Cormie, "Movements of the Spirit in History," 238–60, especially 249–50, available at http://www.koed.hu/talitha/lee.pdf. See also http://www.choike.org/2009/eng/. The author wishes to thank Lee Cormie for suggesting these resources.

36. For an early overview of some of these groups, see Marie Price, "Ecopolitics and Environmental Nongovernmental Organizations in Latin America," *Geographical Review* 84:1 (Jan. 1994): 42–58.

37. Aurora Donoso, "Ecological Debt: The Desecration of Life," available at www.deudaecologica.org/a_sacralife.html. For a description of how the Human

Genome Diversity Project gathered DNA samples from indigenous persons for patentable pharmaceuticals, see Hilary Cunningham and Stephen Scharper, "Human Genome Project Patenting Indigenous People" (Third World Network), available at http://www.dartmouth.edu/~cbbc/courses/bio4/bio4-1996/HumanGenome3rdWorld.html.

38. Forum on Religion and Ecology Website, "Indigenous Groups, Engaged Projects," available at http://fore.research.yale.edu/religion/indigenous/projects/uwa_defense.html.

39. Ibid.

40. Ibid.

41. Ibid.

42. Forum on Religion and Ecology Website, "Hinduism, Engaged Projects," available at http://fore.research.yale.edu/religion/hinduism/index.html.

43. Ibid. See also George A. James, "Ethical and Religious Dimensions of Chipko Resistance," in *Hinduism and Ecology: The Intersection of Earth, Sky, and Water,* ed. Christopher Key Chapple and Mary Evelyn Tucker (Cambridge, Mass.: Center for the Study of World Religions; Harvard University Press, 2000), 499–530.

44. Forum on Religion and Ecology website, "Buddhism, Engaged Projects," available at http://fore.research.yale.edu/religion/buddhism/index.html; see also Susan Darlington, "Not Only Preaching—The Work of the Ecology Monk Phrakhru Nantakhun of Thailand," in *Forest, Trees and People Newsletter* 34 (1997): 17–20, and her "Tree Ordination in Thailand," in *Dharma Rain: Sources of Buddhist Environmentalism,* ed. Stephanie Kaza and Kenneth Kraft (Boston: Shambhala Publications, 2000), 198–205.

45. Forum on Religion and Ecology website, "Buddhism, Engaged Projects."

46. Ibid.

47. Ibid.

48. Ibid.

49. See Sarah McFarland Taylor, "Reinhabiting Religion: Green Sisters, Ecological Renewal, and the Biography of Religious Landscape," in *Worldviews* 6:3 (2002): 227–52. For a lively integration of Thomas Berry and Brian Swimme's work within a social justice framework, see the work of Jim Conlin, especially *At The Edge of Our Longing* (Toronto: Novalis, 2004).

CHAPTER 7

Liberation Science and the Option for the Poor

Protecting Victims of Environmental Injustice

KRISTIN SHRADER-FRECHETTE

Robbins, Illinois, is one of the poorest towns in the United States. Part of South Side Chicago, this African American community is full of small, old, clapboard houses, narrow front yards, and cracked sidewalks. Its unemployment and poverty levels are far above the national averages, and its per capita income is about $7,000 a year. Robbins's seven thousand minority residents are too poor to support a single gas station, Laundromat, or fast-food franchise in their community. Its thirty-four churches outnumber its twenty-six tax-paying businesses. Partly because local property taxes generate only $250,000 each year, Robbins is $6 million in debt. Although its residents are socially, economically, and educationally powerless, the town leads the nation in one area. Besides being home to some of the highest-polluting chemical industries and manufacturers in the United States, it is host to dozens of incinerators that burn waste, trucked in from wealthier communities in the East. Robbins, Illinois, is like many other poor communities in the United States, and it is an example of a place where the option for the poor could be lived out but is not. Instead, Robbins is an example of how environmental injustice is yet one more scourge of poverty and how it may run rampant in poor communities. In this essay we will see how this is so and the effects it has on residents, then we will see another example of how people of good will, exercising the option for the poor, can stop environmental injustice before it happens.

Because South Side Chicago has some of the worst pollution in the United States, more than a decade ago the American Public Health Association recommended that no new incinerators be built there. But state Environmental Protection Agency (EPA) officials continue to ignore these recommendations, and five new incinerators are planned for this poor, minority community. While wealthy neighborhoods can pay attorneys and scientists to help them avoid such health threats, Robbins's residents cannot. In their community, heavily polluting facilities are sited near retirement homes, public housing, and even schools. The latest Robbins incinerator was opened in 1998 by a Pennsylvania company to burn Pennsylvania garbage. It alone annually spews out 1000 pounds of lead and 4400 pounds of mercury, as well as cadmium, other heavy metals, dioxins, and furans into Robbins's air. The result? Many poor, minority children in South Side Chicago are born with cancer. They are at least six times more likely to be hurt by this pollution than adults. Overall in the United States, children of color (aged five to fourteen) are four times more likely than white children to die from diseases like asthma. They are three times more likely to be hospitalized for it, despite their lesser access to health care. Their cancer rates also are disproportionately higher, partly because they are forced to breathe dirtier air and drink dirtier water.[1]

Wealthy people can pay to keep incinerators out of their neighborhoods. They can pay for electrostatic air filters on their furnaces and for reverse-osmosis filters on their water systems. Their lower cancer rates show the effects of their economic protections. Even average-income people can pay for pitchers with Brita water filters. Living in the dirtiest areas and working at the dirtiest jobs, the poor have none of these protections. Social structures thus oppress them twice. *First,* they render them poor and powerless through educational, economic, and tax policies. *Second,* preying on their poverty and powerlessness, oppressors expose them to disproportionate pollution—health-threatening wastes generated in producing products, mainly for the wealthy. Oppressors *first* steal the labor and income of the poor. Once they are powerless, oppressors *next* steal their very lives and health.

OVERVIEW: LIBERATION SCIENCE AND
ENVIRONMENTAL INJUSTICE

How should believers respond to this dual oppression? Liberation theology is one answer. It is the gospel response and reflection of those who
have committed themselves to a prophetic option—expressing preference
for, solidarity with, and compassion for the poor and the powerless. Liberation theology "has its point of departure in an experience," an experience "of dehumanizing poverty and of social and political oppression"
suffered by the poor—like the residents of Robbins.[2] Once believers become aware of this dehumanizing poverty and oppression, how might
they use their talents to implement their commitment to liberation theology? How might scientists and engineers, in particular—or even ordinary college students in any discipline—practice what might be called
"liberation science"? This is science that contributes to liberating the
poor, science that helps ensure that the poor do not bear disproportionate
health threats from the pollution and waste of a society that, in many
ways, has abandoned them.

Focusing on environmental injustice, this essay provides one answer
to the preceding questions. "Environmental injustice" refers to the disproportionate burden of societal pollution—and consequently the disproportionate burden of death and disease borne by poor people and minorities,
especially children. Because they are socially, economically, and educationally less powerful than other groups in society, poor and minority communities often are targeted for the most noxious and dangerous facilities,
just as the residents of Robbins are. Their same lack of power also places
them in the most hazardous and polluted workplaces. As a consequence,
they breathe dirtier air, drink dirtier water, and therefore lead shorter,
unhealthier lives. Oppression takes not only their money but their very
lives, the very resources of air and water given by God in common to all.[3]

Obviously the greatest burdens of environmental injustice, poverty,
and oppression fall on those in developing nations. However, for scientifically literate believers who must live and work in the United States,
one option is to use liberation science to serve the poor in their own nation, and later to employ what they have learned at home to serve the

poor abroad. This essay suggests how believers might use liberation science in such service. It (1) quickly surveys U.S. environmental injustice and shows why recognizing its severity ought to provoke a response of faith and compassion, suffering with the poor, and helping to liberate them. Focusing on how a largely black, poverty-level community in Louisiana was targeted for a dirty and dangerous facility, next the essay (2) illustrates how science is often and typically misused in environmental-impact assessments that oppress the poor through environmental injustice. Finally, the essay (3) outlines one prominent way in which scientifically literate believers might help liberate victims of environmental injustice in their own nation—and thus gain valuable tools for the much-needed, more difficult task of practicing liberation science abroad.

U.S. ENVIRONMENTAL INJUSTICE AND THE NEED FOR LIBERATING POOR PEOPLE AND MINORITIES

In most areas of the world, poverty and powerlessness threaten people's lives not only because the poor lack money, jobs, education, and political power, but because their very powerlessness makes them a target for life-threatening societal pollution. Minorities and poor people generally bear greater health risks partly because poverty and racism force them to live where homes are cheapest and pollution tends to be highest. Proportionately more landfills, power plants, toxic-waste dumps, bus and rail yards, sewage plants, and industrial facilities are sited in the neighborhoods of poor people and minorities. As a result, these areas bear higher levels of contaminated air, contaminated tap water, cancer, and infectious disease.[4]

Examining the 593 sites on the EPA national toxic-waste-cleanup priority list (Superfund), a U.S. National Cancer Institute (NCI) study found that in counties with Superfund sites, cancer death rates are higher, blacks live closer to the sites, and blacks have higher cancer rates than whites.[5] Dr. Glenn Paulson summarized the NCI results this way: "If you know where the chemical industry is, you know where the cancer hotspots are" and where poor people and minorities live.[6]

Of course, environmental injustice is not the only reason for poorer health among minorities and poor people. Fewer educational and employment opportunities, less access to medical care, and less medical insurance are among the other factors that put them at greater health risk. Nevertheless, their environmental injustice risks are significant. A 2004 U.S. National Academies of Science report shows that universal U.S. health insurance could save 18,000 lives each year.[7] For comparison, note that environmental and health scientists claim that up to 240,000 of the 600,000 annual U.S. cancer deaths are attributable to preventable environmental pollution and occur disproportionately among poor people and minorities, especially their children.[8] Even the most conservative of all estimates—from the U.S. Centers for Disease Control (CDC) and NCI—show that pollution causes at least 60,000 annual, premature, preventable, U.S. cancer fatalities alone[9]—far more U.S. deaths than are attributable to lack of universal health insurance. Yet this cancer-death figure includes no pollution-related fatalities from noncancer causes, such as heart attacks or asthma deaths induced by particulate air pollution. For instance, NCI studies show that each 10 micrograms of fine particulate pollution alone causes an 18 percent increase in heart-related deaths, an 8 percent increase in lung-related deaths, and a 4 percent increase in overall deaths.[10] CDC statistics show cancer and heart disease each contribute to about a third of all U.S. deaths. This means that, since Chicago's average annual particulate air pollution is about 17 ug/m³, particulates alone cause roughly 3000 annual, preventable, heart-related Chicago deaths—8 per day—apart from deaths caused by cancer. Even before counting fatalities from other environmental and airborne causes, particulate air pollution alone causes about 10 percent of all Chicago deaths, mostly from heart attacks.[11]

What is most troubling about cancer and other premature deaths is not merely that so many of them are, as the U.S. Office of Technology Assessment put it, "environmentally induced and theoretically preventable."[12] Most worrisome is that this burden of death and disease is borne disproportionately by the poorest and most vulnerable among us. As the American Public Health Association (APHA) puts it, "Exposure to environmental risks varies based on race and . . . income."[13]

The prominent medical journal *Lancet* pointed out that on average whites live six years longer than African Americans in the United States. The essay also noted that, for most causes of death, the mortality differentials between the two groups are increasing, not decreasing. Even worse, the article charged, is that the United States is the only Western developed nation whose government does not collect mortality statistics by class—that is, by income and education. When the author looked at class-based mortality data for the only diseases (heart and cerebrovascular ailments) on which the U.S. government collects class-related information, the class data showed an even wider disparity than the race data. If the author is correct, then the health of poor people and minorities is getting worse—in part because of environmental injustice.[14]

In the United States, the percentage of people of color living in counties with commercial hazardous-waste facilities is three times higher than in counties without these facilities.[15] U.S. people of color also live, in greater concentrations, in areas that have above-average numbers of air-polluting facilities and that fail to meet federal air-quality attainment standards. In the United States, 52 percent of whites, but 71 percent of Hispanics, live in counties with high ozone concentrations. Only 5 percent of whites, but 10 percent of African Americans and 15 percent of Hispanics, live in air that violates all four air-quality standards (carbon monoxide, sulfur dioxide, nitrogen dioxide, and particulate matter). Similar statistics hold for other areas of the world. In the UK, for instance, half of all waste incinerators are in neighborhoods comprising the poorest 10 percent of the country.[16]

As a result of environmental injustice, U.S. black and Hispanic children have much higher incidences of death and disease than do white children. Among poverty-level U.S. black children, nearly one-third have blood-lead levels above the recommended health standard. CDC studies show that blood-lead levels are consistently higher for black than white children, for younger than older children, and for children in lower, than higher, income families. They reveal that 8 percent of poverty-level children are lead poisoned, as compared with only 1 percent of children above the poverty level. About 11 percent of black children are lead poisoned, as compared with about 2 percent of white children.[17]

Even when different racial and socioeconomic groups are exposed to the same levels of pollutants, APHA data show that minority and poor children are likely to be more severely affected than white or non-poverty-level children. Besides lack of health care, poorer economic conditions also encourage poorer nutrition, poorer housing, and thus greater susceptibility to environmental pollution. Repeatedly researchers have shown that mortality is strongly related to a nation's *income inequality*, rather than to median income, *per capita income,* or actual poverty levels. In short: what kills people is income inequality, not mainly poverty. One reason may be that, the greater a nation's societal and economic inequality, the more the rich can pay to avoid threats like pollution, often by dumping them on the poor. The poor, however, cannot avoid them. In democratic societies with greater economic equality, pollution typically decreases because more people can speak for and protect themselves, and others are less able to exploit them or force them to bear higher levels of pollution, transferred from the wealthier sectors. As the Robbins case illustrates, a good example of such U.S. transfers is the largely minority, South Side of Chicago. Because it is impoverished, residents there are forced "to make ends meet" by accepting garbage, including toxic wastes, from many states far away. These wastes are then incinerated, causing massive air pollution from heavy metals, air toxins, and particulates.[18]

Of all developed nations, pollution and public health effects of income inequality are worst in the United States. It has the shortest average life expectancy—and the highest levels of income inequality, infant mortality, poverty, and percentage of children in poverty—of any Western industrialized nation.[19] Such statistics—and the fact that income inequality rather than poverty increases mortality—help explain why U.S. poor people and minorities face more serious health threats than those in other developed nations, even where everyone is exposed to the same levels of pollutants.

- The U.S. death rate for one- to four-year-old children is double that of nations like Finland.
- Even when one controls for the higher U.S. murder rate, the U.S. death rate for fifteen- to twenty-five-year-olds is double that of countries like the Netherlands, Japan, Sweden, and the United Kingdom.
- The U.S. infant-mortality rate is triple that of places like Singapore, and more than double the rate of democratic nations like Sweden, Japan, and Iceland.
- If U.S. infant-mortality rates were as good as those in Singapore, 2212 U.S. babies would be saved each year.
- Even Beijing, China. has an infant-mortality rate that is 4.6 per 1000 live births, as compared with New York City's 6.5, and the U.S. rate of 7, per 1000.[20]

Health disparities like these suggest that U.S. poor people and minorities are more vulnerable than others to the same levels of pollution. Yet the preceding statistics show that poor people and minorities typically bear higher levels of pollution. Also, nearly three times the percentage of U.S. blacks, as whites, are at the poverty level. Partly as a result, blacks have higher incidences of death and disease, especially black children.[21] For all cancers combined, black U.S. males have about a 50 percent higher cancer mortality rate than white males, and black U.S. females . have about a 30 percent higher cancer mortality rate than white females. Even after one controls for other variables—like crime, medical coverage, and income—this inequality in mortality is only reduced, not eliminated. Such data suggest that universal health insurance, alone, will not equally protect U.S. minorities and poor people from cancer and other diseases. The solution is not to eliminate all toxic dumps or hazardous facilities but to minimize and equalize their burdens so that poor people and minorities do not bear most of them. As the APHA has repeatedly noted, racism and environmental injustice (disproportionate pollution) need to be confronted as factors in why U.S. minorities and poor people continue to bear higher health risks.[22]

Although many adults have defenses against premature disease and death caused by air, water, and other pollution, children often do not.[23] Children's developing organ systems, incomplete metabolic processes, and only partially developed detoxification systems are less able to withstand most toxins. Yet per unit of body mass, children take in more air, water, and food, and thus more pollutants, than do adults. Also, because many pollution regulations focus on cancer and only on adults, they typically ignore pollution-induced developmental and neurological disorders in children.[24]

As a recent *New England Journal of Medicine* study of 90,000 identical twins concluded, and as the World Health Organization (WHO) says, only "a small fraction of all childhood cancers" are associated with heredity, genetics, infections, and viruses. Instead, environmental pollutants appear "to play a major role."[25] The WHO says air pollution alone is associated with up to half of all childhood cancers.[26] The National Childhood Cancer Foundation, the Children's Oncology Group, and the U.S. National Academy of Sciences (NAS), among other groups, say childhood cancer incidence and childhood developmental-neurological disorders are increasing rapidly. Each year, adult U.S. cancers increase by 1 percent, while childhood cancers increase by about 1.4 percent—40 percent faster. According to the NAS, each year in the United States, approximately 12,500 children are diagnosed with cancer, and about half die within five years. Childhood leukemias and tumors of the brain, nervous system, lymphatic system, kidneys, bones, and muscles are the most common. The U.S. NAS says cancer causes more deaths of children, aged one to fifteen, "than any other disease, more deaths than asthma, diabetes, cystic fibrosis, and AIDS combined." Yet this annual 12,500 figure does not include the significant numbers of noncancer, pollution-induced disorders, including neurological and developmental injuries, endocrine disruption, genetic defects, birth defects, and heart, lung, and respiratory disorders.[27]

While 6000 U.S. children die annually from cancer, 3000 are killed by automobiles. Another 2600 are murdered each year, and 1400 children die annually from child abuse. Given these statistics, why do news reports give relatively little attention to pollution-induced childhood diseases like cancers? One answer may be that the same corporations who are major polluters, like General Electric (GE), also control the news media. GE, for instance, owns NBC, and repeated media analyses show that GE/NBC, like other media outlets, skews news reports to underestimate effects of pollution. The reason? Corporations save money by not controlling pollution.[28]

- Among pesticides listed as reproductive toxins by the state of California, two-thirds are still in use. Parental exposure—especially among Hispanics—has been linked to their children's cancers, and to birth defects such as cleft palate, limb malformations, heart defects, facial and eye deformities, and incomplete bone development in the skull.[29]
- Most major classes of pesticides, including the organochlorines, organophosphates, carbamates, chlorophenoxy herbicides, and pyrethroids adversely affect children's developing nervous systems, compromise their immune systems, and exacerbate their risks of infection and disease.[30]
- U.S. NAS studies show that "exposure to neurotoxic compounds at levels believed to be safe for adults can result in permanent loss of brain function if it occurs during the prenatal and early childhood period of brain development."[31]

- For some pesticides, like organophosphate compounds, a lethal dose in immature animals can be only 1 percent of the lethal dose for adults.[32]
- Because of children's greater exposures and heightened vulnerability, the U.S. NAS says that following even U.S. government pesticide standards does not adequately protect children.[33]

Besides pesticides, children are especially at risk from industrial neurotoxins in air pollution, like that in South Side Chicago.[34] This is partly because of their increased rates of respiration, their smaller airways, and their developing organs. Even in the United States, children are the largest and most vulnerable subgroup of the population that is harmed by air pollution.[35] A 2005 WHO study showed that current levels of air pollution, from sources like coal plants, oil refineries, manufacturing facilities, waste incinerators, and automobiles, are implicated in many childhood health threats. These include increased childhood mortality, lower birth weight, premature birth, intrauterine growth retardation, sudden infant-death syndrome, cancer, and birth defects. Scientists also say current U.S. levels of air pollution cause statistically significant U.S. increases in childhood inflammation, decreased immune function, impaired lung function, allergic responses, cardiac disease, and respiratory disease.[36]

As early as the 1960s, physicians showed that a 10 percent increase in particulate pollution, alone, can cause a 1 percent increase in infant mortality. But little was done to reduce particulates, and the nation has not followed most of the air pollution recommendations of the APHA. The result? Breathing problems now account for one-third of all U.S. infant deaths, and this is likely to continue to increase. Asthma is now the leading cause of childhood school absenteeism and the most common chronic childhood disease; in the last decade, U.S. asthma has increased by 40 percent—costing the nation about $6.2 billion in annual damage.[37] Similar problems exist in Europe, where 30 million people currently have asthma.[38] Airborne particulate pollution, alone, now causes about 6.4 percent of annual U.S. deaths for children aged zero to four. Living only two months in a highly polluted city can increase infant mortality by 10 percent. About 27 million U.S. children under age thirteen, and half the pediatric asthma population, live in areas that violate EPA's ozone standards. What happens to these children? In 2005 Harvard, Yale, and New York University scientists showed that for every 10 parts-per-billion daily ozone increase, deaths increase 10 percent over the subsequent three days. For carbon monoxide, each 1 part per million increase in background rates increases risk of low birth weight by 19 percent.[39]

As already mentioned, even if all environmental laws were enforced, children would not be adequately protected from pollutants. Children are thus the most vulnerable members of poor and minority communities exposed to disproportionate pollution. The American Academy of Pediatrics warned recently that federal air-pollution standards have "little or no margin of safety for children engaged in active outdoor activity."[40]

- Columbia University researchers showed that even before they are born, children risk birth defects, genetic injuries, decreased birth weight, decreased length, and decreased head circumference because of mothers' exposures to carcinogens in ambient air.[41]
- The U.S. CDC showed recently that between one in five and one in eight U.S. women have blood-levels of mercury—from pollution—that are high enough to cause neurological and developmental defects in their unborn children.[42]
- Researchers have documented doublings of respiratory-related hospital admissions for preschoolers when even one local pollution source (a steel mill) was operating rather than closed.[43]
- During peak particulate-pollution months, although hospital admissions for adult respiratory problems can increase 40 percent, those for children can increase 300 percent.[44]
- Mortality rates also increase markedly as a function of air pollution, especially from ozone, sulfur dioxide, and particulates.[45]

Most U.S. water standards likewise fail to protect children and other vulnerable groups because they are based on health effects for average adults. Yet based on average body weight, infants and children drink two to three times as much water as adults. And even inadequate U.S. water standards are not always enforced.[46] The EPA says 600,000 U.S. children annually drink tap water that violates its standards.[47] Those who drink the dirty water are largely children of poor people—those who cannot afford water filters on their faucets.[48]

SCIENCE MISUSED TO OPPRESS THE POOR

How does flawed science contribute to environmental injustice problems like those just cited? In the United States, often it occurs in environmental-impact assessments. Since 1969 the U.S. National Environmental Policy Act has mandated that an environmental-impact assessment must be done for any building project, regulated by the federal government, that has environmental or public health impacts. Examples include siting a nuclear power plant, a toxic waste dump, or expanding a manufacturing facility. Every year in the United States, roughly 2500–3000 environmental-impact assessments are produced, in virtually every state. Most of these assessments are written by corporations wishing to site or expand some plant. The law requires that a draft of the assessment be completed, that it be released to the public and to the affected community, and that the community have weeks or months to respond (to the federal government) regarding the adequacy of the assessment. Addressing resulting citizen comments, the government authorizes a final, corrected environmental-impact assessment. On its basis, officials either approve, disapprove, or amend the project in question. As the preceding section suggests, most hazardous facilities are sited in poor or minority communities. Why? One reason is that poor and minority communities are those least able either to criticize the draft environmental-impact assessment or to pay outside scientific consultants to respond to it. As a result, extremely flawed science is often used to justify placing additional noxious facilities in already heavily polluted, largely poor or minority communities—like Robbins, Illinois. The same facilities would quickly be disallowed in wealthier communities.[49]

Consider a recent case, a proposal by a multinational corporation, Louisiana Energy Services (LES), to build a uranium-enrichment facility to produce fuel for commercial nuclear reactors. LES proposed putting the highly polluting plant in an African American community in Homer, Louisiana. Widely regarded as the first major U.S. environmental justice victory, it is a good example of how a poor, minority community was able to prevent its being targeted for noxious pollution. Except for its being an environmental justice success story, the Homer case is fairly typical of those in which environmental injustice occurs. Most poor communities, however, do not have the outside resources to help them avoid oppression. One of the poorest towns in the United States, Homer has a per capita income of only about $5000 per year. Members of the local community were able to stop the facility only because of unpaid scientific help from outside experts, some of whom were this author and her doctoral students. After they helped stop the Louisiana facility in 1997, LES proposed building in another black community in Tennessee. Again LES was defeated after local poor and minority people received pro bono help from outside experts. As of summer 2006, the multinational corporation is now attempting to site the plant near Eunice, New Mexico—an area with a 20 percent poverty rate and 50 percent minority population, mostly Hispanics and Native Americans. Both figures are nearly double the U.S. poverty and minority population averages.[50]

How has LES used poor science in attempting to site its facilities among the poor? The draft environmental-impact assessment for the Homer facility argued (1) that it was safe and would have minimal environmental and health impacts;[51] (2) that there was an industrial need for the nuclear-fuel products of the facility;[52] and (3) that U.S. companies would use most of the enriched uranium it produced.[53] The draft environmental-impact assessment likewise argued (4) that it would be "a major socioeconomic asset" to the community;[54] (5) that costs to this community, because of the plant, would be "minimal";[55] and (6) that the facility would provide many local jobs.[56] Finally the assessment argued (7) that the plant's gas-centrifuge technology would be more energy-efficient than current gas-diffusion technology used by the U.S. government,[57] and (8) that it was located at an ideal site, given the companies' suppliers and distributors.[58]

Working through the dense, three-inch-thick draft environmental-impact assessment and scores of other scientific studies, the author and her students, as pro bono scientists, were able to show that all the major draft assessment claims 1–8 were likely erroneous. Using probabilistic risk assessment, they were able to show that claim 1 was wildly false; that the corporate assessors underestimated the facility's accident risks; that building it would expose the public to dangerous radioactive material, much of which was unregulated; that local children would bear the highest radioactive risks; and that the corporate assessors had used outdated scientific information, omitted most accident scenarios from their analyses, and ignored quantification of many hazardous impacts. As a result, the assessors massively underestimated risks from the proposed LES facility. Using benefit-cost analysis and simple fact-checking in scientific journals, the author and her students also showed that claims 2–6 were false. The corporate assessors had blatantly ignored existing, adequate U.S. enriched-uranium supplies. They had done no distributive analysis of costs and benefits. Also the students and professor showed that the proposed LES facility would have to sell most of its products abroad; would cause net economic losses for the local black community; would force the town to increase taxes to provide needed services to the facility; and yet would provide profits mainly to foreign investors. They also showed that the plant would provide virtually no employment for the community because nearly all jobs at the facility required a highly skilled, highly educated workforce—unlike workers available in Homer. They likewise revealed that virtually none of the goods and supplies needed for the facility would be purchased inside the state. Finally, they also were able to show that corporate claims 7 and 8 were false. Instead, using refereed articles in the engineering-science literature, they argued that the facility's proposed gas-centrifuge technology was outmoded, unreliable, and rejected by the U.S. government as not cost-effective. As a consequence, the pro bono scientists were able to show that, because of existing liability laws, U.S. taxpayers likely would be responsible for massive cleanup costs later at the proposed facility. Using LES records, the pro bono scientists also were able to show that the company lied; that the Homer site was far from the companies' supplies and distributors, compared with many other proposed sites; and that the company's own memoranda showed it selected the Homer site largely because its residents were powerless to oppose the proposed facility.[59]

Simply by carefully examining the hundreds of pages in the draft environmental-impact assessment, this author and her students also were able to show that the enrichment corporation (wishing to site the proposed facility) employed disclosure procedures that violated minority rights to free informed consent. As classically defined in the ethics and risk literature, informed consent requires full risk disclosure, full subject understanding of the risk, voluntarily acceptance of it, and being competent to assess it.[60] The LES Corporation, however, never disclosed the actual radiological nature of the facility to anyone. Instead its employees canvassed citizens, asking if they would like to have a "manufacturing facility" nearby. LES likewise violated the criterion of voluntariness (for free informed consent) because it polled only white residents living a great distance away from the proposed facility. It did not seek the opinions of any of the minority residents who made up the population living within five miles of the proposed site. LES then claimed that local residents consented to the plant. The company also covered up the radiological risks and health threats to be imposed by the facility, failed to reveal that the onsite radiological wastes would not be covered by U.S. government regulations, and thus again violated the disclosure required for free informed consent. Likewise it did not reveal that the products of the multinational facility would likely be used abroad, not in the United States. Nor did it reveal that these multinational products would compete with higher-quality, less-expensive U.S. fuel-products, while Louisiana residents would bear the health and environmental risks of the outmoded facility. As a result, the pro bono scientists were able to show that attempts to site the Louisiana facility amounted to environmental injustice, taking advantage of a poor community that was alone powerless to protect itself. Both the factual-scientific and ethical arguments in the draft environmental-impact assessment were fatally flawed.[61]

SCIENCE USED TO LIBERATE THE POOR

In criticizing the biased science and ethics used in the draft Louisiana environmental-impact assessment, pro bono scientists were able to show that, once these errors were corrected, there was no justification for the proposed facility—apart from making profits at the expense of the powerless poor. Even if there had been a need for the plant, they were able to show that Louisiana was not the geographically appropriate location, and corporate assessors massively underestimated the health hazards associated with the proposed facility. In short, only flawed science and ethics "justified" the siting. Once they were corrected, the siting was indefensible—an obvious case of environmental injustice.

Because the vast preponderance of draft environmental-impact assessments are done by scientists with conflicts of interest—those who work for the corporation wishing to build or modify some facility—many of the studies employ flawed science. Typically they use whatever they can get away with in order to obtain the necessary government permits for their profit-making projects. Such a conflicted system of U.S. permitting thus means that, unless a community either is well educated itself, or able to pay outside scientists to assess the draft environmental-impact assessment, it can easily be oppressed by polluters who are able to jeopardize community health. Yet only wealthy, well-educated communities generally can either pay others to protect them, or themselves navigate the legal intricacies of the assessment system. This means that poor communities must rely solely on the free services of others. Most poor people do not receive any help, and because they do not, they pay with their health and the health of their children. They bear the lion's share of society's environmental and health burdens, the dangerous crumbs from the tables of the rich.

If people have a will to serve and to share their gifts, it is not difficult for them to provide the expertise that is needed to protect mostly poor and minority victims of environmental injustice. How? The corporate-funded science used in draft environmental-impact assessments typically is done by those with only an undergraduate degree. It is designed to be accessible to the average layperson. This means that, for someone with only minimal technical expertise, criticizing most draft assessments is relatively easy to do. One reason is that typical environmental-impact assessment errors are simple. These include using small sample sizes or short-term studies to assess potential negative health effects. Other flawed assessment science employs incomplete benefit-cost analyses, so that alleged economic benefits of a facility are overstated. Assessors also frequently ignore basic scientific literature in assessing risks, and it is an easy matter for a committed layperson merely to survey the scientific literature. Biased assessors also frequently assume that absence of evidence for some harm is evidence of its absence. Consider, for instance, the case of biased assessors using small sample sizes in their environmental-impact assessments. These small samples often give false assurances of safety because, statistically, they provide virtually no chance of detecting some negative health effect from a facility, product, or pollutant. For example, suppose a facility will annually cause 1 in every 1000 people (who are exposed) to have cancer. Because typical industry studies use sample sizes under 50 and last only for a few weeks, they are unlikely to detect such effects. Consider a recent analysis of chemical-industry (including all pesticide industry) environmental-impact assessments, done by the U.S. EPA Science Advisory Board (SAB), on which the author serves. The SAB discovered that *all* chemical-industry safety studies of its products and pollutants used low-power, small-sample studies of fewer than 50 subjects. Their net effects were to obtain false-negative conclusions, therefore false assurances of safety. On the contrary, the SAB said that sample sizes of at least 2500 subjects, not 50, would be needed for reliable testing of chemicals and their effects on humans.[62]

Other misuses of science, designed to show that some facility or pollution is safe when it is not, include employing some biased, largely theoretical "model" to calculate some impact or effect, while ignoring actual empirical data about the effect. Assessors likewise often use counterfactual assumptions to generate optimistic data that have no real-world relevance. Frequently they also actually suppress data that give conclusions contrary to what their corporate employers want.[63]

Because such misuses of science are so obvious to people with even minimal technical training, the author has found that most undergraduates, even those who are not science majors, are able to find many scientific errors in most environmental-impact assessments. Working with the professor and each other, they easily know enough to do the work of "liberation science." In a one-semester, undergraduate college course, most average, nonscience majors easily can be trained to examine assessments and to look for telltale signs of flawed science. Every year about forty undergraduates at the University of Notre Dame each choose a draft environmental-impact assessment, work closely with the professor to evaluate it critically, supply their findings to the affected poor or minority community, and respond to government decision-makers about the flaws in that particular draft assessment. Often these student results have provided the basis for forcing the government to protect the health of poor people and minorities—Latinos in New Mexico, Native Americans in Nevada, blacks in Tennessee, and so on. This course-based project work thus is "win-win" on at least five levels. *First,* poor and minority communities receive free help and hope. *Second,* Notre Dame students become baptized into liberation science, a baptism that often shapes them for life. *Third,* more privileged citizens learn a new way to share their gifts of education with those less fortunate. *Fourth,* government officials are forced to address the flawed science used by those who practice environmental injustice. And *fifth,* democratic citizenship begins to work as it should. All these benefits arise merely because students use liberation science to implement their religious beliefs and to answer the government's call for responses to draft environmental-impact assessments. Most importantly, students learn they can make a difference in the world.[64]

IMPLEMENTING LIBERATION SCIENCE

Environmental injustice represents a massive source of poverty and oppression, even in wealthy nations like the United States.[65] Yet this injustice often can be prevented if sufficient numbers of committed, technically capable Christians critically evaluate the science employed in most environmental-impact assessments. Often special interests misuse science to justify imposing disproportionate health burdens on the poor and the powerless. By evaluating the assessments and thus standing with the poor and the powerless, believers can practice not only good citizenship but also liberation science. Through liberation science, believers can share their time, opportunities, talents, and technical expertise—not just their money—with the poor.

This scientific sharing also is part of basic Catholic tenets about justice. As Thomas Aquinas noted, "In cases of need, all things are common property. . . . whatever certain people have in superabundance is due, by natural law, to the purpose of succoring the poor."[66] The environmental injustice and disproportionate deaths, outlined above, seem obvious cases of need. If so, all things—including believers' educational opportunities, intellectual gifts, and technical skills—are also common property. They are common property not only because others' need for them is great, as Aquinas noted. People's talents and opportunities also are common property, to be used for "the purpose of succoring the poor," because they are not mainly things that have been earned or merited. If not, they are not mainly property, to which their possessors alone hold the only claim. Instead these talents and opportunities are as much gifts of God as are air and water. They are meant for the benefit of all. Faced with the needs of others and the giftedness of life, liberation science is one way for ordinary people to share their gifts.

NOTES

1. Asthma statistics are from American Public Health Association (APHA): *Priority 2005 Issue: Health Disparities* (Washington, D.C.: APHA, 2005), 26; *Priority 2005 Issue: Environmental Disparities* (Washington, D.C.: APHA, 2005), 28; *Priority 2005 Issue: Racial/Ethnic Disparities* (Washington, D.C.: APHA, 2005), 34. Statistics also come from M. White et al., "Exacerbations of Childhood Asthma and Ozone Pollution in Atlanta," *Environmental Research* 65 (1994): 56–68. M. Weitzman et al., "Racial, Social and Environmental Risks for Childhood Asthma," *American Journal of Diseases of Children (AJDC)* 144 (Nov. 1990): 1189–94. J. Schwartz et al., "Predictions of Asthma and Persistent Wheeze," *American Review of Respiratory Disease* 142 (1990): 555–62. J. Cunningham et al., "Race, Asthma and Persistent Wheeze in Philadelphia School Children," *American Journal of Public Health* 86 (Oct. 1996): 1406–9. U.S. Centers for Disease Control (CDC), "Asthma Mortality and Hospitalization among Children and Young Adults," *Morbidity and Mortality Weekly Report* (May 3, 1996). The Robbins case is taken from Kristin Shrader-Frechette, *Environmental Justice: Creating Equality, Reclaiming Democracy* (New York: Oxford University Press, 2002), 71–74. See also Kristin Shrader-Frechette, *Taking Action, Saving Lives* (New York: Oxford University Press, 2007).

2. Ignacio Ellacuria, "Liberation Theology and Socio-Historical Change in Latin America," in *Towards a Society That Serves Its People,* ed. John Hassett and Hugh Lacey, trans. James R. Brockman (Washington, D.C.: Georgetown University Press, 1991). See also Gustavo Gutiérrez, *A Theology of Liberation* (Maryknoll, N.Y.: Orbis Books, 1973); Jon Sobrino, *Spirituality of Liberation* (Maryknoll, N.Y.: Orbis Books, 1978).

3. See Shrader-Frechette, *Environmental Justice.*

4. See, for example, R. Calderon et al., "Health Risks from Contaminated Water," *Toxicology and Industrial Health* 9:5 (Sept.–Oct. 1993): 879–900; Robert Bullard, ed., *Unequal Protection* (San Francisco, Calif.: Sierra Club Books, 1994); B. Bryant, ed., *Environmental Justice* (Washington, D.C.: Island Press, 1995). Additional documentation is in Shrader-Frechette, *Taking Action,* chap. 1.

5. Jack Griffith, R. C. Duncan, W. B. Riggan, and A. C. Pefforn, "Cancer Mortality in U.S. Counties with Hazardous Waste Sites and Ground Water Pollution," *Archives of Environmental Health* 44:2 (1989): 69–74.

6. Quoted in Stuart Auerbach's "N.J.'s Chemical Belt Takes Its Toll: $4 Billion Industry Tied to Nation's Highest Cancer Death Rate," *Washington Post,* Feb. 8, 1976. See also U.S. Centers for Disease Control, *2001 Incidence and Mortality Data, National Program of Cancer Registries, State vs. National* (Atlanta, Ga.: CDC, 2001), 58–59; available at http://apps.nccd.cdc.gov/uscs/.

7. Institute of Medicine, *Insuring America's Health* (Washington, D.C.: National Academy Press, 2004), 8, provides 18,000 figure.

8. See Paul R. Ehrlich and Anne H. Ehrlich, *Betrayal of Science and Reason* (Washington, D.C.: Island Press, 1996): 154; and K. Bridbord et al., *Estimates of the Fraction of Cancer in the United States Related to Occupational Factors* (Bethesda, Md.: NCI, National Institute of Environmental Health Sciences, and National Institute for Occupational Safety and Health, 1978).

9. U.S. Department of Health and Human Services and NCI, "Health Status Objectives," *Cancer* 16:1 (1991): 416–40.

10. C. Arden Pope et al., "Cardiovascular Mortality and Long-Term Exposure to Particulate Air Pollution," *Circulation* 109 (2003): 71–77; see http://ehp .niehs.nih.gov/article/fetchArticle.action?articleURI=info%3Adoi%2F10.1289 %2Fehp.7938 for air-pollution deaths induced by particulates. M. L. Bell, D. L. Davis, N. Gouveia, L. Cifuentes, and V. H. Borja-Aburto, "Mortality, Morbidity, and Economic Consequences of Fossil Fuel–Related Air Pollution in Three Latin American Cities," *Epidemiology* 15:4 (July 2004): S44–S45; M. L. Bell and D. I. Davis, "Reassessment of the Lethal London Fog of 1952," *Environmental Health Perspectives* 109 (June 2001): 389–94; D. L. Davis, L. Deck, P. Saldiva, and J. Correia, "The Selected Survivor Effect in Developed and Developing Countries Studies of Air Pollution," *Epidemiology* 10:4 (July 1999): S107; L. Cifuentes, V. H. Borja-Aburto, N. Gouveia, G. Thurston, and D. L. Davis, "Assessing the Health Benefits of Urban Air Pollution Reductions Associated with Climate Change Mitigation (2000–2020)," *Environmental Health Perspectives* 109 (June 2001): S419–25; D.L. Davis, T. Kjellstrom, R. Slooff, A. McGartland, D. Atkinson, W. Barbour, W. Hohenstein, P. Nagelhout, T. Woodruff, F. Divita, J. Wilson, and J. Schwartz, "Short-Term Improvements in Public Health from Global-Climate Policies on Fossil-Fuel Combustion," *Lancet* 350:9088 (Nov. 1997); M. L. Bell, D. L. Davis, and G. Sun, "Analysis of the Health Effects of Severe Air Pollution in Developing Countries," *Epidemiology* 13:4 (July 2002): 298; A. D. Kyle, T. J. Woodruff, P. A. Buffler, and D. L. Davis, "Use of an Index to Reflect the Aggregate Burden of Long-Term Exposure to Criteria Air Pollutants in the United States," *Environmental Health Perspectives* 110 (Feb. 2002): S95–102; L. Cifuentes, V. H. Borja-Aburto, N. Gouveia, G. Thurston, and D. L. Davis, "Climate Change: Hidden Health Benefits of Greenhouse Gas Mitigation," *Science* 293:5533 (Aug. 2001): 1257–59.

11. Cancer statistics are from National Institutes of Health, *Cancer Rates and Risks* (Washington, D.C: NIH and NCI, 2000). Cancer statistics are confirmed in S. Devesa, W. Blot, B. Stone, B. Miller, R. Tarone, and J. Fraumeni, "Recent Cancer Trends in the United States," *Journal of the National Cancer Institute* 87:3 (1995): 175–82; SEER, *Cancer Statistics Review, 1973–1997* (Washington, D.C.: National Cancer Institute, National Institutes of Health, 1998); Samuel S. Epstein, "Reversing the Cancer Epidemic," *Tikkun* 17:3 (May 2002): 56–66; Robert T. Greenlee, M. B. Hill-Harmon, Taylor Murray, and Michael Thun, "Cancer Statistics," *CA Cancer J. Clin* 1 (2001): 15–36; Samuel Epstein,

The Politics of Cancer Revisited (New York: East Ridge Press, 1998); Samuel Epstein, *Cancer-Gate* (Amityville, N.Y.: Baywood, 2005); Debra Davis and David Hoel, eds., "Trends in Cancer Mortality in Industrial Countries," *Annals of the New York Academy of Sciences* 609 (1990): 0077–8923; Institute of Medicine and Lovell Jones, John Paretto, and Christine Coussens, eds., *Rebuilding the Unity of Health and the Environment* (Washington, D.C.: National Academy Press, 2005), 2, 15, 43–44. The 60,000 estimate is from the Institute of Medicine, *Making Better Drugs for Children with Cancer* (Washington, D.C.: National Academy Press, 2005), 18. See, for example, D. L. Davis and P. S. Webster, "The Social Context of Science: Cancer and the Environment," *Annals of the American Academy of Political and Social Science* 584 (Nov. 2002): 13–34; D. L. and H. L. Bradlow, "Can Environmental Estrogens Cause Breast Cancer?," *Scientific American* 273:4 (Oct. 1995): 166; F. Valent, D. A. Little, R. Bertollini, L. E. Nemer, G. Barbone, and G. Tamburlini, "Burden of Disease Attributable to Selected Environmental Factors and Injury among Children and Adolescents in Europe," *Lancet* 363 (2004): 2032–39. Regarding the tumor-suppressor gene, see Anton Berns, "Tumour Suppressors: Timing Will Tell," *Nature* 424:6945 (2003): 140; Institute of Medicine, *Making Better Drugs for Children with Cancer* (Washington, D.C.: National Academy Press, 2005), 51; Stanford University Hospital and Clinics, *Cancer Overview,* available at http://cancer.stanford.edu/information/cancerOverview.html; National Cancer Institute (NCI); the American Cancer Society (ACS); the North American Association of Central Cancer Registries (NAACCR); the National Institute on Aging (NIA); the Centers for Disease Control and Prevention (CDC), including the National Center for Health Statistics (NCHS) and the National Center for Chronic Disease Prevention and Health Promotion, "Annual Report to the Nation on the Status of Cancer, 1973–1999," *Cancer* 94:10 (May 15, 2002): 2766–92. See also http://www.nih.gov/news/pr/may2002/nci-14.htm; National Institute of Health, *1987 Annual Cancer Statistics Review* (Bethesda, Md.: National Cancer Institute, 1987): 1.4–1.8; National Cancer Institute, *Surveillance, Epidemiology, and End Results, Cancer Statistics Review, 1973–1994* (Bethesda, Md.: NCI, 1994). See NIH, *Cancer Rates and Risks* (Bethesda, Md.: U.S. National Institutes of Health and U.S. National Cancer Institute, 2000). See also *Rolodex-Cancer* (Washington, D.C.: U.S. Centers for Disease Control and Prevention, 2000); American Cancer Society, *Cancer Facts and Figures 2000* (Atlanta, Ga.: American Cancer Society, 2000); American Cancer Society, *Cancer Facts and Figures 2005* (Atlanta, Ga.: American Cancer Society, 2005). Chicago particulate releases are from the U.S. EPA, *Toxic Release Inventory,* available at http://scorecard.goodguide.com/env-releases/us-main-map.tcl. Chicago cancer statistics are from Illinois Department of Public Health, *Illinois Cancer Statistics Review* (Springfield, Ill.: IDPH, 2003), 2–1. The calculations are as follows. If NCI says 10 ug of particulate pollution causes a 0.18 increase in heart deaths, then Chicago's 17 ug average annual particulate pollution causes a (1.7)(0.18) annual increase in heart deaths, which totals about 11,500 per year. If x = average annual Chicago heart deaths not from particulate pollution, then (1.7)(0.18)x = average annual deaths from Chicago's average particulates, and therefore x + (1.7)(0.18)x = 11,500, which means x + .306x = 11,500. This equation means, in return that 1.31x = 11,500, and thus that x = 11.500/1.31. This equation means, in turn, that x(average annual Chicago heart deaths not from particulates) = 8779. But 11,500 − 8779 = 2,721 average annual Chicago heart deaths, just from particulate pollutants. Institute of Medicine, *Insuring America's Health* (Washington, D.C.: National Academy Press, 2004), 8.

12. J. C. Lashof et al., Health and Life Sciences Division of the U.S. Office of Technology Assessment, *Assessment of Technologies for Determining Cancer Risks from the Environment* (Washington, D.C.: Office of Technology Assessment, 1981), 3, 6ff. See also, for example, D. L. Davis and P. S. Webster, "The Social Context of Science: Cancer and the Environment," *Annals of the American Academy of Political and Social Science* 584 (Nov. 2002): 13–34; D. L. Bradlow and H. L. Bradlow, "Can Environmental Estrogens Cause Breast Cancer?," *Scientific American* 273:4 (Oct. 1995): 166.

13. American Public Health Association, *Priority 2005 Issues: Fact Sheets, Health Disparities, Environmental Disparities, Racial/Ethnic Disparities,* 26, 28, 34.

14. Vincente Navarro, "Race or Class versus Race and Class: Mortality Differentials in the United States," *Lancet* 336 (1990): 1238–40.

15. B. Goldman, and L. Fitton, *Toxic Wastes and Race Revisited* (Washington, D.C.: Center for Policy Alternatives, 1994).

16. Paul Farmer, *Pathologies of Power* (Berkeley: University of California Press, 2005). For statistics, see European Public Health Alliance, *Air, Water Pollution and Health Effects* (Brussels: EPHA, 2006); available at http://www.epha.org/r/54. D. R. Wennette and L. A. Nieves, "Breathing Polluted Air," *EPA Journal* (March/April 1992): 16–17.

17. American Public Health Association, *Priority 2005 Issues: Fact Sheets, Health Disparities, Environmental Disparities, Racial/Ethnic Disparities,* 26, 28, 34; and D. Brody et al., "Blood Lead Levels in the U.S. Population: Phase 1 of the Third National Health and Nutrition Examination Survey (NHANES III, 1988 to 1991)," *Journal of the American Medical Association* 272:4 (July 27, 1994): 277–83. See H. Needleman, and D. Bellinger, "The Health Effects of Low-Level Exposure to Lead," *Annual Review of Public Health* 12 (1991): 111–40; CDC, "Update: Blood Lead Levels—United States, 1991-1994," *Morbidity and Mortality Weekly Report* 46:7 (Feb. 21, 1997).

18. Bruce P. Kennedy et al., "Income distribution and Mortality," *British Medical Journal* 312 (April 20, 1996): 1004–7; George A. Kaplan et al., "Inequality and Income and Mortality in the United States," *British Medical Journal* 312 (April 20, 1996): 999–1003. See American Public Health Association,

Priority 2005 Issues: Fact Sheets, Health Disparities, Environmental Disparities, Racial/Ethnic Disparities. For Chicago incinerator data, see Shrader-Frechette, *Environmental Justice,* 71ff.

19. American Public Health Association, *Priority 2005 Issues: Fact Sheets, Health Disparities, Environmental Disparities, Racial/Ethnic Disparities*; Michael Wolff, Peter Rutten, Albert Bayers, and the World Bank Research Team, *Where We Stand* (New York: Bantam, 1992), 23; U.S. Census, 2003; Kevin Phillips, *Wealth and Democracy* (New York: Broadway, 2002), 151–55; Kevin Phillips, "The Progressive Interview," *The Progressive* 66:9 (Sept. 2002): 33–37; Lawrence Mishel, Jared Bernstein, and John Schmitt, *The State of Working America* (Ithaca, N.Y.: Economic Policy Institute, Cornell University Press, 2001). See also Thomas Piketty and Emmanuel Saez, "Income Inequality in the United States, 1913–1998" (Working Paper no. W8467, National Bureau of Economic Research, Washington, D.C., 2001).

20. Death rates for one- to fifteen-year-olds are in Wolff et al., *Where We Stand,* 15–116. For infant-mortality data, see American Public Health Association, *Priority 2005 Issues: Fact Sheets, Health Disparities, Environmental Disparities, Racial/Ethnic Disparities,* 33; and U.S. Central Intelligence Agency, *The World Factbook* (Washington, D.C.: CIA, 2004), available at https://www.cia.gov/library/publications/the-world-factbook/index.html; U.S. Centers for Disease Control, *Infant Mortality Fact Sheet* (Washington, D.C.: CDC, 2005), available at http://www.cdc.gov/nchs/pressroom/04facts/infant.htm; Wolff et al., *Where We Stand,* 112–13; Nicholas D. Kristof, "Health Care? Ask Cuba," *New York Times,* Jan. 12, 2005, A23, available at nytimes.com/2005/01/12/opinion/12kris.htm?hp.

21. S. L. Syme, and L. Berkman, "Social Class, Susceptibility, and Sickness," *American Journal of Epidemiology* 104:1 (July 1976): 1–4; see also earlier notes, Institute of Medicine, *Insuring America's Health,* 8, and American Public Health Association, *Priority 2005 Issues: Fact Sheets, Health Disparities, Environmental Disparities, Racial/Ethnic Disparities,* 34.

22. American Public Health Association, *2000 Policy Statements,* "The Precautionary Principle and Children's Health"; American Public Health Association, *Priority 2005 Issues: Fact Sheets, Health Disparities, Environmental Disparities, Racial/Ethnic Disparities*; and Institute of Medicine, *Hidden Costs, Value Lost* (Washington, D.C.: National Academy Press, 2003); Institute of Medicine, *Guidance for the National Healthcare Disparities Report* (Washington, D.C.: National Academy Press, 2002); Institute of Medicine, *A Shared Destiny* (Washington, D.C.: National Academy Press, 2003); Institute of Medicine, *The Unequal Burden of Cancer* (Washington, D.C.: National Academy Press, 1999); Institute of Medicine, *Unequal Treatment* (Washington, D.C.: National Academy Press, 2002). See also Melissa Marino, "Racial Disparity in Colorectal Cancer Deaths," Vanderbilt Medical Center, Nashville, Tenn., April 16, 2004; L. A. G. Ries, B. A.

Miller, B. F. Hankey, et al., *SEER Cancer Statistics Review, 1973–1991: Tables and Graphs* (Bethesda, Md.: National Cancer Institute, 1994), NIH publ. no. 94-2789; V. L. Freeman, Ramon Durazo-Arvizu, La Shon Keys, Marc Johnson, Kristian Schofernak, "Racial Differences in Survival among Men with Prostate Cancer," *American Journal of Public Health* 94:5 (May 2004): 803–9; Adam Wagstaff, Flavia Bustreo, Jennifer Bryce, and Marian Claeson, "Child Health," *American Journal of Public Health* 94:5 (May 2004): 726–37; R. M. Campanelli, "Addressing Racial and Ethnic Health Disparities," *American Journal of Public Health* 93:10 (Oct. 2003): 1624–27; S. A. Ibrahim, S. B. Thomas, and M. J. Fine, "Achieving Heath Equity," *American Journal of Public Health* 93:10 (Oct. 2003): 1619–22; P. D. Mail, S. Lachenmayr, M. E. Auld, and K. Roe, "Eliminating Health Disparities," *American Journal of Public Health* 94:4 (April 2004): 519–20; American Public Health Association, *Priority 2005 Issues: Fact Sheets, Health Disparities, Environmental Disparities, Racial/Ethnic Disparities,* 34.

23. UNICEF, *State of the World's Children,* 2005 (New York: UNICEF, 2005); Natural Resources Defense Council, *Our Children at Risk* (Washington, D.C.: NRDC, 1997).

24. American Public Health Association, *2000 Policy Statements,* "The Precautionary Principle and Children's Health," available at http://www.apha.org/advocacy/policy/policysearch/default.htm?id=216 (policy number 200011).

25. WHO, *Effects of Air Pollution on Children's Health* (Bonn: WHO, 2005), 144; Paul Lichtenstein, Niels Holm, Pia Verkasalo, Anastasia Iliadou, Jaakko Kaprio, Markku Koskenvuo, Eero Pukkala, Axel Skytthee, and Kari Hemminki, "Environmental and Heritable Factors in the Causation of Cancer," *New England Journal of Medicine* 343:2 (2002): 78–85.

26. WHO, *Effects of Air Pollution on Children's Health,* 155.

27. Cancer statistics are from the Institute of Medicine, *Making Better Drugs for Children with Cancer,* 1, 5. See National Research Council, *Offspring* (Washington, D.C.: National Academy Press, 2003), 237; and Institute of Medicine, *Infant Formula* (Washington, D.C.: National Academy Press, 2004).

28. American Public Health Association, Policy Statement no. 2005-5, "Protecting Human Milk from Persistent Toxic Chemical Contaminants," available at http://www.apha.org/advocacy/policy/policysearch/default.htm?id=1321. For analysis of the GE case and other media control by polluters, see Shrader-Frechette, *Taking Action, Saving Lives,* chaps. 2–3. For analysis of childhood cancers and other pollution-related diseases, see Shrader-Frechette, *Taking Action, Saving Lives,* chap. 1.

29. Memorandum from Ann Katon to Ralph Lightstone, *Simplification of Adverse Effects Information for SB 950 Chemicals* (Sacramento: California Rural Legal Assistance Foundation, March 10, 1995).

30. D. J. Ecobichon et al., "Neurotoxic Effects of Pesticides," in *The Effects of Pesticides on Human Health,* ed. S. R. Baker and Chris Wilkinson (Princeton,

N.J.: Princeton Scientific, 1990), 131–99; R. Repetto and S. Baliga, *Pesticides and the Immune System* (Washington, D.C.: World Resources Institute, 1996); J. Barnett and K. Rogers, "Pesticides," in *Immunotoxicity and Immunopharmacology,* ed. J. H. Dean et al. (New York: Raven Press, 1994), 191–213; P. T. Thomas et al., "Immunologic Effects of Pesticides," in *The Effects of Pesticides on Human Health,* 261–95, esp. 266; P. R. McConnachie and A. C. Zahalsky, "Immunological Consequences of Exposure to Pentachlorophenol," *Archives of Environmental Health* 46 (July/Aug. 1991): 249–53.

31. National Research Council, *Pesticides in the Diets of Infants and Children* (Washington, D.C.: National Academy Press, 1993), 61.

32. J. M. Spyker and D. L. Avery, "Neurobehavioral Effects of Prenatal Exposure to the Organophosphate Diazinon in Mice," *Journal of Toxicology and Environmental Health* (1977): 989–1002.

33. National Research Council, *Pesticides in the Diets of Infants and Children,* 61.

34. California Air Resources Board, *Study of Children's Activity Patterns* (Sacramento, Calif.: CARB, Sept. 1991), 66a–67. See subsequent note and H. Needleman and P. Landrigan, *Raising Children Toxic Free* (New York: Farrar, Straus and Giroux, 1994). Woodruff T. Bates et al., "The Relationship between Selected Causes of Postneonatal Infant Mortality and Particulate Air Pollution in the United States," *Environmental Health Perspectives* 105:6 (June 1997): 608–12; P. H. Saldiva et al., "Association between Air Pollution and Mortality Due to Respiratory Diseases in Children in São Paulo, Brazil," *Environmental Research* 65 (1994): 218–25; Bobak M. Bates et al., "Air Pollution and Infant Mortality in the Czech Republic," *Lancet* 340 (1992): 1010–14; H. Knobel et al., "Sudden Infant Death Syndrome in Relation to Weather and Optimetrically Measured Air Pollution in Taiwan," *Pediatrics* 96:6 (Dec. 1995): 1106–10; D. L. Davis, *Urban Air Pollution Risks to Children: A Global Environmental Health Indicator* (New York: World Resources Institute, Oct. 1999); Lipsett M. Bates, "The Hazards of Air Pollution to Children," in *Environmental Medicine,* ed. S. Brooks et al. (St. Louis, Mo.: Mosby, 1995); R. Etzel, "Air Pollution Hazards to Children," *Otolaryngology—Head and Neck Surgery* (Feb. 1996): 265–66.

35. Centers for Disease Control, "Populations at Risk from Air Pollution," *Morbidity and Mortality Weekly Report* 42:16 (April 30, 1993).

36. See, for example, Committee of the Environmental and Occupational Health Assembly of the American Thoracic Society, "Health Effects of Outdoor Air Pollution," *American Journal of Respiratory and Critical Care Medicine* 153 (1996): 3–50; D. Bates, "The Effects of Air Pollution in Children," *Environmental Health Perspectives* 103, supp. 6 (Sept. 1995): 49–54; D. Spektor et al., "Effects of Concentration and Cumulative Exposure of Inhaled Sulfuric Acid on Trachea-Bronchial Particle Clearance in Healthy Humans," *Environmental Health Perspectives* 79 (1989): 167–72; M. Lippman, "Health Effects of Ozone," *Journal*

of Air Pollution Control Associations 39:5 (1989): 672–95; J. Last, "Effects of Inhaled Acids on Lung Biochemistry," *Environmental Health Perspectives* 79 (1989): 115–19; M. Utell, and J. Samet, "Air Pollution in the Outdoor Environment," in *Environmental Medicine,* ed. S. Brooks et al. (St. Louis, Mo.: Mosby, 1995), 462–69; A. Pope et al., "Health Effects of Particulate Air Pollution," *Environmental Health Perspectives* 103:5 (May 1995): 472–78; L. Van Bree et al., "Lung Injury during Acute and Subchronic Exposure and Recovery," *American Review of Respiratory Disease* 145:4 (April 1992): A93; P. Lioy et al., "Persistence of Peak Flow Decrement in Children Following Ozone Exposures Exceeding the National Ambient Air Quality Standard," *Journal of Air Pollution Control Associations* 35 (1985): 1069–71; R. Detels et al., "The UCLA Population Studies of CORD," *American Journal of Public Health* 81:3 (1991): 350–59; K. Pinkerton et al., "Exposure to a Simulated 'Ambient' Pattern of Ozone Results in Significant Pulmonary Retention of Asbestos Fibers," *American Review of Respiratory Disease* 137:4 (April 1988): 166; J. Raub et al., "Effects of Low Level Ozone Exposure on Pulmonary Function," *Advances in Modern Environmental Toxicology* 5 (1983): 363; Q. C. He et al., "Effects of Air Pollution on Children's Pulmonary Function," *Archives of Environmental Health* 48 (1993): 382–91; G. Hoek and B. Brunekreef, "Acute Effects of a Winter Air Pollution Episode on Pulmonary Function and Respiratory Symptoms of Children," *Archives of Environmental Health* 48 (1993): 328–35; R. Schmitzberger et al., "Effects of Air Pollution on the Respiratory Tract of Children," *Pediatric Pulmonology* 15 (1993): 68–74; A. Pope, "Respiratory Health and PM 10 Pollution," *American Review of Respiratory Disease* 144 (1991): 668–74; M. Raizenne, "Health Effects of Acid Aerosols on North American Children," *Environmental Health Perspectives* 104:5 (May 1996): 506–14; M. Studnicka et al., "Acidic Particles and Lung Function in Children," *American Journal of Respiratory and Critical Care Medicine* 151 (1995): 423–30; L. Neas et al., "The Association of Ambient Air Pollution with Twice Daily Peak Expiratory Flow Rate Measurements in Children," *American Journal of Epidemiology* 141 (1995): 111–222; L. Neas et al., "Fungus Spores, Air Pollutants, and Other Determinants of Peak Expiratory Flow Rate in Children," *American Journal of Epidemiology* 143 (1996): 797–807; G. Hock et al., "Acute Effects of Ambient Ozone on Pulmonary Function of Children," *American Review of Respiratory Disease* 147 (1993): 111–17.

   37. M. Weitzman et al., "Recent Trends in the Prevalence and Severity of Childhood Asthma," *Journal of the American Medical Association* 268:19 (Nov. 18, 1992): 2673–77; E. Friebele and M. Weitzman et al., "The Attack of Asthma," *Environmental Health Perspectives* 104:1 (Jan. 1996): 22–25; K. Weiss et al., "An Economic Evaluation of Asthma in the United States," *New England Journal of Medicine* 326:13 (March 26, 1992): 862–66; Center for Disease Control, "Asthma Mortality and Hospitalization among Children and Young Adults— United States, 1980–1993," *Morbidity and Mortality Weekly Report* (May 3,

1996); George D. Thurston, "Summertime Haze Air Pollution and Children with Asthma," *American Journal of Respiratory and Critical Care Medicine* 155 (Feb. 1997): 654–60; M. White et al., "Exacerbations of Childhood Asthma and Ozone Pollution in Atlanta," *Environmental Research* 65 (1994): 56–68; I. Romieu et al., "Effects of Air Pollution on the Respiratory Health of Asthmatic Children Living in Mexico City," *American Journal of Respiratory and Critical Care Medicine* 154 (1996): 300–307.

    38. See European Public Health Alliance, *Air, Water Pollution and Health Effects.*

    39. WHO, *Effects of Air Pollution on Children's Health,* 20, 23. See earlier notes for APHA air-pollution recommendations. American Lung Association, *Danger Zones* (Washington, D.C.: American Lung Association, 1995); Center for Disease Control, "Asthma Mortality and Hospitalization among Children and Young Adults—United States, 1980–1993." Ozone data are in preceding notes.

    40. American Academy of Pediatrics Committee on Environmental Health, "Ambient Air Pollution: Respiratory Hazards to Children," *Pediatrics* 91:6 (1993): 1210–13.

    41. F. P. Perera, *Progress Report to the Colette Chuda Environmental Fund for the Molecular Epidemiological Study of Effects of Environmental Pollution on Women and the Developing Fetus* (New York: School of Public Health, Columbia University, 1994).

    42. CDC, *Blood Mercury Levels in Young Children and Childbearing-Aged Women* (Washington, D.C.: CDC, 2004), 7; available at http://www.cdc.gov/mmwr/preview/mmwrhtml/mm5343a5.htm. "One in Five Women Carries Too Much Mercury," *OMB Watch* 7:4 (Feb. 22, 2006); available at http://www.ombwatch.org/node/2801.

    43. A. Pope, "Respiratory Hospital Admissions Associated with PM10 Pollution in Utah, Salt Lake, and Cache Valleys," *Archives of Environmental Health* 46 (1991): 90–97.

    44. See previous note and D. V. Bates, and R. Sizto, "Hospital Admissions and Air Pollutants," *Environmental Research* 43 (1987): 317–31; R. T. Burnett et al., "Effects of Low Ambient Levels of Ozone and Sulfates on the Frequency of Respiratory Admissions," *Environmental Research* 65 (1994): 172–94; G. D. Thurston et al., "Respiratory Hospital Admissions and Summertime Haze Air Pollution," *Environmental Research* 65 (1994): 271–90; C. Braun-Fahrlander et al., "Air Pollution and Respiratory Symptoms in Preschool Children," *American Review of Respiratory Disease* 145 (1992): 42–47; J. Jaakkola et al., "Low Level Air Pollution and Upper Respiratory Infections in Children," *American Journal of Public Health* 81 (Aug. 1991): 1060–63; E. von Mutius et al., "Air Pollution and Upper Respiratory Symptoms in Children," *European Respiratory Journal* 8 (1995): 723–28; J. H. Ware et al., "Effects of Ambient Sulfur Oxides and Suspended Particles on Respiratory Health of Preadolescent Children," *American*

Review of Respiratory Disease 133 (1986): 834–42; D. Dockery et al., "Effects of Inhalable Particles on Respiratory Health of Children," *American Review of Respiratory Disease* 139 (1989): 587–94; J. Schwartz et al., "Acute Effects of Summer Air Pollution on Respiratory Symptom Reporting in Children," *American Journal of Respiratory and Critical Care Medicine* 150 (1994): 1234–42.

45. D. Bates, "Observations on Asthma," *Environmental Health Perspectives* 103, supp. 6 (Sept. 1995): 243–52; M. White et al., "Exacerbations of Childhood Asthma and Ozone Pollution in Atlanta," *Environmental Research* 65 (1994): 56–68; J. Schwartz, D. Dockery, et al., "An Association between Air Pollution and Mortality in Six U.S. Cities," *New England Journal of Medicine* 329:24 (Dec. 9, 1993): 1753–59.

46. L. Plunkett et al., "Differences between Adults and Children Affecting Exposure Assessment," in *Similarities and Differences between Children and Adults,* ed. P Guzelian (Washington, D.C.: International Life Sciences Institute, 1992).

47. EPA, *Fact Sheet, National Primary Drinking Water Regulations for Lead and Copper* (Washington, D.C.: EPA, May 1991), 3; also available in *Fed. Reg.* 26,470 (June 7, 1991). See M. Shannon, and J. Graef, "Lead Intoxication in Infancy," *Pediatrics* 89:1 (Jan. 1992): 87–90; M. Shannon and J. Graef, "Hazard of Lead in Infant Formula," *New England Journal of Medicine* 326:9 (1992): 137.

48. WHO, *Water for Life* (Geneva: WHO, 2005).

49. For an overview of environmental-impact assessment, see Kristin Shrader-Frechette, *Risk Analysis and Scientific Method* (Boston: Kluwer, 1985), 15–54; and Shrader-Frechette, *Risk and Rationality* (Berkeley: University of California Press, 1991), 5–7, 53–65.

50. This case is discussed in Shrader-Frechette, *Environmental Justice: Creating Equality, Reclaiming Democracy,* 71–93. For up-to-date information on the LES attempt to build the plant in New Mexico, see Public Citizen, *LES-Proposed Uranium Enrichment Facility Near Eunice, New Mexico* (Washington, D.C.: Public Citizen, 2006); available at http://www.citizen.org/cmep/energy_enviro _nuclear/newnukes/les/.

51. U.S. Nuclear Regulatory Commission (NRC), *Final Environment Impact Statement for the Construction and Operation of Claiborne Enrichment Center Homer Louisiana,* NUREG-1484, vol. 1 (Washington, D.C.: U.S. NRC, Office of Nuclear Material Safety and Safeguards, Aug. 1994), xxvi, 4-35, 4-53, 4-54, 4-56; Shrader-Frechette, *Risk and Rationality,* 71.

52. U.S. Nuclear Regulatory Commission (NRC), *Final Environment Impact Statement for the Construction and Operation of Claiborne Enrichment Center Homer Louisiana,* 1-5 through 1-9, 4-77.

53. Ibid., 1-5.

54. Ibid., 4-77 through 4-84, 4-86.

55. Ibid., 4-86.

56. Ibid., 4-77.

57. Ibid., 1-5.

58. Ibid., 2-3 through 2-19.

59. Shrader-Frechette, *Environmental Justice: Creating Equality, Reclaiming Democracy,* 71–93. For arguments in favor of the facility, see Henry Payne, "Environmental Injustice," *Reason* 29:4 (Sept. 1997): 53–57. See also Daniel Wigley and Kristin Shrader-Frechette, "Environmental Justice: A Louisiana Case Study," *Journal of Agricultural and Environmental Ethics* 9:1 (1996): 61–82.

60. Ruth Faden and Tom Beauchamp, *A History and Theory of Free Informed Consent* (New York: Oxford University Press, 1986); Tom Beauchamp and James Childress, *Principles of Biomedical Ethics* (New York: Oxford University Press, 1994).

61. Shrader-Frechette, *Environmental Justice: Creating Equality, Reclaiming Democracy,* 71–93.

62. Science Advisory Board, U.S. Environmental Protection Agency, *Comments on the Use of Data from the Testing of Human Subjects,* EPA-SAB-EC-00-017 (Washington, D.C.: U.S. EPA, 2000). See also Christopher Oleskey, Alan Fleischman, Lynn Goldman, Kurt Hirschhorn, Philip J. Landrigan, Marc Lappe, Mary Faith Marshall, Herbert Needleman, Rosamond Rhodes, and Michael McCally, "Pesticide Testing in Humans," *Environmental Health Perspectives* 112:8 (June 2004): 914–19.

63. Shrader-Frechette, *Taking Action, Saving Lives: Public Health, Human Rights, Environmental Justice,* chap. 3.

64. The syllabus for the course, in which many Notre Dame undergraduates do pro bono environmental justice work every semester, is at http://www.nd.edu/~kshrader/courses/14120/2006-5-fall-ej-syllabus.pdf. For further discussion of the students' environmental justice work, see Heidi Schlumpf, "Expert Witness . . . An Interview with Kristin Shrader-Frechette," *U.S. Catholic* 71:4 (April 2006): 18–23. For examples of environmental justice papers coauthored with students, see, for instance, Sean Walsh and Kristin Shrader-Frechette, "Environmental Justice and Procedural Safeguards," *University of Arizona Law Review* 42:2 (Summer 2000): 525–40, which was written to help protect a New Mexico Latino population; and the paper coauthored with Dan Wigley (note 59), written to help protect the Louisiana African American population that is discussed in this essay.

65. See Shrader-Frechette, *Taking Action, Saving Lives: Public Health, Human Rights, Environmental Justice,* chaps. 4–6, for answers to various objections to the preceding arguments.

66. Aquinas, *Summa Theologiae* Ia IIae, q. 66, art. 7; available at http://www.newadvent.org/summa/306607.htm.

CHAPTER 8

Teaching and Transformation

Liberal Arts for the Homeless

F. CLARK POWER AND
STEPHEN M. FALLON

As is true of the occupation of any Christian, our teaching at the University of Notre Dame bears a great relation to our responsibility to exercise a preferential option for the poor, and vice versa. We write this chapter with uneasy consciences, insofar as much of our work teaching a Great Books curriculum at Notre Dame disproportionately serves the privileged in our society and in our church. The Golden Dome that crowns our campus symbolizes the success of a once struggling immigrant Catholic population. Despite its historical origins in an attempt to extend the resources of universities to working men and women, Great Books liberal arts education—with its focus on the classics of literature, philosophy, theology, music, and science—has most often been offered to the children of society's elite. Moreover, the Great Books canon has for the past two decades been attacked as presenting a biased, Eurocentric, white male perspective. Indeed, some have viewed our curriculum as an indoctrination in Western hegemonic values.

We argue in this chapter that, properly conceived, a Great Books education constitutes a powerful pedagogy for the dispossessed in the United States. The challenge for Notre Dame and other universities that recognize the value of the Great Books approach is to make the approach available to the poor. We as a university faculty cannot be content merely to teach the privileged to be conscious of poverty and injustice in our society. If we trust in the power of the education that we are giving to the best and brightest of our undergraduates, we ought to find a way to bring that education to those at the margins of our society. Whom we educate matters every bit as much as how we educate. We do not believe that the university's responsibilities to the poor in society are a specifically Catholic issue. Justice, which is a universal moral principle, demands that education be offered to all members of society. Given that education leads to power in a democratic society, we have a special obligation to distribute our society's educational resources to bring about full equality. This means that the poor in our society, whose needs are the greatest, should receive an equitable share of our society's educational opportunities. In a word, justice dictates a preference for the poor. Our Catholic institutional identity only intensifies our sense of commitment to this moral imperative. Our Catholic identity also makes more salient and painful the contradiction between our ideals and our reality.

In this chapter, we will describe the World Masterpieces class, which we have been offering since 1999 to guests at the Center for the Homeless. Our experience in undertaking this modest initiative raises important questions about what the preferential option for the poor means for us as a Catholic university. We have never thought of the World Masterpieces course simply as personal service but as a corporate Notre Dame initiative. We have seen ourselves as agents of the university helping to realize the university's educational mission. The program has been made possible by institutional support. On the other hand, we reluctantly admit that this course, like its students, balances precariously at the margins. It has yet to find its way into the mainstream of university life; it is without a real home at Notre Dame.

GREAT BOOKS AND IDEOLOGY

Judging by appearances, a case might be made that teaching in a Great Books program at a wealthy university contributes to the subjugation, not the liberation, of the poor. Some of the most visible defenders of liberal arts education, such as William Bennett and Allan Bloom, have fed the popular perception of Great Books programs as supporting the status quo. But appearances can be, of course, deceiving, and, in our view, the criticism that Great Books education is inherently biased against the oppressed is itself uninformed and unfair, whether viewed in terms of historical origins, content, or effect.

The Great Books movement originated at New York City's Columbia University in the 1920s. Convinced that working men and women were equal to and would benefit from the challenges posed by great works in the arts, humanities, and social sciences, the founders of the movement developed a curriculum to be offered in evening seminars to those who otherwise would not have access to university instruction. The demand for and success of the Great Books seminars justified the founders' confidence. Not surprisingly, the success of the venture left its mark on university curricula, as the Great Books seminars proved the inspiration for the core curricula at Columbia, the University of Chicago, and elsewhere. Our own department began in 1950 as a pilot program for a new core curriculum at Notre Dame. Since the 1920s, the Great Books seminar has led a double life, inside and outside the university. In both settings, its aims are democratic, working against a rigid hierarchy that places teacher above student, mediating to a passive audience the esoteric knowledge of the specialist. In place of the lecture, the Great Books seminar promotes shared inquiry. The texts we read were written for intelligent, educated audiences, not for specialists, and the Great Books seminar attempts to read them in that spirit.

To read through the Great Books curriculum is to be disabused of the notion that the texts constitute or promote a monolithic intellectual vision that might underwrite an oppressive political regime. Instead, the works present deeply divergent perspectives on fundamental questions of meaning and value. The works of Plato, Aristotle, Augustine, Aquinas, Julian of Norwich, Descartes, Hobbes, Locke, Smith, Marx, Nietzsche, Woolf, and others on our Great Books list make for a combative conversation, not the transmission of particular ideology. Moreover, Great Books lists have extended in recent years to include more works by women, minority, and non-Western authors. We welcome and we have been advocates for these changes. For example, our students now read Ellison's *Invisible Man,* which offers a challenging perspective previously absent from the list.

To those who fear that reading the Great Books promotes a politics of oppression, we would note that the greatest advocates for justice and social reform in our day have been inspired by works in the supposedly reactionary traditional canon. Martin Luther King Jr.'s "Letter from Birmingham Jail," which arguably deserves a place among the classic speeches of all time, draws on the Bible, Plato's *Apology*, Thomas Aquinas's *Summa Theologica*, the Declaration of Independence, and other great texts to make a case for measured civil disobedience as both an American and a Christian response to America's racist history. As E. D. Hirsch argued, largely to deaf ears, in *Cultural Literacy*, classic texts inspired the Black Panthers as well.[1] Hirsch's point remains a valid one. Classic texts, as the language of the enfranchised and the elite in our society, give access to power. They can liberate the mind to see possibilities, to question conventions and authority, and to articulate the otherwise inarticulate aspirations of the dispossessed.

A GREAT BOOKS PEDAGOGY FOR THE POOR

The Hebrew word for the poor is *anawim*, which in the Hebrew Bible means literally "little breaths." Thinking of the poor as "little breaths" calls attention as much to a lack of power and influence as it does a lack of material goods. Donald Trump declared bankruptcy, but Donald Trump never lacked influence. He was never poor. One direct response to poverty is to help the *anawim* find their breath, their voice. By this we mean more than advocating for the poor. To advocate means to speak for another. In biblical terms we may think of advocacy as the stronger putting their breath behind the weaker. Advocacy is a necessary but not sufficient response to poverty. Ultimately we must enable the poor to breathe for themselves, to find their own voice in society. Breathing finds its full embodiment in the spoken word. God's act of creation is depicted in Genesis as involving God's breath or God's wind, which then becomes God's word.

The creation story reminds us not only of the power of the word but also of the origin of that power in God. To enable the poor to breathe and speak for themselves is to participate in the ongoing creative activity of God. This understanding of human activity as rooted in divine activity has, we believe, serious implications for our work. On the one hand, we must accept our own responsibility to the poor. On the other hand, we must acknowledge our limitations and poverty of spirit. We are like God, but we are all poor and lacking in breath.

Within the framework that we are developing, education is all about breath and words. Education leads to power, especially in today's world. The most effective way of maintaining dominance is to restrict the access to education or to educate in ways that lead to conformity and dependence on powerful others. Education should lead to autonomy, which means not only self-rule but the democratic rule of free and reasonable selves who govern together according to principles of mutual respect and commitment to the common good.

It is thus not enough to provide education for the poor; we need to think about the kind of education provided. Generally the poor are offered what is called "vocational education," which is oriented to acquiring a competence in a particular occupation, such as computer repair, welding, or hairstyling. Vocational education is, indeed, extremely important because it is directly linked to opportunities for interesting and well-paying jobs. On the other hand, vocational education is by nature limited to the acquisition of specific skills. Vocational education is not an adequate preparation for full cultural membership and political effectiveness.

We cannot think of better preparation for citizenship than the liberal arts education offered in the Notre Dame Great Books program. Crucial to the success of the program is not simply reading great books but reading great books with an open mind. Typically university professors help students to read texts by offering a particular interpretation of the text. Generally students appreciate such assistance because the books are difficult and are open to different kinds of readings. In Notre Dame's Program of Liberal Studies, faculty are discouraged from suggesting to students what a text means. In fact, lecturing that goes beyond brief introductory comments is all but forbidden in Great Books seminars.

The primary pedagogical reason for this is not to curb the faculty's imposition of their own points of view but to encourage students' own engagement with the texts. By interpreting texts for them, faculty give students shortcuts that diminish the whole experience of grappling with a text's meanings. Students should not be spared the hard work of careful reading and understanding. Even well-meaning faculty, who simply offer students a (not *the*) reading of a text, fail to appreciate how their authority gets in the way of their students' learning. All too often, whatever the faculty member says is taken as the truth. Although faculty cannot avoid reaching their own conclusions about a text, they should avoid making what may be taken as authoritative pronouncements on the text.

Because seminar pedagogy breaks down the hierarchical relationship between faculty and students, we sometimes describe the Great Books pedagogy as radically democratic. The Program of Liberal Studies' real teachers are the authors of the Great Books; everyone else is a student.[2] The rules for our Great Books seminars limit discussion to the text under consideration or to the texts that faculty and students have read together. This levels the playing field of seminar discussion by eliminating faculty digressions on contextual scholarship and other primary sources that our students have not read.

This democratization of teaching has the intended effect of empowering students as readers and interpreters. Students gain confidence as they gain competence. Although our approach evokes the *sola scriptura* sense of Protestant individualism, the seminar discussion is a communal enterprise. Members of the seminar help each other to sort out more and less adequate readings. Although it is rare for members of a class to agree on all points of interpretation, most seminars do lead to a base of common understanding and to an appreciation of resolving differences through discourse. Seminars strengthen faith in a democratic process rooted in free and reasoned communication.

Our view of Great Books pedagogy clearly challenges those who prize or criticize Great Books programs as based in a conservative ideology that maintains inequalities of wealth, status, and power. The fact that the kind of liberal arts education that we espouse has been made available only to the most elite members of society should not mislead us about the transformative power of the Great Books pedagogy and Great Books themselves. It is not coincidental that Program of Liberal Studies students have the highest rates of participation in community service programs while they are at Notre Dame and the highest rates of voluntary service after graduation. Whether the Program of Liberal Studies inspires service to the poor or whether it attracts idealistic students, Program students exhibit a degree of civic engagement unparalleled in any other major in the university. The challenge, as yet unmet by secular and Christian organizations alike, is to make the Great Books approach available not only to students who meet the high admission standards of a university such as Notre Dame, but also to those who may never have dreamed of pursuing higher education.

THE WORLD MASTERPIECES PROGRAM

We now turn to the story of the World Masterpieces class, which began in 1998. We had for some time been thinking of ways in which we might follow the example of our students and become involved in some form of community service. Clark suggested that our service should in some way be related to our expertise. Steve countered that opportunities for such service might more easily present themselves to Clark, an educational psychologist, than to himself, a specialist in Milton and Renaissance literature. The matter rested until a colleague brought to our attention a *Harper's* article in which Earl Shorris described a class in the humanities that he initiated for adults below the poverty line in New York City. Shorris's article was based on a chapter of his 1997 book, *New American Blues: A Journey through Poverty to Democracy.*[3] A graduate of the University of Chicago during the Hutchins era, when students in the college followed a rigorous Great Books curriculum, Shorris makes a strong case for a Great Books education as "an answer to the problem of poverty in the United States." He argues very simply that a Great Books education in the humanities fosters human development and political participation.

While researching the nature of American poverty, he interviewed Viniece Walker, a prisoner in the Bedford Hills Correctional Facility in Westchester County. In response to his question about how to eliminate poverty, Ms. Walker replied profoundly simply, "You've got to teach the moral life of downtown." By downtown she meant high culture: plays, museums, concerts, literature. Ms. Walker was saying that to grasp politics, to enter the public world, the poor first had to learn to reflect and to claim ownership of civic life. Art and the humanities were a gateway to reflection and to ownership. As Shorris put it, "The poor did not need anyone to release them; an escape route existed. But to open this avenue to reflection and politics a major distinction between the preparation for the life of the rich and the life of the poor had to be eliminated."

Shorris's *New American Blues* offers both an intellectual and a practical response to the elitist view of university education put forth by his classmate Allan Bloom in *The Closing of the American Mind,*[4] a book that Bloom discussed with our Program of Liberal Studies (PLS) faculty prior to its publication in 1987. Although we agreed with part of Bloom's criticism of American popular culture, we were dismayed by his view that liberal arts education should be preserved for the elite few. While the term *liberal arts* originated as a reference to the arts of free or privileged men who had leisure to explore them, the term has come in a democratic age to refer to the liberating effect of the arts, which can prepare any man or woman for full participation in the community's cultural and political life.

Unfortunately, as we noted earlier, most Great Books programs are located within private universities and are, therefore, inaccessible to most Americans. On the other hand, the Great Books movement began with adult discussion groups involving individuals from all walks of life. Shorris's course in New York City, taught by a cadre of volunteer professors, retrieved the democratic impulse in the Great Books movement and convinced us not that the Great Books were for everyone—we already believed that—but that the Program of Liberal Studies could and should reach out to the poor in our own city of South Bend, Indiana.

We turned for help to the then director of the Center for the Homeless, 1983 PLS graduate Lou Nanni. Under Nanni's leadership, the center, which began with financial support from the university, had become nationally recognized for its comprehensive, long-term care that helped move individuals from the streets to employment and good housing. Responding enthusiastically, Nanni suggested that we recruit our students from those who had finished the initial treatment phase offered by the center.

Because the life circumstances of guests of the center often change quickly and unpredictably, we decided to offer a sequence of three eight-week units. Students earn a credit at the completion of each unit and new students are recruited for each unit. We organized the units thematically beginning with the theme of "justice and tyranny," moving to "self-discovery," and concluding with "God and nature." We took most of our texts from the undergraduate seminar lists and added a few contemporary selections, such as Martin Luther King Jr.'s "Letter from Birmingham Jail" and Doris Lessing's "The Old Chief Mshlanga."

Nanni recommended that we offer the course for credit, as Shorris had done. Awarding credit, although largely symbolic, was more important than we originally realized. We discovered that students from the center wanted to prove to themselves and to the outside world that they could perform as well as traditional Notre Dame students. They wanted assurance from us that they were getting as rigorous an education as the other undergraduates. They also wanted to belong to the Notre Dame community, a community with a national identity but with few ties to the downtown area where the center was located. Our colleagues in the Program of Liberal Studies and the Notre Dame administrators thought that the idea of giving credit free of charge was a wonderful idea, and with the assurance that we would uphold the high standards of the program, we had little trouble cutting through the red tape of admissions and registration procedures. No doubt the fact that the World Masterpieces course was relatively cost-free expedited the process. W. W. Norton & Company initially donated copies of its two-volume anthology, *World Masterpieces,* for our first-year class and subsequently gave us two hundred sets for future courses. Other expenses have been modest, mainly for refreshments, for copies of books and essays not contained in the Norton text, and for concert and theater tickets. We originally met expenses through T-shirt sales, gifts from our alumnae/i, donated theater and concert tickets from Notre Dame and St. Mary's, and free use of a van from the Center for Social Concerns. After a year, we received a modest budget of approximately five thousand dollars annually from the College of Arts and Letters, which allowed us to get some administrative assistance, purchase tickets to some local events, and attend an opera in Chicago.

At the time we began the course, one administrator cautioned us about donating our teaching time. He believed that the World Masterpieces course deserved the same financial support as the other courses in the undergraduate curriculum. If we really wanted our course to be a genuine extension of the university into the local community, then we should be paid for teaching it. Some colleagues in the program also questioned our voluntary commitment but from another angle. They rightly noted that the course made substantial demands on time and energy that could have been spent on more immediate needs within the regular undergraduate program. Some also questioned whether our involvement of undergraduates as van drivers, child care providers, and ethnographers compromised the time that they should be giving to their own studies.

These questions and objections never really gave us pause. We were in a hurry to get the class started and wanted to make as few demands on the university as possible. We did not feel guilty about asking students to help us because most of our students regularly worked in service projects throughout the school year and because this project was related to their major. We felt that the time we took for the class came largely out of our personal time, some of which would have been devoted to our research. In retrospect, we concede that our colleagues raised valuable and far-reaching questions about the place that the class should have within the department and the college. Although the two of us were in a position to donate our time, most of our colleagues in the program were not so privileged. Many were overextended with university and family responsibilities. The untenured needed to devote themselves fully to their teaching and research. One untenured faculty member taught a World Masterpieces class at the YWCA, and three other colleagues led seminars in their areas of specialization (music, poetry, and history of science). What we had hoped would be a collective project involving the whole department after a couple of years came to be perceived as belonging to the two of us. Finally, the college cut back on its support when the post-9/11 drop in the stock market led to drastic budget cuts throughout the university.

We will return to the question of whether we should seek university funding for teaching the World Masterpieces course at the conclusion of this chapter. In order to make a case for funding, we need to assess what the course contributes to the homeless and to the university. This will bring us back to a consideration of what the preferential option for the poor means for a research university like Notre Dame.

We have been asked many times since we started the course how we would evaluate its outcomes. How many students have gone on for postsecondary education after leaving the center? How many students who took the course found regular jobs and stayed off the streets? Are the students more politically engaged as a result of the course? Not only do we not have the data necessary to answer these questions, we feel that the questions themselves do not reach deeply enough into our students' or our own experience of the course. The number of students we teach at any one time is small, from eight to fifteen students. No two students have exactly the same profile. Some students have an undergraduate degree, while others dropped out of high school. Most struggle with addictions, many are in treatment for various kinds of mental illness. To meet these needs, the Center for the Homeless provides excellent psychological and educational services for its guests.

It is very difficult to isolate the contribution of our course to most outcome variables. On the other hand, we can learn something about the effects of the course simply by asking the students. When *New York Times* reporter Ethan Bronner provocatively asked the class why they were studying the classics like Plato's *Apology* instead of preparing themselves for jobs, a student shouted back, "You cannot live by bread alone." There is a profundity to that comment that might be easily overlooked. The homeless guests search for truth, justice, and beauty as much as or more than the rest of us. Many of our students know far better than we what money can and cannot buy. Here are a few comments on the course from our students at the Center to Bronner as they appeared in his *New York Times* article:

Socrates makes clear that you have to have the courage to examine yourself and to stand up for something. A lot of us have justified our weaknesses for too long a time.

When you come out of the fog of addiction, you thirst for knowledge. You feel there is so much you missed. For 20 years, I never had a goal beyond where my next glass of vodka was coming from. When Socrates talks about the pleasure of knowledge, I know exactly what he means.

It is hard to find beauty when you are in the situation we are in. But I have come to realize through the reading that, in some ways, everybody is homeless. You can be sitting in your fancy penthouse apartment looking out at the world but your life can be hollow. Now my mind is active, I have picked up a lost thread. Who knows? Maybe one day I'll write the great American novel.[5]

In these and other statements, our students call attention to energy that comes from intellectual engagement and self-examination. The value of the World Masterpieces course for students is not so much about the particular content of the course but about the sustenance of the spirit. Music has been an important component of the course not because students learn something about musical composition or a great composer, but because they experience the beauty of a performance and partake of the "downtown" that once seemed so remote.

In proving their competence to others, our students also proved it to themselves. Becoming homeless, losing one's job and one's family is a terrible blow to one's sense of self-esteem. Succeeding with such a challenging curriculum helped our students to gain confidence. The seminar context of the class gave the students an opportunity to develop their skills of interpretation and expression. We would like to think that our presence as seminar leaders made some difference. Our role, as we noted before, was not to impart information, but to direct the discussion through asking questions and calling attention to key passages. Although we always tried to encourage our students, we kept our demands high. The students all felt that the course asked a lot of them. Their sense of accomplishment at the end was well earned.

Years ago following a seminar class, one of the most articulate members of the class heatedly admonished a fellow student, "You keep taking potshots at these books without taking the time to understand what the author is trying to say. You can't begin to criticize a book until you make the effort to get inside it and live it."

Students from the Masterpieces class have "lived" the books themselves and out of that experience brought forth new and significant insights into the texts. For example, while reading the *Odyssey*, we posed for class discussion the dilemma that Calypso put to Odysseus: Should Odysseus stay on the island and have immortal life with a beautiful goddess, or return home and finish the rest of his days with an aging wife? Bill replied that the choice was clear; Odysseus should return home. We were stunned at the lack of debate. "Why wouldn't you choose immortality?" Breaking into a wide smile, Bill explained, "Look around the room, we are all alcoholics and drug addicts. If we could live forever, we'd never stop drinking or using drugs. It is knowing that you only have so much time to live that forces you to face up to what you are doing with the little time that you have." In a later conversation while we were discussing the opening scenes in Shakespeare's *Tempest,* another student addressed the class: "This book was written about us; look around the room—all of us have been shipwrecked by life."

Most educational evaluations rightly focus on the effects on the students. Yet by focusing exclusively on students, we ignore how teaching transforms the teacher. Moreover, we know that good teaching is never unidirectional. This is particularly true of seminar teaching in a Great Books program where we say and believe that our real teachers are the authors of the texts we read. Every Great Books seminar offers a unique encounter not only with those gathered around the table but also with the author of the text.

HOMELESSNESS

During the third year of the program, we took two students, Joe and Alice, to Indianapolis to help us present a seminar on our class to a conference on community and the arts. The conversation drifted to their previous lives. Joe told us that he had drifted all over the country since he dropped out of high school. He explained that he never had had an experience of being at home and just did not know how to be at home in any one place. Alice, who had lived most of her life in the South Bend area, said that she too was homeless by nature. "I've just never at any time— even in my childhood—felt a sense of home," she told us. Like Joe, whenever she felt that she was "settling in," she would suddenly pick up and leave. They were changing, however, they confided. The Center for the Homeless had given them the hope that their days of wandering were over. Shortly after our trip, Alice began working for a local construction company. Ironically, her first job was building a home for others as part of Habitat for Humanity. Joe left the center hours after returning from our Indianapolis trip and has not been heard from since.

Before that conversation with Joe and Alice, we had thought of homelessness as a manifestation of extreme poverty generally accompanied by addiction and mental illness. We had not considered the possibility that homelessness was fundamentally a spiritual condition, marked by a radical rootlessness. Even some of the most penetrating descriptions of homelessness fail to consider homelessness as an internal state. For example, the sociologists David Snow and Leon Anderson note that there are three separate dimensions of homelessness: a residential dimension, a familial support dimension, and a moral worth dimension. The residential dimension is the most obvious: homeless people lack conventional permanent housing and end up sleeping in shelters or in places, like park benches, not intended as dwellings. The familial support dimension is often overlooked: the homeless lack the relational bonds of affection, support, and belonging. The moral worth dimension is the least well understood. Stigmatized as irresponsible and without character, the homeless represent the antithesis of American values.[6]

Unfortunately, responses to homelessness focus primarily on the residential dimension, often at the expense of the other dimensions, particularly the third. Care-taking approaches to the homeless tend to confirm their sense of disconnection, powerlessness, and low moral worth. Moreover, care-taking approaches do not come to grips with the spiritual dimension. The World Masterpieces seminar moves in a very different direction.

One classic text that addresses the spiritual dimension of homelessness in a particularly moving way is the *Confessions of St. Augustine*. When we first discussed the *Confessions* with the Masterpieces class, Kate, a recovering heroin addict, argued that in her judgment Augustine understood addiction and recovery better than anyone she had ever met. The passage that most captivated Kate was Augustine's struggle in the garden, which culminated in his conversion:

> Thus I was sick at heart and in torment, accusing myself with a new intensity of bitterness, twisting and turning in my chain in the hope that it might be broken, for what held me was so small a thing! But it held me . . . The lower condition, which had grown habitual was more powerful than the better condition which had not tried. . . . And she [Continence] smiled upon me and her smile gave me courage as if she were saying, "Why do you stand upon yourself and so not stand at all? Cast yourself upon Him and be not afraid. He will not draw away from you and let you fall. Cast yourself without fear. He will receive you and heal you."[7]

Like Augustine, Kate was experiencing a conversion herself. Also like Augustine, her conversion was, in part, a response to the chant *tolle, lege,* "take up and read." The closing paragraphs of Book 8 of Augustine's *Confessions* spoke as directly to Kate as had chapter 13 of Romans for Augustine. The message was a deceptively simple one: "cast yourself upon him and be not afraid." Kate had tried unsuccessfully to combat her addiction until she recognized the futility of her struggle and put herself into God's hands.

Kate described her homelessness as an outward expression of her inner estrangement. Before she could become free of her addiction and gain control of her life, she had to know herself as God knew her. In the *Confessions,* Augustine speaks of homelessness as alienation from self. The *Confessions* tell the story of his estrangement and conversion. At either end of this narrative, from the first chapter reflecting on his birth to the eighth chapter recounting his confession, Augustine describes the journey of the Prodigal Son as an inner movement of the soul. In chapter 1, he speaks of humankind's experience of estrangement and return.

> Not with our feet or by traversing great distances do we journey away from you or find our way back. That younger son of yours in the Gospel did not hire horses nor carriages, nor did he board ships, nor did he take wing in any visible sense nor put one foot before the other when he journeyed to the foreign land to squander at will the wealth you, his gentle father, had given him at his departure. Gentle you were then, but gentler still with him when he returned in his need. No, to be estranged in a spirit of lust, and lost in its darkness, that is what it means to be far away from your face.[8]

Later in Book 8, Augustine repeats these words but ends by referring explicitly to his own conversion and return: "For to travel and to reach journey's end—was nothing else but to want to go there, but to want it valiantly and with all my heart." Augustine thus framed his own life story as an enactment of estrangement and return, not a movement through space but a movement of the heart.

Looking at his self-understanding from a psychological perspective, one can say that Augustine's identity crisis led him to both a psychological and a theological insight. His psychological insight was that his identity could not simply be discovered. Although he could know things about himself, his identity could not be reduced to a set of talents, dispositions, or traits. When he looked within he saw ambiguity, paradox, conflicting desires, and motives beneath his consciousness. He recognized that his identity rested not on what he could observe but on a fundamental decision to turn to or away from God and to live his life accordingly. Augustine's theological insight was that God had already chosen him and given him the grace to respond to that choice. Augustine's quest for self-knowledge led to God and to a life based on God's will.

Augustine wrote his *Confessions* for all readers in search of themselves. Often our role as teachers amounts to little more than acting like the children who chanted in the garden, "Tolle, lege." In his book on teaching, *De Magistro,* Augustine asked, "Who is so foolishly curious that he would send his child to school in order to learn what the teacher thinks?" Education begins and ends with the students' development—how the students come to know themselves in relationship to what is ultimately true, beautiful, and good. Augustine criticized his early liberal arts education for leading him to vanity—to external honors and acclaim—but not to the truth about himself or God. Augustine's early education was not a liberal arts education in the fullest sense—the arts did not liberate him—but helped to keep him the prisoner of his own addiction. The arts did not address Augustine's spiritual homelessness but distracted him from his homecoming. In his *Confessions,* Augustine gives us a new approach to reading and to liberal arts education more generally. Through a book that teaches us how to read, he takes us with him in his journey out of addiction and homelessness to liberation and an abiding home with God.

The Masterpieces opened our eyes to the reality of the homelessness that we all share. This is a homelessness of the spirit, a homelessness that leads us to recognize our deepest desire for unity with God. It is a homelessness that connects us with the *anawim* without failing to acknowledge the special burdens of those who suffer material deprivation, social isolation, and moral condemnation.

The preferential option for the poor has as much to do with identity as it does politics. The poor are not simply others in need of the help of the powerful. All of us are *anawim* without sufficient breath, without a true home. Power, wealth, privilege, education, and mental and physical health do not in the final analysis define us as persons or bring us lasting fulfillment or happiness. The preferential option for the poor, in our view, leads to a radically democratic liberal arts education oriented to self-discovery in community. The self to be discovered from a Christian perspective is utterly dependent on God and utterly graced by God. A politics of standing with the *anawim* follows from this basic insight. It is a politics that not only protects the *anawim* from exploitation and neglect, but treats the *anawim* as fellow travelers as entitled to the goods of the earth as those who accidentally possess them.

CONCLUDING REFLECTIONS

In recent years, the gap between rich and poor in America has been widening. The University of Notre Dame has profited tremendously from this redistribution of wealth and power. As the university has increased in stature and in standing with the privileged of American society, the question of Catholic character has been raised with an increased sense of urgency. Some have decried the declining percentage of Catholics on the faculty as the most visible indicator of our secularization. But surprisingly little concern has been voiced about the soul of the university and the spiritual dangers of our new material prosperity. To its credit the university has given some financial support to agencies serving the poor in the city of South Bend, such as the South Bend Center for the Homeless and the Northeast Neighborhood Association. The university's Center for Social Concerns may well be the best organization for undergraduate volunteer service in the country. Our experience with the World Masterpieces course suggests to us that as far as we have come as a university, we need to go further. We need to do more than set up special programs. We need to make sure that at the heart of what we do as a university, at the heart of our teaching and research, we are visibly connected with the poor. We need somehow to make the poor the beneficiaries of the best that we have to offer. We also have to establish a working environment at the university that brings us closer to the poor. The preferential option for the poor should be expressed at the center of our collective life; it should influence all that we do.

The World Masterpieces course is one way in which we, as a university, can be with the poor in a way that affects our daily lives. Although the course involves a relatively small group of people, it has captured the imagination of many of our undergraduate students. Now about thirty of our students are teaching a variation of it, the "Junior Great Books Seminar," to middle and high school students in local public and Catholic schools, as well as at the local juvenile correctional facility. Our ability to build upon or even sustain what we are doing will depend on increased financial support from the university. Whatever becomes of the World Masterpieces course and the Great Books seminars, they have opened up a meaningful way in which we as a university might identify with the poor. Other programs may prove to be more worthy of university support than ours. What is most important is that we as a university community see the poor as central to our identity as a just and Catholic university.

NOTES

1. See E. D. Hirsch, *Cultural Literacy: What Every American Needs to Know* (Boston: Houghton Mifflin, 1987).

2. See the Program of Liberal Studies website at http://pls.nd.edu/about/.

3. See Earl Shorris, *New American Blues: A Journey through Poverty to Democracy* (New York: Norton, 1997).

4. See Allan Bloom, *The Closing of the American Mind* (New York: Simon and Schuster, 1987).

5. Ethan Bronner, "For the Homeless, Rebirth through Socrates," *New York Times*, sec. 1, March 7, 1999.

6. David A. Snow and Leon Anderson, *Down on Their Luck: A Study of Homeless Street People* (Berkeley: University of California Press, 1993), 7–9.

7. Augustine, *The Confessions of St. Augustine,* trans. John K. Ryan (Garden City, N.Y.: Doubleday, 1960), 199–201.

8. Ibid., 61.

CHAPTER 9

A Hollywood Option for the Poor

GERARD THOMAS STRAUB

My encounter with the poor was unexpected, but even more unexpected is the way that encounter has changed my life. I was a Hollywood television producer. The poor not only changed my life, they changed the way I live and the work I do.

In April 2003 I was at the University of Notre Dame to screen my film on global poverty, *When Did I See You Hungry?*, and to speak about why I gave up my television career in order to document the life of the poor in India, Kenya, Brazil, the Philippines, Jamaica, and Mexico. There I met Gustavo Gutiérrez. How a son of Hollywood, who spent much of his life producing spicy soap operas, could wind up being given a hand-carved crucifix by this Peruvian father of liberation theology is a story so improbable that a Hollywood writer would be hard pressed to have made it up.

FROM EMPTINESS TO JOY

My journey away from show biz toward solidarity with the poor took a twisting, unpredictable road, eventually leading to the empty seventeenth-century Church of Sant' Isidoro in Rome, Italy, in March 1995. I had not entered the church to pray. I had long since abandoned my Catholic faith and embraced atheism, though I still harbored a faint hope that God did in fact exist. I entered the church because I was tired. I was simply looking for a cool, quiet place to rest. I had just completed a long trip from Los Angeles that drained my enthusiasm for the month in Italy, France, and Holland that lay before me. My flight to Rome was a last-ditch effort to salvage a novel I had been writing for three years. I was broke. If I could not finish the novel I would have to return to commercial television to earn some money. My self-imposed exile from Hollywood and New York, where I produced soap operas, including the wildly popular *General Hospital,* was about to end.

In the late 1980s I was a producer at CBS Television City in Hollywood but hated what I was doing. For me, producing a soap opera was nothing more than a socially acceptable form of prostitution. I longed to explore the depth of my soul. I withdrew from commercial television, picked up my pen, and began my search for the God I assumed did not exist. Through the vehicle of a novel, I decided to create a fictional world that would give me enormous freedom to delve deeply into my problems with God and religion. I toiled in obscurity for four difficult years, working incessantly on a dark, brooding epistolary novel whose main character was so overwhelmed by life and his failure to find God that he decided to kill himself. The book was a series of letters to his ten-year-old daughter. My depressed character spent months composing letters, which he planned to have delivered to his daughter after her twenty-first birthday. *Dear Kate,*[1] published in 1992, received a handful of positive reviews, but it was mostly ignored, selling only about 350 copies, at least 25 of which I personally purchased. The book was a 479-page angry scream at God and the Catholic Church into which I was born. Don't read it.

After delivering my novel to the publisher, my literary focus shifted to the connection between creativity and spirituality. For the next three years I struggled with a novel whose main character was an unemployed, unpublished writer obsessed with the lives of Vincent van Gogh and Saint Francis of Assisi. The artist represented creativity, and the saint symbolized spirituality. I was far more interested in Vincent than in Francis. Van Gogh's life and his religious and artistic struggles intrigued me. Vincent, the son of a pastor, had only one desire as a young man. The future artist desired to follow Christ and serve God. His literal interpretation of the gospel compelled him to give away all his possessions and to be poor among the poorest of miners, ministering to their temporal and spiritual needs. But the radical way van Gogh lived his faith caused the leaders of his denomination to derail his plans for ordained ministry. Vincent turned to art. In contrast, I considered the life of Saint Francis—the son of a wealthy cloth merchant who went from rowdy playboy and soldier to saint, and bore the wounds of the crucified Christ in his own flesh—to be little more than a pious, medieval fairy tale with little to say to the modern skeptic.

Over the years my search for God evolved into a pursuit of reasons to deny the existence of God. I found plenty. The lives of many believers, no matter what faith tradition they followed, were filled with enough hypocrisies, absurdities, and contradictions to nullify their claims of knowing and following God. Moreover, the rising tide of mindless fundamentalism within all faiths ignited outbursts of bloody violence in the name of God around the world, including the United States, where fundamentalist Christians killed doctors who performed legal abortions. Still, in the dark recesses of my mind, I harbored the faintest of hopes that God did exist, and that God's existence actually mattered. My work on this novel-in-progress, entitled *The Canvas of the Soul,* eventually led me to Europe; I wanted to walk in the footsteps of the saint and the artist before abandoning the novel that seemed to be going nowhere—just like me. And that trip turned my life upside down . . . or right side up.

I found myself seated in the empty church in Rome, and there an empty church and an empty man became an intersection of grace. The church was silent. I was merely resting. But something happened, something highly unexpected: God broke through the silence, and without warning, everything changed. I felt the overwhelming presence of God. I didn't see any images or hear any words. What I felt was beyond images and words. I felt immersed in a sea of love. I knew—not intellectually, but experientially—that God was real, that God loved me, and that the hunger and thirst I had felt for so long could only be satisfied by God. In the quiet of the dark church, I read the words of Psalm 63 and my soul leapt with joy:

> God, you are my God, I am seeking you,
> my soul is thirsting for you,
> my flesh is longing for you,

a land parched, weary and waterless;
I long to gaze on you in the Sanctuary,
and to see your power and glory.

Your love is better than life itself,
my lips will recite your praise;
all my life I will bless you,
in your name lift up my hands;
my soul will feast most richly,
on my lips a song of joy, in my mouth praise.

In that moment of revelation, I was transformed from an atheist into a pilgrim. I went from denying God to wanting to experience more and more of God. A few days later, after a long conversation with a Franciscan priest from Ireland, I went to confession. The next day I received the Eucharist at Mass; from that day on, attendance at daily Mass has become the foundation of my life.

A JOURNEY INTO POVERTY

Saint Francis of Assisi became my spiritual guide. Day after day, the medieval, fairy-tale saint, who I believed had nothing to say, showed this modern skeptic how to enter the heart of God. The walled, hillside town of Assisi became my spiritual home and opened the mystical windows of my soul. I did continue my trip, visiting all the important places in van Gogh's life: Arles, Saintes-Maries-de-la-Mer, Auvers-sur-Oise, St. Remy, Paris, and Amsterdam. But none of those exotic, exciting places could match the wonder of what I experienced within myself as I sat alone inside the Church of Sant' Isidoro in Rome. Since that trip in 1995, I have returned to Assisi seven more times, spending a total of more than nine months within her hallowed walls. The place is still magical and my heart longs to be there. Once home, I set aside my novel on Vincent and Francis, took up instead the lives of Francis, Clare, and my own spiritual pilgrimage, and completed *The Sun and Moon over Assisi*.[2]

While writing *The Sun and Moon over Assisi*, the hardest thing for me to understand was not only Saint Francis's love of the poor but poverty itself. It made no sense. I spent my life chasing money and fame. To help me understand, a Franciscan friar suggested I spend time with the friars working among the poor in one of the worst slums in America. After a few days at the Saint Francis Inn in the Kensington section of Philadelphia everything I ever thought about the poor and poverty was turned inside out. A friend who worked on *Good Morning America* helped me make a film about this amazing soup kitchen. The friars allowed me to live with them while I wrote the script. By God's grace, *We Have a Table for Four Ready* has aired on many PBS stations across America, and people of all faiths—and no faith—have responded by contacting the Saint Francis Inn and sending donations sufficient to make possible building a new kitchen to better serve the poor.

Another turn in the road placed me in Rome where I met Giacomo Bini, OFM, the minister general of the Order of Friars Minor. I told him that I wrestled with the subject of poverty, understanding it on a theological level, but not having a practical vision of how it should impact my life. I proposed to him the idea of spending time with friars who ministered to the poorest of the poor around the world. I wanted to document, in black and white photographs, the life of people living in poverty and a Christian response to it. Father Bini endorsed my project and gave his authorization for the friars to host and guide me.

Within ten days I had landed in Calcutta, India, where I was greeted by a Franciscan friar from Ireland. We would travel together visiting the poor in Chennai, Bangalore, Guwahati, and Rangjuli; however, on arrival in Calcutta, I was so horrified by what I saw during the night ride from the airport to the church, in the heart of a large slum, that I couldn't sleep. Streets were lined with homeless people, every inch of sidewalk covered with sleeping bodies. One young boy, perhaps five years old, slept naked on the ground. We drove past decayed buildings and people standing around large fires burning in barrels. Cows and wild dogs shared roads with ancient cars, trucks, and ox-drawn carts. It looked worse in daylight. The next day I was so overwhelmed that I could barely lift the camera. I had stepped into a vast unknown with no idea that the project would be so physically, emotionally, and spiritually challenging.

Back at home I found it extremely difficult to process what I had witnessed in India. It was the Thanksgiving/Christmas season, and I was overwhelmed by the vast array of goods on display at the malls, unable to disengage from the images of poverty I had captured on film. Even a trip to the supermarket left me beleaguered by the sheer abundance of our choices.

I traveled next to Nairobi, Kenya. In a nation of 43 million, at least 5 percent of Kenyans live as squatters, occupying very small strips of land—rarely wider than twenty feet—on which they build illegal huts. In Kagoshi, near Mount Kenya, 1500 people live in the gutter along a narrow strip of land adjacent to the road. Crime in Nairobi abounds. Almost half the population is unemployed. Power outages are commonplace. Phones work sporadically. Infrastructures are crumbling. Illness from tainted food and water is constant. For persons fleeing poverty and starvation in Africa, forced migration becomes a way of life.

I walked through Nairobi's slums where thousands of people live without running water, toilets, or electricity. I saw mile upon mile of misery and disease. To be a migrant in Africa is to be a nonperson, unwanted and unneeded. After five days of witnessing the misery of extreme poverty, famine, drought, hunger, illness, suffering, and death, I reached the limits of my endurance and asked the friars to send me home a few days early. In Kenya I saw no wildlife, only life wildly out of balance.

After similar distressing trips to Mexico, Jamaica, and the Philippines, the photo/essay book was completed, but my need to be among people living in poverty was only beginning. *When Did I See You Hungry?* was published in 2002.[3]

I thought my travels among people living in desperate poverty had ended, but I received a letter from a man from San Luis Obispo, California, telling me how much *The Sun and Moon over Assisi* had helped him. The letter meant so much to me that I decided to call him and thank him for writing. I told him about the poverty book and how I harbored a dream of turning the black-and-white photographs into a short film. I was stunned when he offered to help finance the project, and when Martin Sheen agreed to narrate the film. The film version of *When Did I See You Hungry?*[4] led, with the help of numerous friends and supporters who shared their creative talents and financial resources, to the creation of the San Damiano Foundation. The foundation raised enough funds to produce five films in the first three years, and our vision was refined to one simple phrase: putting the power of film at the service of the poor.

The San Damiano Foundation's second film took me into a nightmare I thought had been eradicated in the Middle Ages. I traveled to the

Amazon region of Brazil with Jim Flickinger. He is a lawyer who had a successful practice in Grand Rapids, Michigan, until he decided to do something about the poverty he saw in the Amazon. He founded Amazon Relief, a charitable organization that works to break the cycle of poverty that imprisons people in slums cluttered with mazes of poorly constructed shacks. In these small dwellings, about the size of a two-car garage, ten to twenty people live in crowded, suffocating conditions. The shacks are built on stilts, elevating them over pools of percolating raw human waste. The stench is nauseating, and a wide array of diseases is prevalent. Mosquitoes transmit malaria and dengue fever. People live without drinkable water or sanitation. They share their humble homes with snakes, bats, spiders, and a horde of large, ugly insects, and never find relief from stifling heat and humidity. Living in this dreadful environment are countless malnourished children who face profound hunger. Amazon Relief operates schools that create special educational programs for children from the jungle or who live in absolute poverty. Two schools funded by Amazon Relief serve over 650 children, teaching reading, writing, and basic hygiene, and feeding them nutritious daily meals.

If the suffering and pain in these sprawling slums were not enough, leprosy is yet another distressing factor in the equation of life in the Amazon. Amazon Relief aids a large leprosarium, housing scores of people whose hands, arms, legs, and faces have been eaten away by an unspeakably loathsome disease. Amazon Relief provides specially designed lightweight carts that give some degree of mobility to people who suffer with this debilitating disease, and supplies shelter, food, medicine, and clothing for many of the forty-five thousand people with leprosy in the Amazon, offering them an alternative to begging on the streets for survival.

It was an honor to make the film *Embracing the Leper*[5] about Jim Flickinger's ministry. At college showings students are shocked by the sight of people with leprosy, and many vow to help make a difference in the lives of the poor in their cities. Jim Flickinger reports that the film has greatly helped him raise funds for his ministry.

After chronicling the plight of people living in abject poverty in nine nations, I am ashamed to admit that I was blind to the brutally poor in my own backyard. After seeing the San Damiano Foundation's first two films, the head of the Union Rescue Mission in Los Angeles invited me to make a film about the mission. As I drove to the mission for the first time, I was struck by the number of homeless people I saw camped on the streets. Immediately I knew I wanted to explore the world of the urban homeless, and spent a year making this film.

Rescue Me is a two-part documentary on the poor and homeless of Skid Row in downtown Los Angeles and the heroic work of the Union Rescue Mission.[6] The URM offers food, shelter, and rehabilitation programs. The film's painful and disturbing images force us to face things we would rather pretend do not exist. Skid Row is a nightmarish fifty-block area in downtown Los Angeles where more than ten thousand people, including a shocking number of women and children, live in cardboard boxes or overcrowded missions. Yet amid this stark reality, on full display on the mean streets of Skid Row, the URM, a place where love abounds, stands ready to offer a helping hand and a way to a better life. This film is about suffering and rejection, grace and redemption, and helping people without a home find a way home.

A DETOUR INTO MIGRATION

After I finished *Rescue Me,* Daniel Groody, CSC, invited me to travel with him through Mexico, visiting dusty towns south of the border from Nogales, Arizona. I went from Skid Row to the border of death. The trip was a crash course on the plight of migrants, many of whom die crossing the brutal, vast Arizona desert as they struggle to enter the United States for back-breaking, low-paying jobs unwanted by U.S. citizens. I committed to making a film, *Endless Exodus,*[7] with Father Groody, and over the next six months we shot over fifty hours of footage in El Salvador and Mexico, and along the border in Arizona and California.

Since 1995 thousands of migrants have died trying to cross the nearly two-thousand-mile-long border between the United States and Mexico.[8] To be an immigrant without legal U.S. status is to live a life of punishing journeys, fatigue, fear, and anxiety. Uncertainty and physical suffering come with the territory of a desert crossing without shelter, shade, or adequate water. Migrants without legal U.S. status are ignored and scorned by those with deaf ears and hardened hearts, and forced to face a wall of ingratitude and the emotional toll of being unwanted and unloved. As they hunt for a better life they are in turn hunted, handcuffed, and returned to their prison of poverty. To be an immigrant often means dying in the desert. In light of the terrorist attacks of 9/11, we can appreciate the need to maintain secure borders, but they must not be borders between life and death. Nationalism must not supersede the gospel.

I am beginning to learn the truth that in some respects we are all migrants, struggling to cross the borders of our own selfishness to be embraced by God's limitless love. Part of this migration involves moving out of our own self-centeredness and sin, and crossing the desert of self-surrender to enter a God-centered paradise of self-giving love.

I am also beginning to learn that Christ offers good news to the lowly, the hurting, the ailing. He is at home with the exiled; he shelters the scorned. If Christ walked in the flesh among us today, I believe he would be in the hot, dry Arizona desert giving water to those physically dying of thirst and hope to those thirsting for a better life. In the process of looking for Jesus, I am starting to discover his presence, in a mysterious way, among those who are being crucified, rejected, alienated, and oppressed. I find him in the cruel, barren desert, in dark neighborhood corners, waiting for help. I am discovering that, in standing shoulder to shoulder with the poorest of the poor, I find not only the crucified Christ but also the richness of something fresh and liberating. Resurrection comes close to describing this experience. I am finding that it is not enough to be for the poor, but that somehow I must also learn to stand with them and be against their poverty, a poverty created by injustice and selfishness.

With these spiritual and theological considerations in mind, I cringe when I hear the term *illegal alien*. The ugly word *alien* is not in compassion's vocabulary. Compassion is the lifeblood of true human community, refusing to segregate people into friends and enemies, neighbors and outsiders. But compassion is far removed from pity and sympathy. Compassion grows from awareness that we are all part of one body, and that when one suffers, we all do. The emotion of compassion requires a transformation into concrete action as a response to the suffering of others. Pity must become love; sympathy must become empathy. The poor need charity and justice, a true justice that will help lift them out of poverty. As Catholic social thought teaches, and the preferential option for the poor reiterates, the true moral fiber of any society is revealed in how it cares for its weakest members.

TRANSFORMATION AND CONVERSION: NEW LIVES AND COMMUNITIES

The message of love from the crucified and transfigured Christ compels us to judge no one, to exclude no one. The incarnation, life, death, and resurrection of Christ teach that there are no limits to forgiveness and sharing. In breaking the bread of our lives we share with others our hearts, hopes, dreams, thoughts, time. Goodness, from a Christian perspective, does not come from morality but from communion with God and neighbor; it is from the womb of mercy that loving communities are born.

Through my journey into the world of the poor, I have become increasingly intrigued by the interplay of image and spirit. The film *When Did I See You Hungry?* reveals the unseen suffering caused by severe poverty throughout the world, making visible what was invisible to us. Viewers are moved out of themselves and into the drama of survival—and many have shared that they begin to see the world in a different way. That is the power of art, the profound impact of image and spirit on people, transforming, by God's grace, their lives.

Because of my experiences with the poorest of the poor, I have come to believe that the most tangible way to love God is to relieve the pain and suffering of others. Each act of mercy and kindness brings us closer to the reality of God. As we seek to know God we set about creating community founded on welcome and respect, embracing the most vulnerable among us, doing our utmost to narrow the gap between rich and poor which grows wider every year, and strive to give the common good priority of place over our individual good. Prayer enables me to see Christ present in and among the poor. Praying creates an awareness of God that elicits a response. Prayer fosters relationships—with God and each other.

Saint Francis of Assisi spent roughly half his time in prayer and deep contemplation, often in remote mountaintop hermitages. The saint's quiet time gave focus and direction to his outward ministry, providing him strength and courage to complete it. From our time spent in prayer and reflection we also become equipped to execute Christ's exhortation to feed the hungry, shelter the homeless, visit the sick and imprisoned, extend a helping hand to the poor, and embrace the leper. From Christ's perspective, how we care for the poor is the only authentic indicator of how much we love God.

Both the Hebrew and Christian Testaments reveal God's preferential love for those the world ignores and rejects. The essence of Christ's message is this: make every stranger, no matter how poor or dirty, no matter how weak or unlovable, our neighbor. Prayer and compassion are the wings of Christian life. Prayer prompts us to reach out in compassion to the suffering and weak, and helps us embrace all of humanity. In prayer, we discern how we must respond to people living in poverty and persecution. Prayer guides and sustains us as we reach out to them in action and advocacy.

Living among the poor has taught me that we are all beggars. None of us is self-sufficient. By ourselves, we are incomplete. Our needs are always beyond our capacities. Prayer and contemplation free us from a self-serving mindset and prepare us to lead a life of service to others. We live in a world of stark inequality and injustice. So did Jesus. Jesus had a deep concern for the suffering and marginalized. So should we. For the follower of Jesus, compassion is not an option but an obligation—a sign that our lives have been transformed by the healing presence of Christ.

After spending much time among the poor one fact becomes crystal clear: the reality of God is strongly present in the horrible slums and places of deepest poverty in developing nations. The spiritual lesson is equally clear: God has not abandoned the poor; often it is the poor who know best the richness of God. I am not endorsing poverty. Far from it. The physical poverty I have witnessed is injustice on a grand scale. It must be eliminated; human dignity must be restored.

Another kind of poverty, poverty of spirit, does not refer to an economic condition. It reflects the human reality that we are poor before God and radically dependent on God for everything. Poverty of spirit stands in stark contrast to the unbridled pursuit of comfort, power, pleasure, and riches which permeates a society that prizes possessions as a measure of status. Poverty of spirit maintains a continual attitude of dying to self, and dying to self is the only way to be fully alive to God. Being fully alive to God involves doing the work of God in caring for the needs of others, a mark of true piety.

God's love is universal, and it enables us to recognize better the inalienable dignity of every human being regardless of race, religion, or nationality. The inclusivity of the gospel requires us to love everyone especially the neglected and abandoned. The option for the poor challenges us to stand in solidarity with the poor, to identify with their misery, grief, sickness, and even their death. Only then will the poor feel loved and strengthened. In entering into greater relationship with the poor, it is possible for them and us to detect the divine-human solidarity of the God-Man, Christ, with all men and women. Only then can we more adequately reflect the reality that we are God's gift to each other.

Conversion is a key concept in the process of social justice. Jesus speaks loudly, clearly, and often about the importance of love for others. Yet much in our contemporary society shouts a contradictory message. TV, movies, and advertising say: the individual is most important, grab all you can for yourself, consume more, do your own thing, anything goes. But Christianity is a radical religion preaching a far different message. It turns everything upside down, or, more accurately, right side up. How can the gospel penetrate the noise that engulfs our lives? It cannot without ongoing conversion, a continual deepening of our faith. Daily conversion and surrender to Christ enables us to drink more deeply at the well of God's mercy and grace, and in turn to be more merciful to others—especially the poor and marginalized.

THE WORST WAS YET TO COME

My travels through Kenya, India, Jamaica, Brazil, El Salvador, Mexico, and the Philippines brought me face to face with staggering levels of poverty. The horrors of sprawling slums in Nairobi, Calcutta, Juarez, and Manila brought me to tears. The stench of open sewers running through crowded slums was nauseating. Naked kids bathing in the streets in water laced with bacteria, and entire families squeezed into one room without electricity or a toilet were appalling.

But the saddest, most inhumane place I visited is known as the Payatas, a giant garbage dump on the outskirts of metropolitan Manila in the Philippines. The dump is so massive it forms a mountain more than fifty feet high—over seven stories. The dump covers seventy-four acres. The mountain of garbage is home to seventy-five thousand people who live in the dump and off its refuse. The people of Payatas earn their living scavenging through the waste of others. Entire families, including small children, spend long hours picking through the garbage, searching for scraps of recyclable and reusable material to salvage and sell for a few pennies. This is the only life they know: a garbage dump. Scavenging is an arduous and hazardous life. Disease, such as tuberculosis, is rampant. Many children are disabled; most suffer from malnutrition. Their tiny bodies are infested with worms, and covered with wounds received from sharp objects hidden in the garbage.

All day, day in and day out, a relentless chain of garbage trucks makes its slow crawl up the muddy road to the peak. At the base of the mountain is a camp, a hellish hamlet of shacks where the garbage-pickers live. The place is a nightmare, a blight on society. Every day, the poor trek up the mountain to forage for used plastic containers, cardboard boxes, copper wire, aluminum, bottles, bits and pieces of machinery, broken toys, and parts of appliances—anything they can sell to junk shops. It is raw capitalism. The Payatas scavengers are the lowliest of the urban poor. They are our *anawim*, the Hebrew Testament term for the poorest of the poor, those completely overwhelmed by want, without voice or rights in their surrounding community. Scripture makes it abundantly clear that to forget the anawim is to forget God. Jesus made caring for the anawim a litmus test for our love of God.

As I took pictures in the Payatas I felt myself becoming sick from the smell—and from the reality that people are forced to live like wild animals picking at the corpse of obsessive consumerism. The dreadful images I captured during my time in Manila's oldest and largest open pit dumpsite still haunt me. I do not want to forget the people of Payatas, or that I am part of the reason they are forced to live on a mountain of garbage.

Though places like the Payatas deeply disturb me, I have become accustomed to being in the slums, and comfortable with photographing the suffering within them. I have come to feel the presence of God in these dreadful places. I have come to like to be with the poor because they teach me about my own poverty, my own weakness, and help me learn how to become an instrument of mercy, peace, and love.

A SHARE IN POVERTY AND LIBERATION

The incarnation teaches us that God is humble. God lives in our poverty and weakness. Jesus mingled with the poor and outcasts of his society.

He embraced, touched, and loved the poor and rejected. He called them "blessed." For Jesus, the poor and lowly are sacraments, because they offer a direct way to encounter God. The richness of God is revealed in the poverty of Christ. Christ shows us that mercy is more than compassion or justice. Mercy requires us to become one with the poor and hurting, to live their misery as though it were our own. The poor, broken, and rejected are portals through which we enter into the mystery of the cross.

In *Rescue Me,* I observed, "Skid Row opened my eyes to the reality that vulnerability is an essential part of life; security is an illusion. In Skid Row I came to better understand that the road to grace is most often the road of brokenness. Maybe when we ignore or reject the people of Skid Row, we are rejecting our own inner brokenness, our own incapacity to love, and maybe we can be healed by those we reject."

In my travels, I began to see how in turning our backs on the poor we turn our backs on Jesus. We need each other. We need to stand with the poor, walk with them, share a meal with them, talk with them. To learn the causes of poverty, we must spend time with the poor. The mercy we share with broken people is the mercy Jesus returns to us. My exposure to those saddled with dire poverty uncovered my own clinging selfishness. Slowly, I am coming to see that consuming more than I need is stealing from those in need. The daily, ongoing process of conversion continues to help us learn to let go of that which holds us back from God and from our neighbor. An awareness of God's mysterious presence within helps us become more aware of that same presence within others. In our encounters with the poor we must move from pity to love, from charity to justice. Service to the poor and lowly is not optional—it is a requirement for the follower of Christ. If we share in their struggles we can share in their liberation.

A FUTURE NOT OUR OWN

Jesus led me to the poorest, the lowliest, and the lost so that I might give my heart to them. Christ is asking each of us to be his hands, his heart, to reach out to his brothers and sisters who are hurting. Our job is simple, to incarnate the love of God in the heart of darkness. And with God, all things are possible.

During my time in Africa I was reading Evelyn Underhill's *The School of Charity* when this sentence jumped out at me: "Our whole life is to be poised on a certain glad expectancy of God; taking each moment, incident, choice, and opportunity as material placed in our hands by the Creator whose whole intricate and mysterious process moves toward the triumph of the Cross, and who has given each living spirit a tiny part in the vast work of transformation."[9] In my journal, I wrote a response to those words: "Well, I have seen some of the cross these past few months, and I guess it is hard for me to believe my tiny part in the work of transforming the pain into triumph can make any difference. But I must believe, I must allow God to work things out according to his mysterious plan."

It is so easy to give in to a skepticism that says we cannot make a difference in the lives of the poor. The following prayer gives me comfort:

Prophets of a Future Not Our Own

It helps, now and then, to step back and take the long view.
The kingdom is not only beyond our efforts, it is beyond our vision.
We accomplish in our lifetime only a tiny fraction of
the magnificent enterprise that is God's work.
Nothing we do is complete, which is another way of saying
that the kingdom always lies beyond us.
No statement says all that could be said. No prayer fully expresses our faith.
No confession brings perfection. No pastoral visit brings wholeness.
No program accomplishes the church's mission.
No set of goals and objectives includes everything.
This is what we are about: We plant seeds that one day will grow.
We water seeds already planted, knowing that they hold future promise.
We lay foundations that will need further development.
We provide yeast that produces effects beyond our capabilities.
We cannot do everything and there is a sense of liberation in realizing that.
This enables us to do something, and to do it very well.
It may be incomplete, but it is a beginning, a step along the way,
an opportunity for God's grace to enter and do the rest.
We may never see the end results,
but that is the difference between the master builder and the worker.

> We are workers, not master builders, ministers, not messiahs.
> We are prophets of a future not our own. Amen.[10]

When I walked into that empty church in Rome in 1995, I had no idea where God's grace would lead me, no idea I was—as you are too—a prophet of a future not our own. The task before us is enormous, our abilities minuscule. Prayer and poverty of spirit draw us closer to God. With God the task is hardly a task at all—it is a joy. As our love for God increases, it becomes increasingly easier to love each other and all of creation.

NOTES

1. Gerard Thomas Straub, *Dear Kate: A Novel* (Amherst, N.Y.: Prometheus Books, 1992).

2. Gerard Thomas Straub, *The Sun and Moon over Assisi: Personal Encounters with Francis and Clare* (Cincinnati, Ohio: St. Anthony Messenger Press, 2000). Named by the Catholic Press Association the best hardcover spirituality book of 2000.

3. Gerard Thomas Straub, *When Did I See You Hungry?* (Cincinnati, Ohio: St. Anthony Messenger Press, 2002).

4. Gerard Thomas Straub, *When Did I See You Hungry?* (Burbank, Calif.: San Damiano Foundation, 2002).

5. Gerard Thomas Straub, *Embracing the Leper: The Story of Amazon Relief* (Burbank, Calif.: San Damiano Foundation, 2002).

6. Gerard Thomas Straub, *Rescue Me* (Burbank, Calif.: San Damiano Foundation, 2003).

7. Gerard Thomas Straub, *Endless Exodus* (Burbank, Calif.: San Damiano Foundation, 2004).

8. See "Discarded Migrants," available at http://www.cmsm.org/forum /forum_fall10_migrants.html.

9. See Evelyn Underhill, *The School of Charity: Meditations on the Christian Creed* (New York: Morehouse Publishing, 1991).

10. This prayer, often attributed to Archbishop Oscar Romero, was written by Bishop Ken Untener for Cardinal John Dearden. See "The Peace Pulpit, by Bishop Thomas J. Gumbleton, March 28, 2004," *National Catholic Reporter,* available at http://www.nationalcatholicreporter.org/peace/gumb032804.htm.

CHAPTER 10

The Option for the Poor and Community-Based Education

MARY BECKMAN

The option for the poor challenges us to pay attention to those who are most marginalized and most in need in our world. We do this through action that transforms institutions and systems as well as through direct service. It must be done so that not only the lack of those without is filled, but so that the voices of those in need contribute in finding solutions to their unjust situations and, therein, to the plight of the entire human family that remains unwhole as long as any suffer deprivation.[1]

How do we help undergraduate students to understand this challenge? The challenge calls for them to act not only or even primarily on the behalf of others, but to act *with* those whose poverty is being addressed. To become educated toward addressing such a challenge, students hear the stories of people oppressed; they attempt to experience their reality and be open to transformation because of that experience, to see the world anew. They participate with those who are poor in the identification of solutions. And they act in solidarity with others, among them the marginalized themselves, so as to create fairer structures and laws as well as promote better treatment of one by the other. They learn about the causes of marginality and oppression so that they can approach those challenges holistically—that is, in ways that get at the root of forces perpetuating exclusion.

Community-based learning is a pedagogy that lends itself well to this kind of education. The Center for Social Concerns at the University of Notre Dame, which I know best, uses this pedagogy explicitly to help students learn about and practice living out the option for the poor.

COMMUNITY-BASED LEARNING

Community-based learning emerged as a formal pedagogy during the 1970s in the United States under the name "service-learning." Through this pedagogy, students make regular, meaningful contributions in off-campus communities as part of formal academic course work. For example, they may volunteer several hours a week at a shelter for people who are homeless as part of a sociology course on poverty. Simultaneously, they are reading, writing, and discussing in class the issues they are confronting through their community engagement. Community involvement is integrated into the course as a kind of text. Reflection—consideration of the service experience in light of course readings and class discussion—is characteristic of service-learning. Journal assignments are frequently used to encourage analysis and reflection.

In the 1980s, the George H. W. Bush's "thousand points of light" thinking—the idea that each person should volunteer to make the country a better place—gave service-learning momentum. Service-learning is rooted, however, in the work of experiential learning theorists writing in the beginning of the last century, most notably John Dewey. Dewey advocated what is often called active learning. He believed that good learning could be provoked only through engagement with a problem, experiencing some conflict. Emotion, as well as intellect, was an important component of learning, action as well as reflection.[2]

While the literature on community-based learning grounds this pedagogy in the work of educational theorists such as Dewey, it might also be situated in the notion of practical reasoning, especially if the option for the poor is of special concern. "Without the engagement of the concepts via this *way* of thinking," theologian Todd Whitmore writes, "the substance of Catholic social thought can only be sustained via ecclesiastical and curricular fiat."[3] It will not be alive for us. We would likely bring its guidance to our lives only insofar as we interpreted it as providing rules or dictates from the church.

What is this practical, reasoned way of thinking? It is perhaps easiest to understand by referring first to what it is not. Practical reasoning can be contrasted with Aristotle's speculative or theoretical reasoning, which demonstrates "knowledge of things that do not change." In the language of Thomas Aquinas, speculative reasoning is about "necessary things, which can not be other than they are," which, "like universal principles, contain truth without fail."[4]

On the other hand, practical reasoning, from Aquinas, "is busied with contingent matters, about which human actions are concerned."[5] It can be argued that "the reasoning in the social documents addresses areas of life that are subject to change and to less precision than speculative reason."[6] John XXIII described these areas as ones where there is a "pronounced dynamism" in which the "requirements of justice is a problem which will never admit a definitive solution."[7]

Practical reasoning, therefore, is a way of thinking that "seeks to guide variable human practice or action (praxis)."[8] It is not a mode of thought that results in clear-cut, definitive solutions. Thinking in this way requires an acceptance or toleration of a certain messiness of life. Furthermore, it requires not only a consideration of pressing human problems from afar, but an engagement with them.

To engage in practical reasoning requires experience, experience in the world and outside the classroom, experience beyond that of reading books. Experience is a crucial basis on which the critical reflection that will lead to choices about human action must rest. And practical reasoning requires a dialectical engagement with others, with those of different backgrounds, different experiences, in communities, with contested realities, and with consideration of real human dilemmas. All of this can be accomplished through community-based learning.

Over the years, the kinds of activities students do within the framework of service-learning has expanded. Initially, the emphasis was on direct service, for example tutoring children in reading or prisoners preparing for General Educational Development (GED) tests, or acting as a big brother or sister to a young person. These days, however, service-learning implies many ways for students to be civic participants—that is, actively to address injustice or create improvements in their communities. Through community research, for example, students are conducting investigations of various kinds with and for community agencies.[9] It is likely these days that one would find students in service-learning classes engaged in community organizing as well, or working with neighborhood organizations to determine and fulfill their agendas. Many in the field have replaced the label *service-learning* with the term *community-based learning,* as the latter has come to be identified with the valuing of *nondirect* service activities as well as direct service.

A wealth of studies substantiates the contributions of community-based learning to undergraduate education. Community-based learning students do not necessarily do better than their counterparts when it comes to test taking or grade point averages. If, however, community-based learning students are asked to perform tasks that require them to transfer what they have learned to new contexts, they excel.

In 1929 Alfred Whitehead used the term *inert knowledge*[10] to refer to learning that occurred through lectures, followed by tests; it was inert in the sense that it was unusable beyond the classroom. Studies comparing learning outcomes of service-learning students to counterparts who have not experienced this pedagogy have shown consistently that the service-learning students are better able to transfer course learning to contexts outside the classroom. For example, if we teach students in the classroom about the policy-making process of government, those students may be able to describe the process when they take a test. But if taken into a real world setting where policy is to be developed and established, the classroom learning would not be as useful as if they had participated firsthand in some aspects of such policy work, as a community-based learning experience could have made possible.

Thus, a part of the educational rationale for community-based learning is that through it students learn in a context where they can apply what they are learning, and that in so doing they are then better able later to make use of the knowledge in new contexts. Studies have also shown community-based learning students manifest greater depth of analysis and a fuller sense of the complexity of world problems than peers who have not learned through this approach.[11]

According to the service-learning literature, much of the positive educational results from community-based learning can be attributed to four factors: (1) student interest in the subject matter of the course through which the community involvement occurs; (2) writing assignments that encourage reflection; (3) processing the experience through discussion and by connecting it to course materials; and (4) the quality of the student's community involvement. A high quality community setting is one where the student feels challenged, is active, has varied tasks, receives feedback and appreciation, and believes he or she has made a positive contribution.[12] Close relationships with professors lead to many positive outcomes for college students.[13] Service-learning promotes such relationships.

LEARNING CATHOLIC SOCIAL THOUGHT THROUGH COMMUNITY-BASED LEARNING

In a community-based learning course, it is possible to orient readings, written assignments, and discussion to focus on root causes of injustice and oppression, and on the role of structures or systems within society, such as the education and health care systems. Such orientation is necessary for an education about the option for the poor.

If the emphasis in service-learning is on direct service, it may fail "to meet the requirement of dialectical interchange with the persons served"[14] that is central to the challenge of the option for the poor. For example, students at one small eastern college

> did a significant amount of service type volunteering in the wider community . . . but there was no real reciprocity, no invitation to the community . . . to come to [the campus] and witness to the university and therefore no real lessons learned beyond the general ones that poverty is a harsh reality . . . These are indeed important lessons, but if they are the only ones and if volunteer service in the city is the only way that the university relates to the city, then . . . we are left with a kind of paternalism that is inadequate as a model.[15]

Such unidirectional service lacks the mutuality and the dialectical encounters that assist the teaching and learning of Catholic social thought, and specifically the option for the poor.

Fortunately, today community-based learning implies many ways for students to be civic participants. Through community research, for example, students conducting investigations must be accountable to those to whom they provide information in a way that they are not accountable to the homeless person for whom soup is being ladled through direct service at the homeless shelter. The homeless person would not likely be thought of as a boss, for example, as the agency supervisor would likely be for whom a student is collecting information or analyzing data in a community research project. A student likely brings a sense of inadequacy to the research task in a manner that is less likely to occur in a direct service situation. The student researcher is probably trying out for the first time budding research skills that have thus far been used only in the classroom. Thus, the student is not buoyed by his or her own sense of educational privilege in relation to those being served, as might be the case when he or she tutors GED classes through direct service. Nor is this type of community involvement "business as usual," which direct service may be. The novelty raises new challenges for the student. The relationship between the student and the people being served in these alternative forms of community engagement is likely less unidirectional, situated less in unequal privilege, and embodying more mutuality, than in most direct service.

We know how to make use of this pedagogy so as to achieve fairly specific learning goals. If Catholic social thought is part of the content of such courses, we can have confidence that if these courses are done well— if sufficient attention is paid to the quality of the student experience in the community—students will be able to apply what they have learned. So through community-based learning courses crafted with the principle of the option for the poor in mind, students will not only have the opportunity to make sense of this principle, but will also have practice living it out.

COMMUNITY-BASED LEARNING AT THE CENTER FOR SOCIAL CONCERNS: EMPHASIZING OPTION FOR THE POOR

When asked how the principle of the option for the poor has become meaningful to him, University of Notre Dame undergraduate Jesse Flores claims that it has been through service and accompanying reflection: "How has it come to be that the [principle of the option for the poor] embodied in Catholic social teaching [has] ceased to be [an] abstract academic [idea] and become [an] interior conviction that [has] formed and shaped the ways in which I view [such things as] policy decisions? . . . I would say that it has been through . . . my service experiences and reflections that I have become convicted." When Flores says "service experiences and reflections," he is referring to academic courses that involve a community-based learning pedagogy. Though many such courses are offered throughout the university curriculum, he is referring specifically to seminars taken through Notre Dame's Center for Social Concerns.

As an undergraduate, Flores had taken formal classroom-centered courses on Catholic social thought, for example, *Contemporary Issues in Christian Ethics*. For this course, he studied the 1996 welfare reform and its effects on immigrants: "I read *Economic Justice for All* in its entirety,[16] as well as several smaller documents promulgated by the church. I wrote a paper having applied several facets of Catholic social thought to arrive at my conclusion regarding the ethics of the treatment of immigrants through welfare reform." And while he learned a great deal through this course, it is to a different kind of pedagogy that he attributes a more profound education: community-based learning.

Flores's comments below suggest the effectiveness of the community-based learning pedagogy in bringing depth and a sense for complexity to his initial perceptions: "My reflections over the course . . . began with my seeing how lazy some of the kids and their families were. As the weeks progressed, I realized . . . that my initial . . . thoughts were incorrect and that issues were deeper than perceived laziness. Issues of racism and intolerance from their schools, the ways that they were perceived . . . took tolls on their emotions and strength." His summer experience convinced him "that the plight of the poor was institutional *and* personal."

We attribute such results to the incorporation, to varying degrees, of social analysis into all the seminars run by the Center for Social Concerns.[17] The first moment in social analysis, typically intended to be undertaken by a group, involves the identification of an experience for reflection, typically a problem or challenge faced by a community or by a student engaged with a particular community. Also, the participant in social analysis is asked to identify his or her personal response to the experience, and the values upon which the response is based. During the second step, the question "why" is asked about the initial experience. A broad exploration of possible causes is urged. Examination from an economic perspective, a religious perspective, historical, environmental, and so on is important so that those doing the analysis will be able to see the complexity of the issues and the interdependence of causes. Theological reflection—bringing one's faith-based knowledge and insights to bear on the issues—is a next step, followed by a plan of action to address the issue.

Courses offered through the center do not always take students through all steps in this social analysis process, but they do all create opportunities for students to explore the causes of whatever social challenges they are witnessing through their course. In this manner, students are pushed to see root causes and the role of structures, laws, policies, and systems—those institutions outside the control of any individual marginalized person—in every course. We see the results of such analysis in Flores's comments above. He concludes that it is not merely laziness, obviously a first response to his experience, but institutional forces as well. Thus, these community-based learning opportunities create an avenue for students to face the particular challenge posed by the option for the poor of gaining a deep understanding of the causes of a marginalized position.

Brigitte Gynther,[18] another Notre Dame student, indicates the value of questioning causes that this type of social analysis urges: "We often forget things until they take on real meaning to us and then become worth remembering. If someone tells me that [the principle of the option for the poor supports the notion that] all workers have the right to unionize, I am apt to forget this until I learn why this is important." She goes on to explain how community-based learning contributes to this process:

> Why are people who contribute full-time to our society, often doing the most necessary jobs, unable to live decently? What laws allow this? . . . How are people attempting to change these systems? What social change movements are currently occurring? Luckily, [community-based] learning . . . naturally leads to [these questions] and it is the role of the teacher to foster and allow this to occur. . . . A questioning format combined with the witnessing of injustices during [community-based] learning

should combine naturally to lead to the questioning about the underlying systems and change movements that make up learning about the world.

Flores's and Gynther's comments are based largely on their experience in the Center for Social Concern's Summer Service Learning Program (SSLP). This is a three-credit class offered in collaboration with the university's Department of Theology. Through this academic offering, over two hundred students travel to sites across the United States in the summer to engage in local communities for eight weeks. Students are assigned readings, journal writings, and a paper. They finish the course with several class sessions at the university upon their return in the fall. Flores's summer course took him to Austin, Texas, where he was a community organizer working with a Catholic parish. Gynther went to Immokalee, Florida, where she worked with migrant laborers.

The Center for Social Concerns is the university's community-based learning center.[19] With approximately thirty full-time employees and some forty undergraduate and graduate part-time student staff, the center enrolls more than one thousand students into its many community-based learning courses each year. In addition to the summer course in which Flores and Gynther participated, there is a program called the Urban Plunge. This is a forty-eight-hour investigation into urban challenges that over two hundred students participate in during their semester break, in various cities across the United States as part of a one-credit theology course. More than eighteen other one-credit seminars take roughly five hundred students to designated sites in the United States over spring and fall breaks, where issues facing poor children in New York City and challenges experienced by people who are poor in the Appalachia region are among those that students encounter. The International Summer Service Learning Program is a four-credit academic offering that takes more than forty students to over fourteen locations in the developing world where they work, for example, with individuals suffering from AIDS in Cambodia, or with children in an orphanage in Chile.

The experiential dimension of student learning is fundamental to center programs. Experience facilitates students' movement toward informed awareness of moral and ethical challenges facing the world; it provides them with encounters of multiple perspectives against which to test out and reformulate their own beliefs, their personal choices. And obviously it engages them directly with the people for whom the option for the poor is intended, those in various ways on the margins of society.

Community-based learning courses entail, by definition, reflection. It is as if students put a mirror up to their actions so as to see in new ways how they are behaving. They bring to light assumptions that may have been implicit. They consider these reflections in the light of readings and class discussion. Such activity is part and parcel of any legitimate service-learning course.

The special twist of the Center for Social Concerns courses is that reflection includes explicitly theological reflection. In other words, students in center classes are asked to consider their experiences in relation to their religious or faith views. In this manner, the principle of the option for the poor and other aspects of Catholic social thought are brought out as the student attempts to make sense of his or her community engagement, of what he or she reads about the causes of social issues or about policy. These principles are incorporated as explicit content areas in all of the center's courses. Thus, students hear about the principle of the option for the poor in each seminar, and it is stressed centrally in a number of classes. Additionally, Catholic social thought provides benchmarks against which students measure their own responses to the issues with which they are confronted—a lens for analysis, a guiding framework.

Since empirical investigations show there is a strong relationship between the interest the student has in the course material and the meaningfulness and quality of learning, the Center for Social Concerns provides community-based learning opportunities for students in their major fields. For example, one of its eight-week summer student opportunities is with ACCION, a micro-lending institution with offices throughout the United States. This internship is open to business students with finance and marketing backgrounds; they learn about financial opportunities for low-income individuals and businesses in various locations in the United States.

Generally with the support of the Center for Social Concerns, aspects of Catholic social thought are integrated as well into three-credit community-based learning courses offered in disciplines across the campus, of which there are over one hundred sections each year. For example, one professor, economist Charles Wilber,[20] has offered two courses in his discipline in which he integrates Catholic social thought. Wilber explains, "I believe that *how* the course is run is as important as its content. Students learn values from the process of learning. I strive for student participation, problem solving, and experiential learning as integral to a Christian approach to teaching economics." He goes on to describe some of what students in his courses do: "In my economics and ethics class each student has to contribute eight hours of voluntary labor to an organization devoted to working for justice: Holy Family Catholic Worker House, South Bend Homeless Center, Saint Augustine's Soup Kitchen, et al. . . . I ask the students to prepare a six-to-eight-page paper reflecting on this service experience and tying it to the readings in the course." From these efforts, Wilber says, students come to see that "economics and ethics are inextricably mixed in both theory and policy." His courses also are, he says, "successful in showing students the need for understanding how their faith does shape and should shape their responses to economic issues."

Chemistry professor Dennis Jacobs offered a course to chemistry and engineering students entitled "Chemistry in Service of the Community," through which his students test for lead in the paint and soil around homes in a nearby predominantly low-income neighborhood. They instruct family members on how to reduce the possibilities of creating lead hazards through simple house-cleaning methods. These students read documents from the United States Conference of Catholic Bishops and other materials within the broad frame of Catholic social thought which address issues pertaining to the environment, to race, and to class. They are asked to consider how these materials might guide one to respond to the lead hazards facing children in the neighborhood. They think about the policy level as well as personal action and responsibility.

Catholic social thought is written for people who are living their lives through the whole gamut of possible works or professions. It is written not only for the Dorothy Days or Mother Teresas, but for all who live out vocations as lawyers, teachers, artists, entrepreneurs, and the many other professions necessary to support our society. Thus, internships offered in fields linked to students' future work interests are required of the students who study in Notre Dame's Catholic Social Tradition Program. Students spend two to three hours a week at a site where they interview, observe, and engage in workplace activities. The students keep journals. These internships, such as the Center for Social Concerns ACCION internship, are intended to reflect the fields the students hope to enter.

Indeed, the content of Catholic social thought can be presented and explained, but it is in the application and reflection upon it in real life that the learning becomes most effective. As Brigitte Gynther comments, "Catholic social thought only can be truly understood through application. It is meant to be applied, and we learn just as much through analyzing that application as we do through reading that theory." This is the method of community-based learning. It is through crucibles of experience that the option for the poor takes on its possible meanings and becomes usable guidance for living.

INTEGRATING THE OPTION FOR THE POOR ACROSS THE UNIVERSITY

Catholic social thought, including the principle of the option for the poor, can be integrated and highlighted within academic courses and curricula in many ways, and obviously not only through community-based learning. In the university's Catholic Social Tradition Program,[21] a core seminar is required of all students seeking a minor. In this course, one student prepares a short paper on each week's readings and another prepares a response. The class begins with the response, which leads to dialogue between the author and respondent and then eventually the involvement of the entire class. The professor moderates, clarifies, and occasionally briefly presents something denser than the students yet have the skills or knowledge to approach.

According to theology professor Todd Whitmore, the director of Notre Dame's Catholic Social Tradition Program, the pedagogy of this seminar, though it does not take students into the local community, nonetheless reflects attention to principles of Catholic social teaching: "Here we have relative egalitarianism regulated by the principle of subsidiarity: the professor serves a supporting function and involves him- or herself directly only when necessary, and then with the commitment to remove him- or herself from direct participation as soon as the discussion allows." Whitmore also notes, in this example, attentiveness to the principle of the common good: "Equality is not an end in itself, but rather serves the common good, and it may be necessary to shift to more hierarchical modes at certain points. Indeed as long as courses require evaluation of students on the part of the faculty, there will necessarily be an ongoing hierarchical element."[22] The principle of the option for the poor is also considered. "Within the classroom," Whitmore writes, attention to this principle "alerts the professor to the dynamics of the conversation with attention to who is participating and who is not and whether one person's participation is marginalizing someone else."[23]

In an economics course, students are asked to consider how Catholic social teaching principles might be used to help a CEO decide whether or not to move her plant from the east coast of the United States to a country in Asia. They are asked to consider how one might decide which principles to privilege. Is it subsidiarity, which might encourage the CEO to show concern for workers locally? Solidarity, which might support a move to offer livelihoods to Taiwanese labor? Human dignity? Common good? Option for the poor? Students in this course also consider how various other perspectives might influence such decision making—deontological and consequentialist ethical frameworks, market thinking, and so forth.

Regarding curricula, it has been argued that investigations of poverty provide an important content area for students' study if one is interested in the option for the poor principle. As this principle leads us to attempt to see the world from the perspective of those who are poor, any learning opportunities that facilitate this would be valuable in an education in Catholic social thought.

CONCLUSION

The principle of the option for the poor can be brought into a student's educational experience in multiple ways. Community-based learning has the potential to be a particularly meaningful one. This is because it enables the learner to enter into the life experience of people who live on the margins, for example, of working poor or individuals without homes of their own. It requires an integration of this experience with course readings, and engages students in reflection on the connections between those readings, the lived experience of real people to and with whom students make a contribution, and their own faith experience.

If students do only direct service through their community-based learning courses, it is possible they will not engage with those who are poor in such a way as to glimpse the world through their eyes. It is possible then that they will retain their sense of privilege and not open themselves to new ways of seeing. If, however, as is done in courses at the Center for Social Concerns, students are offered additional ways to participate in their communities along with direct service, and if they are encouraged to view their community involvement as action *with,* after first listening, rather than action *for,* the meaning of the option for the poor can come to life for them.

If the reflection that is an essential attribute of community-based learning is characterized by social analysis, students will be challenged to see the larger context in which the social concern they are addressing occurs—the race and class issues that situate lead poisoning of poor children, for example. This too occurs through the Center for Social Concerns community-based learning courses. Through this social analysis, students will also see the multiple causes of social issues, and be urged to get at root causes.

The option for the poor is an explicit content area in center courses. It, as well as the whole body of Catholic social tradition and any other meaningful dimension of one's spiritual life, is part of the theological reflection in these courses. Ultimately, through community-based learning pedagogy, students are given the opportunity to understand the meaning of the preferential option for the poor through word and their own deed.

NOTES

1. U.S. Conference of Catholic Bishops, *A Century of Social Teaching: A Common Heritage, a Continuing Challenge* (Washington, D.C.: U.S. Catholic Bishops Conference, 1990), 6–7.

2. John Dewey, *Democracy and Education* (New York: Macmillan, 1916).

3. Todd D. Whitmore, "Teaching and Living Practical Reasoning: The Role of Catholic Social Thought in a Catholic University Curriculum," *Journal of Peace and Peace Studies* 11:2 (2001): 2.

4. Thomas Aquinas, *Summa Theologica,* I-II, qu. 94, a. 4.

5. Ibid.

6. Whitmore, "Teaching and Living Practical Reasoning," 3.

7. John XXIII, *Pacem in terris,* 155.

8. Whitmore, "Teaching and Living Practical Reasoning," 2.

9. An excellent discussion on this subject can be found in Kerry Strand, Nicholas Cutforth, Randy Stoecker, Sam Marullo, and Patrick Donohue, *Community-Based Research and Higher Education: Principles and Practices* (San Francisco: Jossey-Bass, 2003).

10. Alfred North Whitehead, *The Aims of Education and Other Essays* (New York: Macmillan, 1929), 6–7.

11. See Dwight E. Giles, Jr. and Janet Eyler, *Where's the Learning in Service-Learning?* (San Francisco: Jossey-Bass, 1999). This provides a good summary of the study results on service-learning's effectiveness with students.

12. Ibid.

13. E. T. Pascarella and P. T. Terezini, *How College Affects Students: Findings and Insights from Twenty Years of Research* (San Francisco: Jossey-Bass, 1991).

14. Whitmore, "Teaching and Living Practical Reasoning," 17.

15. Ibid., 14.

16. *Economic Justice for All: A Pastoral Letter on Catholic Social Teaching and the U.S. Economy* (Washington, D.C.: U.S. Catholic Bishops Conference, 1986).

17. See Joe Holland and Peter Henriot, *Social Analysis: Linking Faith and Justice,* rev. ed. (Maryknoll, N.Y.: Orbis Books, 1983).

18. Both Jesse Flores and Brigitte Gynther participated in a panel presentation, "Option for the Poor and Pedagogy: Teaching and Learning Catholic Social Tradition," at a conference on the option for the poor at the University of Notre Dame, Nov. 12, 2002.

19. See the Center for Social Concerns website at http://socialconcerns .nd.edu. Some of the opportunities facilitated by the center would perhaps more accurately be labeled experiential learning or immersion experiences. These can be distinguished from service- or community-based learning in that they do not offer students service opportunities and may not bring them into engagement with individuals and organizations dealing with social challenges. For example, testing for chemicals in a local pond can constitute experiential learning, but if there is no related service or effort with a community related to findings, this might more aptly be called experiential learning. An immersion experience, a form of experiential learning, engages students with a powerful off-campus experience of a social challenge; for example, when students visit urban sites over semester break as part of the Center for Social Concerns' Urban Plunge, they generally engage in service, but if not, they will nonetheless have potent encounters with people who are in various ways dealing with the issues of deindustrialization, poverty, and the like. In the field of community-based learning, there is a fair amount of discussion about definitional differences across institutions. For example, Michigan State University uses "community outreach" when referring to its community-based learning efforts, Cornell uses "participatory action

research" for its community-based research work, and so on. Differences are determined by cultural context, historical factors, etc.

20. Wilber was also a presenter on the panel with Flores and Gynther at the 2002 option for the poor conference at the University of Notre Dame.

21. The web address for the program is http://www.nd.edu/~cstprog/inside page.htm

22. Todd D. Whitmore, "Practicing the Common Good: The Pedagogical Implications of Catholic Social Teaching," *Teaching Theology and Religions* 3:1 (2000): 15.

23. Ibid., 16.

CHAPTER 11

Health, Healing, and Social Justice
Insights from Liberation Theology

PAUL FARMER

If I define my neighbor as the one I must go out to look for, on the highways and byways, in the factories and slums, on the farms and in the mines—then my world changes. This is what is happening with the "option for the poor," for in the gospel it is the poor person who is the neighbor par excellence. . . .

But the poor person does not exist as an inescapable fact of destiny. His or her existence is not politically neutral, and it is not ethically innocent. The poor are a by-product of the system in which we live and for which we are responsible. They are marginalized by our social and cultural world. They are the oppressed, exploited proletariat, robbed of the fruit of their labor and despoiled of their humanity. Hence the poverty of the poor is not a call to generous relief action, but a demand that we go and build a different kind of social order.

—Gustavo Gutiérrez, *The Power of the Poor in History*

Not everything that the poor are and do is gospel. But a great deal of it is.

—Jon Sobrino, *Spirituality of Liberation*

This chapter originally published in Paul E. Farmer, *Pathologies of Power: Health, Human Rights, and the New War on the Poor* (Berkeley: University of California Press, 2004). Reprinted with permission.

MAKING A PREFERENTIAL OPTION FOR THE POOR

For decades now, proponents of liberation theology have argued that people of faith must make a "preferential option for the poor." As discussed by Brazil's Leonardo Boff, a leading contributor to the movement, "the Church's option is a preferential option *for the poor, against their poverty*." The poor, Boff adds, "are those who suffer injustice. Their poverty is produced by mechanisms of impoverishment and exploitation. Their poverty is therefore an evil and an injustice."[1] To those concerned with health, a preferential option for the poor offers both a challenge and an insight. It challenges doctors and other health providers to make an option—a choice—for the poor, to work on their behalf.

The insight is, in a sense, an epidemiological one: most often, diseases themselves make a preferential option for the poor. Every careful survey, across boundaries of time and space, shows us that the poor are sicker than the nonpoor. They are at increased risk of dying prematurely, whether from increased exposure to pathogens (including pathogenic situations) or from decreased access to services—or, as is most often the case, from both of these "risk factors" working together.[2] Given this indisputable association, medicine has a clear—if not always observed—mandate to devote itself to populations struggling against poverty.

It is also clear that many health professionals feel paralyzed by the magnitude of the challenge. Where on earth does one start? We have received endless, detailed prescriptions from experts, many of them manifestly dismissive of initiatives coming from afflicted communities themselves. But those who formulate health policy in Geneva, Washington, New York, or Paris do not really labor to transform the social conditions of the wretched of the earth. Instead, the actions of technocrats—and what physician is not a technocrat?—are most often tantamount to managing social inequality, to keeping the problem under control. The limitations of such tinkering are sharp, as Peruvian theologian Gustavo Gutiérrez warns:

> Latin American misery and injustice go too deep to be responsive to palliatives. Hence we speak of social revolution, not reform; of liberation, not development; of socialism, not modernization of the prevailing sys-

tem. "Realists" call these statements romantic and utopian. And they should, for the reality of these statements is of a kind quite unfamiliar to them.[3]

Liberation theology, in contrast to officialdom, argues that genuine change will be most often rooted in small communities of poor people; and it advances a simple methodology—*observe, judge, act*.[4] Throughout Latin America, such base-community movements have worked to take stock of their situations and devise strategies for change.[5] The approach is straightforward. Although it has been termed "simplistic" by technocrats and experts, this methodology has proved useful for promoting health in settings as diverse as Brazil, Guatemala, El Salvador, rural Mexico, and urban Peru. Insights from liberation theology have proved useful in rural Haiti too, perhaps the sickest region of the hemisphere and the one I know best. With all due respect for health policy expertise, then, this chapter explores the implications—so far, almost completely overlooked—of liberation theology for medicine and health policy.[6]

Observe, judge, act. The "observe" part of the formula implies analysis. There has been no shortage of analysis from the self-appointed apostles of international health policy, who insist that their latest recipes become the cornerstones of health policy in all of Latin America's nations.[7] Within ministries of health, one quickly learns not to question these fads, since failure to acknowledge the primacy of the regnant health ideology can stop many projects from ever getting off the ground. But other, less conventional sources of analysis are relevant to our understanding of health and illness. It's surprising that many Catholic bishops of Latin America, for centuries allied with the elites of their countries, have in more recent decades chosen to favor tough-minded social analysis of their societies. Many would argue that liberation theology's key documents were hammered out at the bishops' conventions in Medellín in 1968 and in Puebla in 1978. In both instances, progressive bishops, working with like-minded theologians, denounced the political and economic forces that immiserate so many Latin Americans. Regarding causality, the bishops did not mince words:

Let us recall once again that the present moment in the history of our peoples is characterized in the social order, and from an objective point of view, by a situation of underdevelopment. Certain phenomena point an accusing finger at it: marginalized existence, alienation, and poverty. In the last analysis it is conditioned by structures of economic, political, and cultural dependence on the great industrialized metropolises, the latter enjoying a monopoly on technology and science (neocolonialism).[8]

What began timidly in the preparation for the Medellín meeting in 1968 was by 1978 a strong current. "The Puebla document," remarks Boff, "moves immediately to the structural analysis of these forces and denounces the systems, structures, and mechanisms that 'create a situation where the rich get richer at the expense of the poor, who get even poorer.'"[9] In both of these meetings, the bishops were at pains to argue that "this reality calls for personal conversion and profound structural changes that will meet the legitimate aspirations of the people for authentic social justice."[10]

Liberation theology has always been about the struggle for social and economic rights. The injunction to "observe" leads to descriptions of the conditions of the Latin American poor, and also to claims regarding the origins of these conditions. These causal claims have obvious implications for a rethinking of human rights, as Gutiérrez explains:

> A structural analysis better suited to Latin American reality has led certain Christians to speak of the "rights of the poor" and to interpret the defense of human rights under this new formality. The adjustment is not merely a matter of words. This alternative language represents a critical approach to the laissez-faire, liberal doctrine to the effect that our society enjoys an equality that in fact does not exist. This new formulation likewise seeks constantly to remind us of what is really at stake in the defense of human rights: the misery and spoliation of the poorest of the poor, the conflictive character of Latin American life and society, and the biblical roots of the defense of the poor.[11]

Liberation theologians are among the few who have dared to underline, from the left, the deficiencies of the liberal human rights movement. The most glaring of these deficiencies emerges from intimate acquaintance with the suffering of the poor in countries that are signatory to all modern human rights agreements. When children living in poverty die of measles, gastroenteritis, and malnutrition, and yet no party is judged guilty of a human rights violation, liberation theology finds fault with the entire notion of human rights as defined within liberal democracies. Thus, even before judgment is rendered, the "observe" part of the formula reveals atrocious conditions as atrocious.

The "judge" part of the equation is nonetheless important even if it is, in a sense, prejudged. We look at the lives of the poor and are sure, just as they are, that *something is terribly wrong.* They are targets of structural violence. (Some of the bishops termed this "structural sin.")[12] This is, granted, an a priori judgment—but it is seldom incorrect, for analysis of social suffering invariably reveals its social origins. It is not primarily cataclysms of nature that wreak havoc in the lives of the Latin American poor:

> All these aspects which make up the overall picture of the state of humanity in the late twentieth century have one common name: oppression. They all, including the hunger suffered by millions of human beings, result from the oppression of some human beings by others. The impotence of international bodies in the face of generally recognized problems, their inability to effect solutions, stems from the self-interest of those who stand to benefit from their oppression of other human beings. In each major problem there is broad recognition of both the moral intolerableness and the political non-viability of the existing situation, coupled with a lack of capacity to respond. If the problem is (or the problems are) a conflict of interests, then the energy to find the solution can come only from the oppressed themselves.[13]

Rendering judgment based on careful observation can be a powerful experience. The Brazilian sociologist Paulo Freire coined the term *conscientization,* or "consciousness raising," to explain the process of coming to understand how social structures cause injustice.[14] This "involves discovering that evil not only is present in the hearts of powerful individuals who muck things up for the rest of us but is embedded in the very structures of society, so that those structures, and not just individuals who work within them, must be changed if the world is to change."[15] Liberation theology uses the primary tools of social analysis to reveal the mechanisms by which social structures cause social misery. Such analysis, unlike many fraudulently dispassionate academic treatises, is meant to challenge the observer to judge. It requires a very different approach than that most often used by, say, global health bureaucrats. It requires an approach that implicates the observer, as Jon Sobrino notes:

> The reality posed by the poor, then, is no rhetorical question. Precisely as sin, this reality tends to conceal itself, to be relativized, to pass itself off as something secondary and provisional in the larger picture of human achievements. It is a reality that calls men and women not only to recognize and acknowledge it, but to take a primary, basic position regarding it. Outwardly, this reality demands that it be stated for what it is, and denounced. . . . But inwardly, this same reality is a question for human beings as themselves participants in the sin of humankind. . . . the poor of the world are not the causal products of human history. No, poverty results from the actions of other human beings.[16]

How is all of this relevant to medicine? It is more realistic, surely, to ask how this could be considered irrelevant to medicine. In the wealthy countries of the Northern Hemisphere, the relatively poor often travel far and wait long for health care inferior to that available to the wealthy. In the Third World, where conservative estimates suggest that 1 billion souls live in dire poverty, the plight of the poor is even worse. How do they cope? They don't, often enough. The poor there have short life expectancies, often dying of preventable or treatable diseases or from accidents. Few have access to modern medical care. In fact, most of the Third World poor receive no effective biomedical care at all. For some people, there is no such thing as a measles vaccine. For many, tuberculosis is as lethal as AIDS. Childbirth involves mortal risk. In an age of explosive development in the realm of medical technology, it is unnerving to find that the discoveries of Salk, Sabin, and even Pasteur remain irrelevant to much of humanity.

Many physicians are uncomfortable acknowledging these harsh facts of life and death. To do so, one must admit that the majority of premature deaths are, as the Haitians would say, "stupid deaths." They are completely preventable with the tools already available to the fortunate few. By the criteria of liberation theology, these deaths are a great injustice and a stain on the conscience of modern medicine and science. Why, then, are these premature deaths not the primary object of discussion and debate within our professional circles? Again, liberation theology helps to answer this question. First, acknowledging the scandalous conditions of those living in poverty often requires a rejection of comforting relativism. Sobrino is addressing fellow theologians, but what he writes is of relevance to physicians, too:

> In order to recognize the truth of creation today, one must take another tack in this first, basic moment, a moment of honesty. The data, the statistics, may seem cold. They may seem to have precious little to do with theology. But we must take account of them. This is where we have to start. "Humanity" today is the victim of poverty and institutionalized violence. Often enough this means death, slow or sudden.[17]

A second reason that premature deaths are not the primary topic of our professional discussion is that the viewpoints of poor people will inevitably be suppressed or neglected as long as elites control most means of communication. Thus the steps of observation and judgment are usually difficult, because vested interests, including those controlling "development" and even international health policy, have an obvious stake in shaping observations about causality and in attenuating harsh judgments of harsh conditions. (This is, of course, another reason that people living in poverty are cited in this book as experts on structural violence and human rights.)

Finally, the liberation theologians and the communities from which they draw their inspiration agree that it is necessary to *act* on these reflections. The "act" part of the formula implies much more than reporting one's findings. The goal of this judging is not producing more publications or securing tenure in a university: "In order to *understand* the world, Latin American Christians are taking seriously the insights of social scientists, sociologists, and economists, in order to learn how to *change* the world."[18] Sobrino puts it this way: "There is no doubt that the only correct way to love the poor will be to struggle for their liberation. This liberation will consist, first and foremost, in their liberation at the most elementary level—that of their simple, physical life, which is what is at stake in the present situation."[19] I could confirm his assessment with my own experiences in Haiti and elsewhere, including the streets of some of the cities of the hemisphere's most affluent country. What is at stake, for many of the poor, is physical survival.

The results of following this "simple" methodology can be quiet and yet effective, as in the small-scale project described in the next section. But careful reflection on the inhuman conditions endured by so many in this time of great affluence can of course also lead to more explosive actions. Retrospective analysis of these explosions often reveals them to be last-ditch efforts to escape untenable situations. That is, the explosions follow innumerable peaceful attempts to attenuate structural violence and the lies that help sustain it. The Zapatistas, who refer often to early death from treatable illnesses, explain it this way in an early communiqué:

> Some ask why we decided to begin now, if we were prepared before. The answer is that before this we tried other peaceful and legal roads to change, but without success. During these last ten years more than 150,000 of our indigenous brothers and sisters have died from curable diseases. The federal, state, and municipal governments' economic and social plans do not even consider any real solution to our problems, and consist of giving us handouts at election times. But these crumbs of charity solve our problems for no more than a moment, and then, death returns to our houses. That is why we think no, no more, enough of this dying useless deaths, it would be better to fight for change. If we die now, we will not die with shame, but with the dignity of our ancestors. Another 150,000 of us are ready to die if that is what is needed to waken our people from their deceit-induced stupor.[20]

APPLYING PRINCIPLES OF LIBERATION THEOLOGY TO MEDICINE

To act as a physician in the service of poor or otherwise oppressed people is to prevent, whenever possible, the diseases that afflict them—but also to treat and, if possible, to cure. So where's the innovation in that? How would a health intervention inspired by liberation theology be different from one with more conventional underpinnings? Over the past decade, Partners in Health has joined local community health activists to provide basic primary care and preventive services to poor communities in Mexico, Peru, the United States, and, especially, Haiti—offering what we have termed "pragmatic solidarity." Pragmatic solidarity is different from but nourished by solidarity per se, the desire to make common cause with those in need. Solidarity is a precious thing: people enduring great hardship often remark that they are grateful for the prayers and good wishes of fellow human beings. But when sentiment is accompanied by the goods and services that might diminish unjust hardship, surely it is enriched. To those in great need, solidarity without the pragmatic component can seem like so much abstract piety.

Lest all this talk of structural violence and explosive responses to it seem vague and far-removed from the everyday obligations of medicine, allow me to give examples from my own clinical experience. How does liberation theology inform medical practice in, say, rural Haiti? Take tuberculosis, along with HIV the leading infectious cause of preventable adult deaths in the world. How might one observe, judge, and act in pragmatic solidarity with those most likely to acquire tuberculosis or already suffering from it?

The "observation" part of the formula is key, for it involves careful review of a large body of literature that seeks to explain the distribution of the disease within populations, to explore its clinical characteristics, and to evaluate tuberculosis treatment regimens. This sort of review is standard in all responsible health planning, but liberation theology would push analysis in two directions: first, to seek the root causes of the problem; second, *to elicit the experiences and views of poor people* and to incorporate these views into all observations, judgments, and actions.

Ironically enough, some who understand, quite correctly, that the underlying causes of tuberculosis are poverty and social inequality make a terrible error by failing to honor the experience and views of the poor in designing strategies to respond to the disease. What happens if, after analysis reveals poverty as the root cause of tuberculosis, tuberculosis control strategies ignore the sick and focus solely on eradicating poverty? Elsewhere, I have called this the "Luddite trap," since this ostensibly progressive view would have us ignore both current distress and the tools of modern medicine that might relieve it, thereby committing a new and grave injustice.[21] The destitute sick ardently desire the eradication of poverty, but their tuberculosis can be readily cured by drugs such as isoniazid and rifampin. The prescription for poverty is not so clear.

Careful review of the biomedical and epidemiological literature on tuberculosis does permit certain conclusions. One of the clearest is that the incidence of the disease is not at all random. Certainly, tuberculosis has claimed victims among the great (Frederic Chopin, Fyodor Dostoyevsky, George Orwell, Eleanor Roosevelt), but historically it is a disease that has ravaged the economically disadvantaged.[22] This is especially true in recent decades: with the development of effective therapy in the mid-twentieth century came high cure rates—over 95 percent—for those with access to the right drugs for the right amount of time. Thus tuberculosis *deaths* now—which each year number in the millions—occur almost exclusively among the poor, whether they reside in the inner cities of the United States or in the poor countries of the Southern Hemisphere.[23]

The latest twists to the story—the resurgence of tuberculosis in the United States, the advent of HIV-related tuberculosis, and the development of strains of tuberculosis resistant to the first-line therapies developed in recent decades—serve to reinforce the thesis that *Mycobacterium tuberculosis,* the causative organism, makes its own preferential option for the poor.[24]

What "judgment" might be offered on these epidemiological and clinical facts? Many would find it scandalous that one of the world's leading causes of preventable adult deaths is a disease that, with the possible exception of emerging resistant strains, is more than 95 percent curable, with inexpensive therapies developed decades ago. Those inspired by liberation theology would certainly express distaste for a disease so partial to poor and debilitated hosts and would judge unacceptable the lack of therapy for those most likely to become ill with tuberculosis: poverty puts people at risk of tuberculosis and then bars them from access to effective treatment. An option-for-the-poor approach to tuberculosis would make the disease a top priority for research and development of new drugs and vaccines and at the same time would make programs to detect and cure all cases a global priority.

Contrast this reading to the received wisdom—and the current agenda—concerning tuberculosis. Authorities rarely blame the recrudescence of tuberculosis on the inequalities that structure our society. Instead, we hear mostly about biological factors (the advent of HIV, the mutations that lead to drug resistance) or about cultural and psychological barriers that result in "noncompliance." Through these two sets of explanatory mechanisms, one can expediently attribute high rates of treatment failure either to the organism or to uncooperative patients.

There are costs to seeing the problem in this way. If we see the resurgence or persistence of tuberculosis as an exclusively biological phenomenon, then we will shunt available resources to basic biological research, which, though needed, is not the primary solution, since almost all tuberculosis deaths result from lack of access to existing effective therapy. If we see the problem primarily as one of patient noncompliance, then we must necessarily ground our strategies in plans to change the patients rather than to change the weak tuberculosis control programs that fail to detect and cure the majority of cases. In either event, weak analysis produces the sort of dithering that characterizes current global tuberculosis policy, which must accept as its primary rebuke the shameful death toll that continues unabated.

How about the "act" part of the formula advocated by liberation theology? In a sense, it's simple: heal the sick. Prompt diagnosis and cure of tuberculosis are also the means to prevent new infections, so prevention and treatment are intimately linked. Most studies of tuberculosis in Haiti reveal that the vast majority of patients do not complete treatment—which explains why, until very recently, tuberculosis remained the leading cause of adult death in rural regions of Haiti. (It has now been surpassed by HIV.) But it does not need to be so. In the country's Central Plateau, Partners in Health worked with our sister organization, Zanmi Lasante, to devise a tuberculosis treatment effort that borrows a number of ideas—and also some passion—from liberation theology.

Although the Zanmi Lasante staff had, from the outset, identified and referred patients with pulmonary tuberculosis to its clinic, it gradually became clear that detection of new cases did not always lead to cure, even though all tuberculosis care, including medication, was free of charge. In December 1988, following the deaths from tuberculosis of three HIV-negative patients, all adults in their forties, the staff met to reconsider the care these individuals had received. How had the staff failed to prevent these deaths? How could we better observe, judge, and act as a community making common cause with the destitute sick?

Initially, we responded to these questions in differing ways. In fact, the early discussions were heated, with a fairly sharp divide between community health workers, who shared the social conditions of the patients, and the doctors and nurses, who did not. Some community health workers believed that tuberculosis patients with poor outcomes were the most economically impoverished and thus the sickest; others hypothesized that patients lost interest in chemotherapy after ridding themselves of the symptoms that had caused them to seek medical advice. Feeling better, they returned as quickly as possible to the herculean task of providing for their families. Still others, including the physicians and nurses, attributed poor compliance to widespread beliefs that tuberculosis was a disorder inflicted through sorcery, beliefs that led patients to abandon biomedical therapy. A desire to focus blame on the patients' ignorance or misunderstanding was palpable, even though the physicians and nurses sought to cure the disease as ardently as anyone else involved in the program.

The caregivers' ideas about the causes of poor outcomes tended to coalesce in two directions: a *cognitivist-personalistic* pole that emphasized individual patient agency (curiously, "cultural" explanations fit best under this rubric, since beliefs about sorcery allegedly led patients to abandon therapy), and a *structural* pole that emphasized the patients' poverty. And this poverty, though generic to outsiders like the physicians from Port-au-Prince, had a vivid history to those from the region. Most of our tuberculosis patients were landless peasants living in the most dire poverty. They had lost their land a generation before when the Péligre Dam, part of an internationally funded development project, flooded their fertile valley.[25]

More meetings followed. Over the next several months, we devised a plan to improve services to patients with tuberculosis—and to test these discrepant hypotheses. Briefly, the new program set goals of detecting cases, supplying adequate chemotherapy, and providing close follow-up. Although they also continued contact screening and vaccination for infants, the staff of Zanmi Lasante was then most concerned with caring for smear-positive and coughing patients—whom many believed to be the most important source of community exposure. The new program was aggressive and community-based, relying heavily on community health workers for close follow-up. It also responded to patients' appeals for nutritional assistance. The patients argued, often with some vehemence and always with eloquence, that to give medicines without food was tantamount to *lave men, siye atè* (washing one's hands and then wiping them dry in the dirt).

Those diagnosed with tuberculosis who participated in the new treatment program were to receive daily visits from their village health worker during the first month following diagnosis. They would also receive financial aid of thirty dollars per month for the first three months; would be eligible for nutritional supplements; would receive regular reminders from their village health worker to attend the clinic; and would receive a five-dollar honorarium to defray "travel expenses" (for example, renting a donkey) for attending the clinic. If a patient did not attend, someone from the clinic—often a physician or an auxiliary nurse—would make a visit to the no-show's house. A series of forms, including a detailed initial interview schedule and home visit reports, regularized these arrangements and replaced the relatively limited forms used for other clinic patients.

Between February 1989 and September 1990, 50 patients were enrolled in the program. During the same period, the clinical staff diagnosed pulmonary tuberculosis in 213 patients from outside our catchment area. The first 50 of these patients to be diagnosed formed the comparison group that would be used to judge the efficacy of the new intervention. They were a "control group" only in the sense that they did not benefit from the community-based services and financial aid; all tuberculosis patients continued to receive free care.

The difference in the outcomes of the two groups was little short of startling. By June 1991, 46 of the patients receiving the "enhanced package" were free of all symptoms, and none of those with symptoms met radiologic or clinical diagnostic criteria for persistent tuberculosis. Therefore, the medical staff concluded that none had active pulmonary tuberculosis, giving the participants a cure rate of 100 percent. We could not locate all 50 of the patients from outside the catchment area, but for the 40 patients examined more than one year after diagnosis, the cure rate was barely half that of the first group, based on clinical, laboratory, and radiographic evaluation. It should be noted that this dismal cure rate was nonetheless higher than that reported in most studies of tuberculosis outcomes in Haiti.[26]

Could this striking difference in outcome be attributed to patients' ideas and beliefs about tuberculosis? Previous ethnographic research had revealed extremely complex and changing ways of understanding and speaking about tuberculosis among rural Haitians.[27] Because most physicians and nurses (and a few community health workers) had hypothesized that patients who "believed in sorcery" as a cause of tuberculosis would have higher rates of noncompliance with their medical regimens, we took some pains to address this issue with each patient. As the resident medical anthropologist, I conducted long—often very long—and open-ended interviews with all patients in both groups, trying to delineate the dominant explanatory models that shaped their views of the disease. I learned that few from either group would deny the possibility of sorcery as an etiologic factor in their own illness, but I could discern no relationship between avowal of such beliefs and compliance with a biomedical regimen. That is, the outcomes were related to the quality of the program rather than the quality of the patients' ideas about the disease. Suffice it to say, this was not the outcome envisioned by many of my colleagues in anthropology.

Although anthropologists are expected to underline the importance of *culture* in determining the efficacy of efforts to combat disease, in Haiti we learned that many of the most important variables—initial exposure to infection, reactivation of quiescent tuberculosis, transmission to household members, access to diagnosis and therapy, length of convalescence, development of drug resistance, degree of lung destruction, and, most of all, mortality—are all strongly influenced by *economic* factors. We concluded that removing structural barriers to "compliance," when coupled with financial aid, dramatically improved outcomes in poor Haitians with tuberculosis. This conclusion proved that the community health workers, and not the doctors, had been correct.

This insight forever altered approaches to tuberculosis within our program. It cut straight to the heart of the compliance question. Certainly, patients may be noncompliant, but how relevant is the notion of compliance in rural Haiti? Doctors may instruct their patients to eat well. But the patients will "refuse" if they have no food. They may be told to sleep in an open room and away from others, and here again they will be "noncompliant" if they do not expand and remodel their miserable huts. They may be instructed to go to a hospital. But if hospital care must be paid for in cash, as is the case throughout Haiti, and the patients have no cash, they will be deemed "grossly negligent." In a study published in collaboration with the Zanmi Lasante team, we concluded that "the hoary truth that poverty and tuberculosis are greater than the sum of their parts is once again supported by data, this time coming from rural Haiti and reminding us that such deadly synergism, formerly linked chiefly to crowded cities, is in fact most closely associated with deep poverty."[28]

Similar scenarios could be offered for diseases ranging from typhoid to AIDS. In each case, poor people are at higher risk of contracting the disease and are also less likely to have access to care. And in each case, analysis of the problem can lead researchers to focus on the patients' shortcomings (for example, failure to drink pure water, failure to use condoms, ignorance about public health and hygiene) or, instead, to focus on the conditions that structure people's risk (for example, lack of access to potable water, lack of economic opportunities for women, unfair distribution of the world's resources). In many current discussions of these plagues of the poor, one can discern a cognitivist-personalistic pole and a structural pole. Although focus on the former is the current fashion, one of the chief benefits of the latter mode of analysis is that it encourages physicians (and others concerned to protect or promote health) to make common cause with people who are both poor and sick.

A SOCIAL JUSTICE APPROACH TO ADDRESSING DISEASE AND SUFFERING

Tuberculosis aside, what follows next from a perspective on medicine that is based in liberation theology? Does recourse to these ideas demand loyalty to any specific ideology? For me, applying an option for the poor has never implied advancing a particular strategy for a national economy. It does not imply preferring one form of development, or social system, over another—although some economic systems are patently more pathogenic than others and should be denounced as such by physicians. Recourse to the central ideas of liberation theology does not necessarily imply subscription to a specific body of religious beliefs; Partners in Health and its sister organizations in Haiti and Peru are completely ecumenical.[29] At the same time, the flabby moral relativism of our times would have us believe that we may now choose from a broad menu of approaches to delivering effective health care services to the poor. This is simply not true. Whether you are sitting in a clinic in rural Haiti, and thus a witness to stupid deaths from infection, or sitting in an emergency room in a U.S. city, and thus the provider of first resort for 40 million uninsured, you must acknowledge that the commodification of medicine invariably punishes the vulnerable.

A truly committed quest for high-quality care for the destitute sick starts from the perspective that health is a fundamental human right. In contrast, commodified medicine invariably begins with the notion that health is a desirable outcome to be attained through the purchase of the right goods and services. Socialized medicine in industrialized countries is no doubt a step up from a situation in which market forces determine who has access to care. But a perspective based in liberation theology highlights the fundamental weakness of this and other strategies of the affluent: if the governments of Scandinavian countries and that of France, for example, then spend a great deal of effort barring noncitizens from access to health care services, they will find few critics within their borders. (Indeed, the social democracies share a mania for border control.) But we will critique them, and bitterly, because access to the fruits of science and medicine should not be determined by passports, but rather by need. The "health care for all" movement in the United States will never be morally robust until it truly means "all."

Liberation theology's first lesson for medicine is similar to that usually confronting healers: There is something terribly wrong. Things are not the way they should be. But the problem, in this view, is with the world, even though it may be manifest in the patient. Truth—and liberation theology, in contrast to much postmodern attitudinizing, believes in historical accuracy—is to be found in the perspective of those who suffer unjust privation.[30] Cornel West argues that "the condition of truth is to allow the suffering to speak. It doesn't mean that those who suffer have a monopoly on truth, but it means that the condition of truth to emerge must be in tune with those who are undergoing social misery—socially induced forms of suffering."[31]

The second lesson is that medicine has much to learn by reflecting on the lives and struggles of poor or otherwise oppressed people. How is suffering, including that caused by sickness, best explained? How is it to be addressed? These questions are, of course, as old as humankind. We've had millennia in which to address—societally, in an organized fashion— the suffering that surrounds us. In looking at approaches to such problems, one can easily discern three main trends: *charity, development,* and *social justice.*

Each of these might have much to recommend it, but it is my belief that the first two approaches are deeply flawed. Those who believe that

charity is the answer to the world's problems often have a tendency—
sometimes striking, sometimes subtle, and surely lurking in all of us—to
regard those needing charity as intrinsically inferior. This is different
from regarding the poor as powerless or impoverished because of historical processes and events (slavery, say, or unjust economic policies
propped up by powerful parties). There is an enormous difference between seeing people as the victims of innate shortcomings and seeing
them as the victims of structural violence. Indeed, it is likely that the
struggle for rights is undermined whenever the history of unequal
chances, and of oppression, is erased or distorted.

The approach of charity further presupposes that there will always be
those who have and those who have not. This may or may not be true,
but, again, there are costs to viewing the problem in this light. In *Pedagogy of the Oppressed*, Paulo Freire writes: "In order to have the continued
opportunity to express their 'generosity,' the oppressors must perpetuate
injustice as well. An unjust social order is the permanent fount of this
'generosity,' which is nourished by death, despair, and poverty." Freire's
conclusion follows naturally enough: "True generosity consists precisely
in fighting to destroy the causes which nourish false charity."[32] Given the
twentieth century's marked tendency toward increasing economic inequity in the face of economic growth, the future holds plenty of false
charity. All the recent chatter about "personal responsibility" from "compassionate conservatives" erases history in a manner embarrassingly expe-
dient for themselves. In a study of food aid in the United States, Janet
Poppendieck links a rise in "kindness" to a decline in justice:

> The resurgence of charity is at once a *symptom* and a *cause* of our society's
> failure to face up to and deal with the erosion of equality. It is a symptom
> in that it stems, in part at least, from an abandonment of our hopes for
> the elimination of poverty; it signifies a retreat from the goals as well as
> the means that characterized the Great Society. It is symptomatic of a
> pervasive despair about actually solving problems that has turned us to-
> ward ways of managing them: damage control, rather than prevention.
> More significantly, and more controversially, the proliferation of charity
> *contributes* to our society's failure to grapple in meaningful ways with
> poverty.[33]

It is possible, however, to overstate the case against charity—it is, after all, one of the four cardinal virtues, in many traditions. Sometimes holier-than-thou progressives dismiss charity when it is precisely the virtue demanded. In medicine, charity underpins the often laudable goal of addressing the needs of "underserved populations." To the extent that medicine responds to, rather than creates, underserved populations, charity will always have its place in medicine.

Unfortunately, a preferential option for the poor is all too often absent from charity medicine. First, charity medicine should avoid, at all costs, the temptation to ignore or hide the causes of excess suffering among the poor. Meredeth Turshen gives a jarring example from apartheid South Africa:

> South African paediatricians may have developed an expertise in the understanding and treatment of malnutrition and its complications, but medical expertise does not change the system that gives rise to malnutrition nor the environment to which treated children return, an environment in which half of the children die before their fifth birthday. Malnutrition, in this context, is a direct result of the government's policies, which perpetuate the apartheid system and promote the poor health conditions and human rights violations.[34]

Second, charity medicine too frequently consists of secondhand, castoff services—leftover medicine—doled out in piecemeal fashion. How can we tell the difference between the proper place of charity in medicine and the doling out of leftovers? Many of us have been involved in these sorts of good works and have often heard a motto such as this: "The homeless poor are every bit as deserving of good medical care as the rest of us." The notion of a preferential option for the poor challenges us by reframing the motto: The homeless poor are *more* deserving of good medical care than the rest of us.[35] Whenever medicine seeks to reserve its finest services for the destitute sick, you can be sure that it is option-for-the-poor medicine.

What about development approaches?[36] Often, this perspective seems to regard progress and development as almost natural processes. The technocrats who design development projects—including a certain Péligre Dam, which three decades ago displaced the population we seek to serve in central Haiti—plead for patience. In due time, the technocrats tell the poor, if they speak to them at all, you too will share our standard of living. (After a generation, the reassurance may be changed to "if not you, your children.") And certainly, looking around us, we see everywhere the tangible benefits of scientific development. So who but a Luddite would object to development as touted by the technocrats?

According to liberation theology, progress for the poor is not likely to ensue from development approaches, which are based on a "liberal" view of poverty. Liberal views place the problem with the poor themselves: these people are backward and reject the technological fruits of modernity. With assistance from others, they too will, after a while, reach a higher level of development. Thus does the victim-blaming noted in the earlier discussion of tuberculosis recur in discussions of underdevelopment.

For many liberation theologians, developmentalism or reformism cannot be rehabilitated. Jorge Pixley and Clodovis Boff use these terms to describe what they consider an "erroneous" view of poverty, in contrast to the "dialectical" explanation, in which the growth of poverty is dependent on the growth of wealth. Poverty today, they note, "is mainly the result of a contradictory development, in which the rich become steadily richer, and the poor become steadily poorer." Such a poverty is "internal to the system and a natural product of it."[37] Developmentalism not only erases the historical creation of poverty but also implies that development is necessarily a linear process: progress will inevitably occur if the right steps are followed. Yet any critical assessment of the impact of such approaches must acknowledge their failure to help the poor, as Leonardo and Clodovis Boff argue:

> "Reformism" seeks to improve the situation of the poor, but always within existing social relationships and the basic structuring of society, which rules out greater participation by all and diminution in the privileges enjoyed by the ruling classes. Reformism can lead to great feats of development in the poorer nations, but this development is nearly always at the expense of the oppressed poor and very rarely in their favor. For example, in 1964 the Brazilian economy ranked 46th in the world; in 1984 it ranked 8th. The last twenty years have seen undeniable technological and industrial progress, but at the same time there has been a considerable

worsening of social conditions for the poor, with exploitation, destitution, and hunger on a scale previously unknown in Brazilian history. This has been the price paid by the poor for this type of elitist, exploitative, and exclusivist development.[38]

In his introduction to *A Theology of Liberation,* Gustavo Gutiérrez concurs: we assert our humanity, he argues, in "the struggle to construct a just and fraternal society, where persons can live with dignity and be the agents of their own destiny. It is my opinion that the term *development* does not well express these profound aspirations."[39] Gutiérrez continues by noting that the term *liberation* expresses the hopes of the poor much more succinctly. Philip Berryman puts it even more sharply: "'Liberation' entails a break with the present order in which Latin American countries could establish sufficient autonomy to reshape their economies to serve the needs of that poor majority. The term 'liberation' is understood in contradistinction to 'development.'"[40]

In examining medicine, one sees the impact of "developmental" thinking not only in the planned obsolescence of medical technology, essential to the process of commodification, but also in influential analytic constructs such as the "health transition model."[41] In this view, societies as they develop are making their way toward that great transition, when deaths will no longer be caused by infections such as tuberculosis but will occur much later and be caused by heart disease and cancer. But this model masks interclass differences *within* a particular country. For the poor, wherever they live, there is, often enough, no health transition. In other words, wealthy citizens of "underdeveloped" nations (those countries that have not yet experienced their health transition) do not die young from infectious diseases; they die later and from the same diseases that claim similar populations in wealthy countries. In parts of Harlem, in contrast, death rates in certain age groups are as high as those in Bangladesh; in both places, the leading causes of death in young adults are infections and violence.[42]

The powerful, including heads of state and influential policymakers, are of course impatient with such observations and respond, if they deign to respond, with sharp reminders that the overall trends are the results that count. But if we focus exclusively on aggregate data, why not declare public health in Latin America a resounding success? After all, life expectancies have climbed; infant and maternal mortality have dropped. But if you work in the service of the poor, what's happening to that particular class, whether in Harlem or in Haiti, always counts a great deal. In fact, it counts most. And from this vantage point—the one demanded by liberation theology—neither medicine nor development looks nearly so successful. In fact, the outcome gap between rich and poor has continued to grow.

In summary, then, the charity and development models, though perhaps useful at times, are found wanting in rigorous and soul-searching examination. That leaves the social justice model. In my experience, people who work for social justice, regardless of their own station in life, tend to see the world as deeply flawed. They see the conditions of the poor not only as unacceptable but as the result of structural violence that is human-made. As Robert McAfee Brown, paraphrasing the Uruguayan Jesuit Juan Segundo, observes, "Unless we agree that the world should not be the way it is . . . there is no point of contact, because the world that is satisfying to us is the same world that is utterly devastating to them."[43] Often, if these individuals are privileged people like me, they understand that they have been implicated, whether directly or indirectly, in the creation or maintenance of this structural violence. They then feel indignation, but also humility and penitence. Where I work, this is easy: I see the Péligre Dam almost every week.

This posture—of penitence and indignation—is critical to effective social justice work. Alas, it is all too often absent or, worse, transformed from posture into posturing. And unless the posture is linked to much more pragmatic interventions, it usually fizzles out.

Fortunately, embracing these concepts and this posture does have very concrete implications. Making an option for the poor inevitably implies working for social justice, working with poor people as they struggle to change their situations. In a world riven by inequity, medicine could be viewed as social justice work. In fact, doctors are far more fortunate than most modern professionals: we still have a sliver of hope for meaningful, dignified service to the oppressed. Few other disciplines can make this claim with any honesty. We have a lot to offer right now. In Haiti and Peru and Chiapas, we have found that it is often less a question of "development" and more one of redistribution of goods and services, of simply sharing the fruits of science and technology. The majority of our efforts in the transfer of technology—medications, laboratory supplies, computers, and training—are conceived in just this way. They end up being innovative for other reasons: it is almost unheard of to insist that the destitute sick receive high quality care as a right.

Treating poor Peruvians who suffer from multidrug-resistant tuberculosis according to the highest standard of care, rather than according to whatever happens to be deemed "cost-effective," is not only social justice work but also, ironically enough, innovative. Introducing antiretroviral medications, and the health systems necessary to use them wisely, to AIDS-afflicted rural Haiti is, again, viewed as pie-in-the-sky by international health specialists but as only fitting by liberation theology. For example, operating rooms (and cesarean sections) must be part of any "minimum package" of health services wherever the majority of maternal deaths are caused by cephalopelvic disproportion. This is obvious from the perspective of social justice but controversial in international health circles. And the list goes on.

A preferential option for the poor also implies a mode of analyzing health systems. In examining tuberculosis in Haiti, for example, our analysis must be *historically deep*—not merely deep enough to recall an event such as that which deprived most of my patients of their land, but deep enough to remember that modern-day Haitians are the descendants of a people enslaved in order to provide our ancestors with cheap sugar, coffee, and cotton.

Our analysis must be *geographically broad*. In this increasingly interconnected world ("the world that is satisfying to us is the same world that is utterly devastating to them"), we must understand that what happens to poor people is never divorced from the actions of the powerful. Certainly, people who define themselves as poor may control their own destinies to some extent. But control of lives is related to control of land, systems of production, and the formal political and legal structures in which lives are enmeshed. With time, both wealth and control have become increasingly concentrated in the hands of a few. The opposite trend is desired by those working for social justice.

For those who work in Latin America, the role of the United States looms large. Father James Guadalupe Carney, a Jesuit priest, put his life on the line in order to serve the poor of Honduras. As far as we can tell, he was killed by U.S.-trained Honduran security forces in 1983.[44] In an introduction to his posthumously published autobiography, his sister and brother-in-law asked starkly: "Do we North Americans eat well because the poor in the third world do not eat at all? Are we North Americans powerful, because we help keep the poor in the third world weak? Are we North Americans free, because we help keep the poor in the third world oppressed?"[45]

Granted, it is difficult enough to "think globally and act locally." But perhaps what we are really called to do, in efforts to make common cause with the poor, is to think locally *and* globally and to act in response to both levels of analysis. If we fail in this task, we may never be able to contend with the structures that create and maintain poverty, structures that make people sick. Although physicians and nurses, even those who serve the poor, have not followed liberation theology, its insights have never been more relevant to our vocation. As international health experts come under the sway of the bankers and their curiously bounded utilitarianism, we can expect more and more of our services to be declared "cost-ineffective" and more of our patients to be erased. In declaring health and health care to be a human right, we join forces with those who have long labored to protect the rights and dignity of the poor.

NOTES

1. Leonardo Boff, *Faith on the Edge: Religion and Marginalized Existence,* 1st ed. (San Francisco: Harper and Row, 1989), 23.

2. The literature on the correlation between poverty, inequality, and increased morbidity and mortality is massive. For reviews, see, for example, P. E. Farmer, *Infections and Inequalities: The Modern Plagues* (Berkeley: University of California Press, 1999); J. Y. Kim, J. V. Millen, A. Irwin, and J. Gershman, eds., *Dying for Growth: Global Inequality and the Health of the Poor* (Monroe, Maine: Common Courage Press, 2000); and R. G. Wilkinson, *Unhealthy Societies: The Afflictions of Inequality* (London: Routledge, 1996). Other major reviews include A. Leclerc, D. Fassin, H. Grandjean, et al., eds., *Les inégalités sociales de santé* (Paris: Éditions la Découverte et Syros, 2000); World Health Organization, *World Health Report 1999—Making a Difference* (Geneva: World Health Organization, 1999); *World Health Report 2000. Health Systems: Improving Performance* (Geneva: World Health Organization, 2000); World Bank, *The Burden of Disease among the Global Poor: Current Situation, Future Trends, and Implications for Strategy* (Washington, D.C.: World Bank, 2000); M. Bartley, D. Blane, and

G. D. Smith, "Introduction: Beyond the Black Report," *Sociology of Health and Illness* 20:5 (1998): 563–77; A. Sen, "Mortality as an Indicator of Economic Success and Failure" (text of the Innocenti Lecture of UNICEF, delivered in Florence, March 1995), *Economic Journal* 108:446 (1998): 1–25; D. Coburn, "Income Inequality, Social Cohesion, and the Health Status of Populations: The Role of Neo-Liberalism," *Social Science and Medicine* 51:1 (2000): 135–46; and K. Fiscella, P. Franks, M. R. Gold, et al., "Inequality in Quality: Addressing Socioeconomic, Racial, and Ethnic Disparities in Health Care," *Journal of the American Medical Association* 283:19 (2000): 2579–84. Other articles review case studies of inequality in access to treatment of specific diseases; see, for example, S. S. Rathore, A. K. Berger, K. P. Weinfurt, et al., "Race, Sex, Poverty, and the Medical Treatment of Acute Myocardial Infarction in the Elderly," *Circulation: Journal of the American Heart Association* 102:6 (2000): 642–48; and of course the sizable body of literature on inequality of access to HIV therapy.

3. Gustavo Gutiérrez, *The Power of the Poor in History* (Maryknoll, N.Y.: Orbis Books, 1983), 44.

4. For a concise history of liberation theology, its historical relevance, and an explanation of key themes and motivations, see Leonardo and Clodovis Boff's slim and helpful volume *Introducing Liberation Theology* (Maryknoll, N.Y.: Orbis, 1987).

5. Base-community movements, also known as "basic ecclesial communities," are disparate and sociologically complex, and I do not aspire to review their idealized or actual impact. But, as this movement has been felt throughout Latin America, I would encourage further reading. For an insider account, see the volume by Father Álvaro Barreiro, *Basic Ecclesial Communities: The Evangelization of the Poor* (Maryknoll, N.Y.: Orbis Books, 1982). A study by John Burdick, *Looking for God in Brazil: The Progressive Catholic Church in Urban Brazil's Religious Arena* (Berkeley: University of California Press, 1993), contains a complementary, scholarly examination of such communities in urban Brazil.

6. There are other clues that liberation theology might have something to offer the healing professions: for one, the more destructive forces hate it. In 1982, for example, advisers to U.S. president Ronald Reagan argued that "American foreign policy must begin to counterattack (and not just react against) liberation theology" (quoted from the Santa Fe document, a Reagan administration working paper; cited in Boff and Boff, *Introducing Liberation Theology*, 86).

7. Recent health care "reforms" in Latin America and other developing regions have followed a neoliberal framework that favors commercialization, corporatization, and privatization of health and social welfare services. Most notable is the enthusiastic exportation of the U.S. model of "managed care." As Neill notes in his critique of these developments, "Managed health care is touted by many experts—usually found in USAID, the World Bank, and various havens of academia—as a tangible model which can be of immense value to developing coun-

tries if applied wisely and efficiently." See K. G. Neill, "Dancing with the Devil: Health, Human Rights, and the Export of U.S. Models of Managed Care to Developing Countries," *Cultural Survival Quarterly* 24:4 (2001): 61–63. This position, of course, ignores the growing body of evidence challenging the unabashed claims that managed-care organizations (MCOs) provide quality care with efficiency and cost-effectiveness—evidence that also points to managed care's role in exacerbating the already large inequities that characterize health care in the United States; see G. Anders, *Health against Wealth: HMOs and the Breakdown of Medical Trust* (Boston: Houghton Mifflin, 1996); D. P. Andrulis and B. Carrier, *Managed Care in the Inner City: The Uncertain Promise for Providers, Plans, and Communities* (San Francisco: Jossey-Bass, 1999); P. E. Farmer and B. Rylko-Bauer, "L' 'exceptionnel' système de santé américain: Critique d'une médecine à vocation commerciale" [The "exceptional" American health care system: Critique of the for-profit approach], *Actes de la Recherche en Sciences Sociales* 139 (2001): 13–30; E. Ginzberg, "The Uncertain Future of Managed Care," *New England Journal of Medicine* 340:2 (1999): 144–46; D. Himmelstein, S. Woolhandler, and I. Hellander, *Bleeding the Patient: The Consequences of Corporate Health Care* (Monroe, Maine: Common Courage Press, 2001); M. E. Lewin and S. Altman, eds., *America's Health Care Safety Net: Intact But Endangered* (Washington, D.C.: National Academy Press, 2000); J. Maskovsky, "'Managing' the Poor: Neoliberalism, Medicaid HMOs, and the Triumph of Consumerism among the Poor," *Medical Anthropology* 19 (2000): 121–46; E. Pellegrino, "The Commodification of Medical and Health Care: The Moral Consequences of a Paradigm Shift from a Professional to a Market Ethic," *Journal of Medicine and Philosophy* 24:3 (1999): 243–66; M. A. Peterson, "Managed Care Backlash," *Journal of Health Politics, Policy, and Law* 24:5 (theme issue) (1999): 873–1218; E. C. Schneider, A. M. Zaslavsky, and A. M. Epstein, "Racial Disparities in the Quality of Care for Enrollees in Medicare Managed Care," *Journal of the American Medical Association* 287:10 (2002): 1288–94. In fact, H. Waitzkin and C. Iriart, in "How the United States Exports Managed Care to Developing Countries," *International Journal of Health Services* 31:3 (2001): 495–505, note that, as the U.S. market has become saturated and MCOs face growing criticism, these corporations

have turned their eyes toward developing countries, especially those in Latin America. In the tradition of tobacco and pesticides, U.S. corporations are exporting to developing countries—in the form of managed care—products and practices that have come under heavy criticism domestically. The exportation of managed care is also receiving enthusiastic support from the World Bank, other multilateral lending agencies, and multinational corporations. . . . developing countries are experiencing strong pressure to accept managed care as the organizational framework for privatization of their health and social security systems. . . . this experience is serving as a model for the exportation of managed care to Africa and Asia. (497)

There is, of course, much money to be made by tapping into the health care and social security funds of the public sector even in poorer developing nations, under the guise of rescuing these countries from inefficient bureaucracies and rising costs by importing neoliberal managed-care solutions. Large segments of the population in Latin America live in poverty and often have minimal or no access to formal health care. The consequences of such health care transformations for the poor and the oppressed in developing countries, as well as for the public health systems they might rely on, are dire, to say the least. "As public health systems are dismantled and privatized under the auspices of managed care, multinational corporations predictably will enter the field, reap vast profits, and exit within several years. Then developing countries will face the awesome prospect of reconstructing their public systems" (Waitzkin and Iriart, 498). For more on health care reforms in Latin America, see F. Armada, C. Muntaner, and V. Navarro, "Health and Social Security Reforms in Latin America: The Convergence of the World Health Organization, the World Bank, and Transnational Corporations," *International Journal of Health Services* 31:4 (2001): 729–68; M. Barraza-Lloréns, S. Bertozzi, E. González-Pier, et al., "Addressing Inequality in Health and Health Care in Mexico," *Health Affairs* 21:3 (2002): 47–56; C. Iriart, E. E. Merhy, and H. Waitzkin, "Managed Care in Latin America: The New Common Sense in Health Policy Reform," *Social Science and Medicine* 52 (2001): 1243–53; A. C. Laurell, "Health Reform in Mexico: The Promotion of Inequality," *International Journal of Health Services* 31:2 (2001): 291–321; E. J. Pérez-Stable, "Managed Care Arrives in Latin America," *New England Journal of Medicine* 340:14 (1999): 1110–12; and K. Stocker, H. Waitzkin, and C. Iriart, "The Exportation of Managed Care to Latin America," *New England Journal of Medicine* 340:14 (1999): 1131–36.

8. J. L. Segundo, *Our Idea of God* (Dublin: Gill and Macmillan, 1980), 16; quoted from Segunda Conferencia General del Episcopado Latinoamericano, Medellín 1968.

9. L. Boff, *Faith on the Edge: Religion and Marginalized Existence,* 20.

10. J. Eagleson and P. Sharper, eds., *Puebla and Beyond: Documentation and Commentary* (Maryknoll, N.Y.: Orbis Books, 1979), 128.

11. Gutiérrez, *The Power of the Poor in History,* 87.

12. J. Sobrino explains, in *Spirituality of Liberation: Toward Political Holiness* (Maryknoll, N.Y.: Orbis Books, 1988), 15, the link between structural violence and structural sin: "God's creation is being assaulted and vitiated. . . . because this reality is not simply natural, but historical—being the result of action taken by some human beings against others—this reality is sinful. As absolute negation of God's will, this sinfulness is very serious and fundamental."

13. J. V. Pixley and C. Boff, *The Bible, the Church, and the Poor* (Maryknoll, N.Y.: Orbis Books, 1989), 242.

14. In the English translation of *Pedagogy of the Oppressed,* the original Portuguese term is retained. In P. Freire's own words, *"Conscientização* is the deepening of the attitude of awareness characteristic of all emergence"—in other words, critical consciousness (New York: Continuum, 1986), 101.

15. R. M. Brown, *Liberation Theology: An Introductory Guide* (Louisville: Westminster John Knox Press, 1993), 45.

16. Sobrino, *Spirituality of Liberation,* 31.

17. Ibid., 13, 15.

18. Brown, *Liberation Theology,* 45.

19. Sobrino, *Spirituality of Liberation,* 32.

20. "Communiqué from the CCRI-CG of the EZLN, January 6, 1994," in S. Marcos and the Zapatista Army of National Liberation, *Shadows of Tender Fury: The Letters and Communiqués of Subcomandante Marcos and the Zapatista Army of National Liberation* (New York: Monthly Review Press, 1995), 58.

21. See Farmer, *Infections and Inequalities: The Modern Plagues,* chap. 1; and P. E. Farmer and E. Nardell, "Nihilism and Pragmatism in Tuberculosis Control," *American Journal of Public Health* 88:7 (1998): 4–5.

22. Even at the dawn of the era of antibiotics, when streptomycin was already available, class divisions were sharp inside Europe's sanatoriums. George Orwell's journal entries from the year before his death of tuberculosis are telling:

> Curious effect, here in the sanatorium, on Easter Sunday, when the people in this (the most expensive) block of "chalets" mostly have visitors, of hearing large numbers of upper-class English voices. I have been almost out to the sound of them for two years, hearing them at most one or two at a time, my ears growing more & more used to working-class or lower-middle-class Scottish voices. In the hospital at Hairmyres, for instance, I literally never heard a "cultivated" accent except when I had a visitor. It is as though I were hearing these voices for the first time. And what voices! A sort of over-fedness, a fatuous self-confidence, a constant bah-bahing of laughter abt [*sic*] nothing, above all a sort of heaviness & richness combined with a fundamental ill-will—people who, one instinctively feels, without even being able to see them, are the enemies of anything intelligent or sensitive or beautiful. No wonder everyone hates us so. (G. Orwell, *The Collected Essays, Journalism, and Letters of George Orwell,* vol. 4, *In Front of Your Nose, 1945–1950* [New York: Penguin Books, 1968], 578; journal entry from April 17, 1949)

For more on the history of tuberculosis in North America, see Georgina Feldberg's helpful review, *Disease and Class: Tuberculosis and the Shaping of Modern North American Society* (New Brunswick, N.J.: Rutgers University Press, 1995);

see also the classic study by R. Dubos and J. Dubos, *The White Plague: Tuberculosis, Man, and Society* (Boston: Little, Brown, 1952). Unfortunately, little has been written of the history of tuberculosis in the regions of the world where it has taken its greatest toll.

23. For an overview of the burden of disease and death caused by *M. tuberculosis,* see P. E. Farmer, D. A. Walton, and M. C. Becerra, "International Tuberculosis Control in the 21st Century," in *Tuberculosis: Current Concepts and Treatment,* 2nd ed., ed. L. N. Friedman (Boca Raton, Fla.: CRC Press, 2000), 475–96.

24. These "twists" are reviewed in Farmer, *Infections and Inequalities: The Modern Plagues,* chap. 9.

25. This story is told more fully in P. E. Farmer, *AIDS and Accusation: Haiti and the Geography of Blame* (Berkeley: University of California Press, 1992), 19–27.

26. For a more detailed discussion of this study, see Farmer, *Infections and Inequalities,* 217–25.

27. P. E. Farmer, "Sending Sickness: Sorcery, Politics, and Changing Concepts of AIDS in Rural Haiti," *Medical Anthropology Quarterly* 4:1 (1990): 6–27.

28. P. E. Farmer, S. Robin, S. L. Ramilus, et al., "Tuberculosis, Poverty, and 'Compliance': Lessons from Rural Haiti," *Seminars in Respiratory Infections* 6:4 (1991): 260. For more on this project, see Farmer, *Infections and Inequalities,* chap. 8.

29. Indeed, one does not need to subscribe directly to the religious tenets of liberation theology in order to make a "preferential option for the poor." Pixley and Boff summarize the widespread starvation, malnutrition, and poverty that are a daily reality for millions (remarking that one does not need "socio-scientific instruments" to prove this) and conclude that "this state of affairs is *morally intolerable,* for those who do not believe in the God of the Bible as much as for those who do" (Pixley and Boff, *The Bible, the Church, and the Poor,* 238, 239). They note the simple facts of the situation and what our response—whether one imbued with faith, or one relying solely on reason—must logically be:

> The energy to find the solution can come only from the oppressed themselves. Wherever there is oppression, there will be struggles to win life-sustaining conditions—struggles between classes, between races, between nations, between sexes. This is simply an observable fact, not a moral imperative or a scientific conclusion. We can see the just struggles of the oppressed going on around us, and we cannot see any other way out of the vast problems that afflict humanity at the close of the twentieth century. (242)

For a more in-depth discussion of these matters, refer to the full argument made by Pixley and Boff (*The Bible, the Church, and the Poor,* 237–43).

30. Perhaps it goes without saying that no physician who bases his or her practice on clinical trials can in good faith buy into the postmodern argument that all claims to truth are merely "competing discourses." But, as Christopher

Norris writes, in both the social sciences and the humanities, the conviction that we ought to find out what really happened is proof

> that we hadn't caught up with the "postmodern" rules of the game, the fact that nowadays things have moved on to the point where there is no last ground of appeal to those old, self-deluding "enlightenment" values that once possessed authority (or the semblance thereof), at least in some quarters. Anyone who continues to invoke such standards is plainly in the grip of a nostalgic desire for some ultimate truth-telling discourse—whether Platonist, Kantian, Marxist or whatever—that would offer a delusory refuge from the knowledge that we are nowadays utterly without resources in the matter of distinguishing truth from falsehood. (C. Norris, *Uncritical Theory: Postmodernism, Intellectuals, and the Gulf War* [Amherst: University of Massachusetts Press, 1992], 13)

Norris's devastating account of intellectuals and the Gulf War (1992) is one of the best critiques of the postmodern foolishness that has gained quite a foothold in universities on both sides of the Atlantic. See also C. Norris, *What's Wrong with Postmodernism: Critical Theory and the Ends of Philosophy* (Baltimore: Johns Hopkins University Press, 1990).

31. C. West, *Prophetic Thought in Postmodern Times* (Monroe, Maine: Common Courage Press, 1993), 4.

32. Freire, *Pedagogy of the Oppressed,* 29.

33. J. Poppendieck, *Sweet Charity? Emergency Food and the End of Entitlement* (New York: Viking Press, 1998), 5.

34. M. Turshen, "Health and Human Rights in a South African Bantustan," *Social Science and Medicine* 22:9 (1986): 891.

35. Samuel Johnson once observed that "a decent provision for the poor is the true test of civilization." Surely this is true, and it serves as an indictment of affluent society. But liberation theology delivers an even more damning indictment, since its proponents argue that we should reserve our highest standards for the poor.

36. My critique of development is by no means original; it draws heavily on a very large literature reaching back almost thirty years. From André Gunder Frank to Immanuel Wallerstein, the more refined versions of dependency theory cannot be lightly dismissed. For more recent reviews of the limitations of development approaches to health care, see Meredeth Turshen's wonderful book *Privatizing Health Services in Africa* (New Brunswick, N.J.: Rutgers University Press, 1999).

37. Pixley and C. Boff, *The Bible, the Church, and the Poor,* 6–7.

38. Boff and Boff, *Introducing Liberation Theology,* 5.

39. G. Gutiérrez, *A Theology of Liberation: History, Politics, and Salvation* (Maryknoll, N.Y.: Orbis Books, 1973), xiv.

40. P. Berryman, *Liberation Theology: Essential Facts about the Revolutionary Movement in Latin America and Beyond* (New York: Pantheon Books, 1987), 91.

41. For an introduction to the notion of health transition, see J. C. Caldwell, S. Findley, P. Caldwell, et al., eds., *What We Know about Health Transition: The Cultural, Social, and Behavioural Determinants of Health. The Proceedings of an International Workshop, Canberra, May 1989* (Canberra: Health Transition Centre, Australian National University, 1990); Gutiérrez, Zielinski, and Kendall have more recently qualified this concept by placing it in broader social context. See E. D. Gutiérrez, C. Zielinski, and C. Kendall, "The Globalization of Health and Disease: The Health Transition and Global Change," in *The Handbook of Social Studies in Health and Medicine,* ed. G. Albrecht, R. Fitzpatrick, and S. Scrimshaw (London: Sage, 2000), 84–99. See also the discussion by W. H. Mosley, J. L. Bobadilla, and D. T. Jamison on the implications of this model for developing countries in "The Health Transition: Implications for Health Policy in Developing Countries," in *Disease Control Priorities in Developing Countries,* ed. D. T. Jamison, W. H. Mosley, A. R. Measham, and J. L. Bobadilla (New York: Oxford Medical Publications, 1993), 673–99.

42. C. McCord and H. Freeman, "Excess Mortality in Harlem," *New England Journal of Medicine* 322:3 (1990): 173–77.

43. Brown, *Liberation Theology: An Introductory Guide,* 44.

44. Carney is said to have been killed after being captured when he participated in an ill-fated guerrilla incursion from Nicaragua into Olancho Province, Honduras.

45. J. G. Carney, *To Be a Revolutionary* (San Francisco: Harper and Row, 1987), xi. Carney goes on to criticize the United States directly, citing the U.S.-backed 1973 military coup d'état in Chile, in which tens of thousands were killed, as his own moment of realization about the extent of the often brutal U.S. involvement in the political and economic affairs of the region: "After the bloody military coup of 1973 in Chile, *it was obvious that the United States would never allow a country that is economically dependent on it to make a revolution by means of elections*—through the democratic process directed by the majority—at least as long as the country has an army that obeys the capitalist bourgeoisie of the country" (311). For an examination of U.S. policy toward progressive movements in Guatemala, El Salvador, and Haiti in a similar light, see P. E. Farmer, *The Uses of Haiti* (Monroe, Maine: Common Courage Press, 1994).

CHAPTER 12

Closing Argument

PAT MALONEY, SR.

At the end of a long career as a trial lawyer I take this opportunity to be a final witness and give testimony to the preferential option for the poor, for while I did not always have this name to give to the overarching motivation of my life's work, I have nevertheless tried to live out my understanding of it. My impending death due to terminal illness has had a way of putting things into perspective and of helping me be present to daily life. One of the great blessings of my situation is that I do not have anything more to prove, no more social benchmarks to attain, no more people to impress, no more political games to play. This is tremendously liberating and allows me the luxury of speaking my mind with impunity. I hope that in this closing argument I can present the challenges and rewards of my profession to those about to embark upon it, for it is a profession in which the harvest of justice can be truly plentiful but, regrettably, the workers on behalf of the poor and marginalized are indeed few.

MOTIVE

With the benefit of hindsight I can see that in some seminal way the impetus of my legal advocacy for others began with my father. A shoe salesman earning about twenty-five dollars a week, he was a kind and good man, but he was also an alcoholic. We were poor because his salary, meager to begin with, did not often make it home intact. We did not want to deny him the pleasure of a good drink, but we did not want him to deny us the necessity of food, clothing, and shelter. Negotiating this as a child planted the seeds of what it meant to lobby on behalf of the needs and rights of others. The seeds took root in my military service during the Second World War as I realized that my fellow Marines, mostly poor or underprivileged like me, were fighting a war that others created. Upon reflection, I believe that being a child of the Depression and a young man of World War II guided the formulation of basic principles such as the value of relationships, an admiration for the downtrodden and disadvantaged, the importance of our nation, and the significance of championing civil rights.

I finished law school in 1950 and took a job with the district attorney's office in Bexar County, Texas. As a prosecutor I often landed in the courtroom of Judge Eugene Williams, who was a great friend to the poor and underprivileged. He was the soul of fairness and dedication to the pursuit of justice while on the bench. His advice to counsel who came before him was "Show me your solution is fair and you'll probably have my support." That I too was an officer of the court with a primary responsibility to see that the results were just penetrated deeply into my modus operandi. It is the poor and marginalized—even more than others—who need a fair judicial system, and it was in the DA's office that I internalized my responsibility and obligation to see that they receive a fair trial regardless of the sometimes incompetent and indifferent representation assigned to them. These lessons laid the foundation for the private practice that I began several years later and have continued throughout my career.

MEANS

In my practice I had the power and the duty to ensure that my clients had the best possible representation. Dedication to this cause, rather than resting upon the potential for a large commercial return, required a moral ethic of protection of the innocent and the maintenance of truth and justice. Making sure my clients were being tried on a level legal playing field was an uphill battle. The rule of law was often against us. Contributory negligence, for example, meant that if there was any negligence, even as little as 1 percent, against the victim, no financial recovery was possible.[1] There were other unpalatable features of our legal system during this time. No women were allowed to serve on juries,[2] and I have found that women make by far the best jurors for the poor and deprived. A poll tax was required in order to serve on a jury,[3] and governmental immunity[4] was rampant. These legal hindrances made the chances of winning a victory in court for a poor plaintiff slim indeed. It took twenty-five years to bring change to these laws legislatively and judicially. There was persistent opposition from the insurance industry and special interest groups. Money, greed, duplicity, and falsehood were their constant tools.

The importance of a case in terms of money and recognition can, and often does, present alternatives that are not in the best interest of the needy and deserving client. A "win at any cost" strategy is a hazard that attends many decisions, but the pursuit of truth is the common denominator that requires personal integrity and individual responsibility. Although an unfavorable verdict is not what client or counsel works and hopes for, there are great lessons to be learned through defeat, among them humility, self-examination, perseverance, and resolve. In one wrongful death case, the jury ruled against my African American client, a recent widow with three small children, at the original trial and at the appellate level. In the midst not only of her grief but also her loss in court, this brave woman counseled my son and me in our remorse over the outcome of the case, "I'm black and I'm used to sorrow, defeat, and unfairness. It's not pleasant, but God will provide." She was the loser and yet was comforting us. I marveled that clients, by and large, were not more consumed with anger and resentment due to their injuries and mistreatment. Some were, of course, but most simply wanted to be fairly heard and obtain justice. I learned that listening well is a trait rarely found and deeply needed.

I represented a teenage boy who spent two years in inpatient treatment for the worst burns the doctors had ever seen in a patient who actually survived them. Through his treatment and multiple surgeries I visited weekly, until I could no longer stand the smell from his chlorine baths and the terrifying pain and agony he endured. When I told him why I would be unable to continue to visit regularly, he replied, "I know, Mr. Maloney. I feel the same way." That reply broke my heart as I learned that you must love your clients in order to wage a fair and effective fight on their behalf, especially in view of the courageous battle they themselves are fighting.

The fight on behalf of the poor against the greed and power of corporations that have essentially unlimited resources is sometimes won. Courage, tenacity, and truth can overcome in a showdown between the public and the powerful, and the common good can be served.[5] Prejudice, racism, and bias can and do infiltrate the justice system just as they can on any street corner. It matters who takes the case when the circumstances are not what they seem to be and there is no one to stand and defend the impoverished. It matters who sits in the jury box. I have developed a respect for juries as a reflection of our great and varied American society, and have profited from their wisdom, dedication, and persistent pursuit of honesty and truth.

Even more than the absence of material goods, poverty means vastly reduced options and a lack of hope. Many live in degradation because they cannot see beyond their circumstances. Without adequate education in basic skills like reading, writing, and verbal communication, improvement of circumstances is difficult. Without fundamental interviewing abilities, a poor personal presentation leads to the conclusion that one is ignorant and therefore unemployable. Doors remain closed, and the alternatives to captivity in the cycle of poverty remain hidden from view. The lack of hope sinks even lower into despair. The lack of judicial options for the poor is evidenced by difficulty in obtaining a jury trial, crowded dockets, the expense of employing expert witnesses, overwhelming confrontation with an opponent who often commands vastly superior resources, and appellate influence that makes victory in court almost incidental because appellate reversals are so frequent.

Like the option for the poor in every other discipline, defending the poor and downtrodden in our legal system requires an attorney to be at least as good as the opposing lawyer, armed with full background information and preparation, and willing to engage the full measure of one's personal talents and dedication. Because the resources on the opposing side are often superior, the lawyer for the poor client must more than match them in skill, endurance, and commitment. It is a sacred trust and nothing but the best will adequately serve the cause of justice.

OPPORTUNITY

Ultimately, what I have tried to do for the poor in the courtroom comes from a faith vision rather than a political strategy, a moral obligation, a means of capitalizing on contingencies from large judgments, or a tactic for image building. It comes from striving to remember that those who suffer are my brothers and sisters and that I have a responsibility before God to do everything I can to alleviate that suffering. My option for the poor comes from a place of gratitude to the God who first reached out to me. God is not fooled by fame, fortune, or power. Status and image mean nothing to God. In the end, in the final courtroom, what will sway the judge is what I did for the least of my brothers and sisters (Mt 25:35–36). A lawyer cannot do everything, and no lawyer wins every case. But I have learned that a lawyer can do an incredible amount of good if he or she is grounded in a commitment to the poor.

I recognize that in today's globalized world much has changed and new lawyers will face challenges that I never dreamed of. But the call to lawyers that runs parallel to these challenges remains unchanged because this world will always have the poor, and the rich and powerful who oppress them. The indispensable role of the lawyer and the legal system is, and will always be, to obtain justice for the powerless when they are oppressed by the privileged. While I am grateful for the big wins, now, at the end of my life, I find myself most thankful and proud of the moral victories in which I have tried to give a voice to the voiceless and alleviate the suffering of the oppressed. At the end of the journey it is not hard to believe that fame, fortune, and power were never very important after all.

To my younger colleagues and colleagues-to-be, and to all who are dedicated to advancing the cause of the poor, I implore you to embrace the future and make it your own in the advocacy for the poor. Bring all your gifts and talents to bear in the fight for justice for the poor and injured against the wrongdoer. Remember that your adversary is very good, resourceful, and trained to protect the wrongdoer. Mostly they are the top of the class, handsomely paid, and have all the advantages of power and wealth. Challenging this opponent is not a task for the weak or timid. You must train to be the very best because your opponent will be the very best. Dedication to and love of the pursuit of truth and justice must be your constant shield.

You will need to craft new solutions to old problems that continue to plague the poor, and find innovative, compelling, and contemporary ways to deal with future concerns and intrusions against them. You, like every generation before you, will continue to look out over an increasingly imperfect world and therefore must commit yourselves to do more than merely exist in it. Your skills will be more formidable than those of any previous generation and therefore you will have the power to do great good.

In my closing argument I have shown motive, means, and opportunity, and I trust that the evidence I have presented is enough to convict me of doing all I could for the "least of these," to live out the option for the poor. It is the legacy I leave; it is my greatest triumph.

NOTES

Pat Maloney, Sr., was one of the great trial lawyers in the United States. In his more than half-century as a personal injury and product liability lawyer he won more than one hundred cases where the verdict exceeded $1 million. He was known as the "king of torts" (Joe Holley, "Personal-Injury Lawyer Pat Maloney Dies at 81," *Washington Post,* Sept. 21, 2005). During his career he was a constant advocate for the injured and the downtrodden. In the last months of his life, already dealing with terminal pulmonary fibrosis, we asked him to write a retrospective piece that would share something of what he had learned in his struggle for justice over time and what advice he would give to new lawyers entering the field. He concluded his final battle on September 11, 2005, at the age of eighty-one. This chapter is a "closing argument" about the relationship he saw between law and the option for the poor.

1. Vincent R. Johnson, Alan Gunn, *Studies in American Tort Law,* 2nd ed. (Durham, N.C.: Carolina Academic Press, 1999), 725.

2. The Supreme Court ruled in *Taylor v. Louisiana* (1975) that "affirmative registration" for women for jury service, in which women were not automatically included on jury lists unless they were registered, violated the Sixth Amendment, which guarantees a jury drawn from a cross section of the community.

3. The Twenty-fourth Amendment to the U.S. Constitution abolished the poll tax in national elections. It was ratified in the states in 1962. In 1964, the U.S. Supreme Court ruled in *Harper v. Virginia Board of Elections* that state poll

taxes violated the Equal Protection Clause of the Fourteenth Amendment on the grounds that wealth was not a valid reason to burden citizens' fundamental right to vote.

4. Federal and state governments have waived some of their immunities through tort claims acts. The Texas Tort Claims Act was passed in 1969. However, there are limits. Only if a plaintiff can show that the government owed him or her a special duty beyond that owed to the public at large, will he or she prevail in a tort suit against the government. Further, Texas law caps the amount of damages a person can recover from the government. Punitive damages are recoverable only in limited instances.

5. See *Gravitt-Ashley v. AT&T and Southwestern Bell.* This case was instrumental in leading to the deregulation of the communications industry in the United States.

Afterword

The Most Important Certainty

MARY J. MILLER

José works all day at the paper recycling plant just east of down town and collects the trash in the building where I worked every night. His rounds took him past my office shortly after 5:00 P.M., and having made it my habit always to try to express appreciation to those in thankless roles, I said thanks and emptied my own wastebasket into his big bin each evening. A little occasional conversation soon became a nightly occurrence, and I noticed that if I happened not to be at my desk when José came by, he came back later to visit with me. He tried to teach me a new Spanish phrase every night, brought me a battered Spanish-English dictionary to use, and eventually taught me to say the Our Father in Spanish. Although José has a sixth-grade education and I was pursuing my master's degree, he was the teacher, and I the student. Economically and educationally we are very different, I suppose, but in all the ways that matter most, the matters of the heart, we are not so different at all.

José came to the United States from Mexico in 1979, and José is poor. He lives in an apartment but does not have a car or a phone. He likes rice and beans but does not eat meat every day. He told me that he does not worry much, and I noticed that he almost always seemed happy. José represents a group of people who have always been a part of the human family. Vastly more important than the two, commonly recognizable, sure things in life, death and taxes, is this special certainty that history and José confirm, and of which Jesus reminded us when he said we would always have the poor among us (Jn 12:8).

John Paul II has stated, "The option or love of preference for the poor is an option or a special form of primacy in the exercise of Christian charity to which the whole tradition of the Church bears witness."[1] Yet the option for the poor extends far beyond the confines of theological thought and theory. It is not merely an ideal limited to the realm of academic parlance, but is, rather, a goal that requests and requires the active participation of all people of good will, with their many gifts and talents, to bring about its implementation in our world where it is so urgently needed.

One need not look far to see that we are indeed in desperate straits, for poverty, as we have learned, has many dimensions. It might be a community in suburban Chicago that lacks adequate resources and knowledge to fight the location of a yet another waste incinerator within its already pollution-choked confines. It could be a developing country, having experienced more than its share of corruption and unrest, striving to make a peaceful political transition. Perhaps there are homeless people who really are interested in literature, art, and music. Maybe one person has been injured by a big corporation that refuses to take responsibility. And it could even be the rag-pickers who live off mountainous heaps of garbage in a teeming international city, or the residents of the infinite number of rural villages in the Third World where medical care is virtually nonexistent.

Try as they may, theologians cannot hope to solve the problem of poverty by themselves, nor should they be expected to. If it takes a village to raise a child, it will surely take all people of good will to join together in the task of making sure that our brothers and sisters in most need around the globe have available to them the resources to live with dignity and passion, and to make their own contributions by fulfilling the calling in their lives.

This volume about the option for the poor is not a volume of theological reflections on the principle. It is not theoretical or ideological. It is practical. This book is a manual or primer, of sorts, that gives us, in exemplary form, a glimpse of what is possible when the option for the poor takes root in the heart, manifests in the life, and grows to become more than a theological abstraction. Although each contributor to this volume is motivated by deeply held values and beliefs, he or she has found vital and creative ways to bring those beliefs to the work of justice in a vast array of academic, vocational, and practical settings: taking theory out of the classroom and making it practical in the community is beneficial for both neighbors and students; there really are alternatives to prestigious law firms and large corporations for new lawyers; maybe it does not take as much cash as we think to be truly happy; and perhaps we should not be so quick to demonize the creation of wealth and to target all corporations as evil entities, for if nothing is produced it will not be long until there is no wealth left to distribute.

Those who labor in disciplines beyond theology may be even more vital to the work of addressing poverty because they encourage and motivate us by showing, in their lives and efforts, that the contribution of each of us, no matter what our expertise, can make a very big difference indeed. The multidimensionality and wide scope of poverty is precisely why a multidimensional and widespread approach is necessary. This volume eliminates our excuses and reaffirms the responsibility that each of us bears to do good to, for, and with the least of these (Mt 25:31–46).

At the core of all work for justice, and well illustrated in this volume, are relationships rooted in love and respect. This is the case for people of all faiths, and none, but is especially true of those who find their motivation in the Christian gospel. David Tracy makes this profoundly simple summary statement, "In my judgment, by rendering explicit the option for the poor as central to their understanding, Christians have a great opportunity to rethink the issue at the heart of Christianity, namely, the relationship between love and justice."[2] It is through the solidarity of relationships built on loving respect that the scars of poverty begin to heal.

A lack of control has historically been a fundamental mark of poverty. The poor lack power over supplies of food and other natural resources, they lack the social and economic status to enable them to exchange goods and services effectively, and they lack the ability to maintain and sustain wellness. The results are not only hunger and thirst but possible starvation, victimizing debt, unfair interest rates, slavery, material loss, unending economic need, vulnerability to chronic and acute disease, homelessness, and social exile.[3] Not much has changed. Today the gulf between rich and poor is greater than it has ever been; where the economic scale used to be broad and contain many levels, it is now weighted very heavily at the top and, sadly, at the bottom. Loving respect begins to elevate those who live with this lack of control to a place where within their grasp is the means to exercise self-determination in matters that concern them.

The impetus for loving respect comes also from the gospel. The story of a blind beggar is told in Mark 10:46–52, and while there are many gems to mine from this narrative, one is of primary importance here. As Jesus passed by on the road, the blind man, wanting something from him and determined to be heard, shouted at him and begged for mercy. Jesus did not allow the man to be marginalized by the crowd who urged him to be quiet, and called the man to him. In a defining moment, Jesus asked the man, "What do you want me to do for you?" (v. 51). Surely Jesus knew that the man was blind and wanted to see again. But he dignified the man, and made him of the highest standing, like anyone else, by not assuming that he knew best what the man needed, by allowing the man to speak for himself, by giving him a voice and the chance to be heard. Jesus gave the blind man loving respect before ever restoring his sight.

Acts of citizenship, kinship, unity, and elevation mean that the poor will not remain forever "other." Solidarity and loving respect for our brothers and sisters in most need at least opens up a hope and a possibility that something other than poverty is possible. These acts are not the exclusive domain of the theologian. Loving respect, kinship, and solidarity are public domain: the university professors who share great literature with the homeless; the students who serve in the community because it is a required element of a course, but find their problem-solving skills sharpened and their hearts stirred in the bargain; the trial lawyer who advocates for the resourceless individual and lobbies for lasting legislative justice; the filmmaker who gives up the glitz of a make-believe world for the crushing reality of global slums; the physician who spends the time to discover which treatments and methodologies work best in a remote village.

Poverty is the work of human hands and has human causes. It has human solutions as well, and the option for the poor implores us to apply our own unique gifts, whatever they may be, toward advancing the solutions. Experience teaches us that it is possible to give from almost nothing. After all, who is it who can say, "I have no more love to give," or "I have no more friendship to give"? We live in the kingdom that has already come, but not in its fullness, and therefore we live in the tension of the already and the not yet. In our experiences of loving and serving the poor and working for an end to poverty, we move the already a little closer to the not yet.

As José was pushing his bin away from my office after one of our nightly visits, I began the ritual of my few Spanish parting phrases. I meant to say, "Cuida te, mi amigo," which means "Take care, my friend," but what came out of my mouth was "Te quiero, mi amigo." My English-speaking brain got confused because "te quiero" sounds like the English "take care," but in reality it is one way, in Spanish, to say "I love you." Without even a moment's hesitation, as he rounded the corner going away from me, and without looking back, José said, "Te quiero mucho, Maria." For an instant I wondered about the misunderstanding I might have inadvertently created, but then immediately realized that what we had just said to each other was true after all, for I have discovered that it is virtually impossible to consider anyone whom I have taken even the briefest time to get to know as completely "other." It is the relationship that makes all the difference in the world, and we are related to each other because we are related to Jesus.

As I look at José, his slim build, gray hair, and brown skin seem to fade until only his eyes remain—eyes of friendship, eyes of a deep connection, eyes that no longer let me look away in ignorance, eyes that will not let me dismiss him as irrelevant or marginal, truly the eyes of conversion. My conversion. As I look into José's face, I see not only him, but I see the face of Jesus, and I will never be the same, for one cannot encounter God and walk away from the experience unchanged. José has demanded nothing of me but my attention and my friendship. But Jesus in his eyes demands much, much more. "Inasmuch as you have done it to the least of these, you have done it to me" (Mt 25:40). As a human person, as a Christian with the weight of the "whole tradition of the church" coming to bear on my life, and as a member of the church in this modern age, I will be the rest of a lifetime fulfilling those demands.

NOTES

1. J. Michael Miller, ed., "Sollicitudo Rei Socialis," in *The Encyclicals of John Paul II* (Huntington, Ind.: Our Sunday Visitor, 1996), 467.

2. David Tracy, "The Christian Option for the Poor," in *Option for the Poor in Christian Theology*, ed. Daniel G. Groody (Notre Dame, Ind.: University of Notre Dame Press, 2007), 124.

3. Susan R. Holman, *The Hungry Are Dying: Beggars and Bishops in Roman Cappadocia* (New York: Oxford University Press, 2001), 168.

Contributors

José O. Aylwin is Chairman of the Program for the Rights of Indigenous Peoples, at the Institute for Indigenous Studies, Universidad de la Frontera, Temuco, Chile. He is the son of former president of the Republic of Chile, Patricio A. Aylwin.

Patricio A. Aylwin is former President of the Republic of Chile. He led the reconstruction of Chile and the reconciliation of its peoples following the military government of General Augusto Pinochet. Continuing his lifetime commitment to promoting justice, he is now President of the Corporation for Democracy and Justice, a nonprofit organization he founded to develop approaches to eliminating poverty and to strengthen ethical values in politics.

Mary Beckman, PhD, is Associate Director of Academic Affairs and Research at the Center for Social Concerns at the University of Notre Dame, where her responsibilities include directing a program in community-based research. An economist and faculty member at Notre Dame, she codeveloped and teaches in the Poverty Studies Interdisciplinary Minor (PSIM). She was a tenured professor in an interdisciplinary position at Lafayette College for many years before assuming her current role at Notre Dame. Her publications can be found in diverse journals including *Review of Radical Political Economics, Journal on Excellence in College Teaching, Women's Studies Quarterly,* and the *Journal of Higher Education Outreach and Engagement.*

242

Matt Bloom is Associate Professor of Management at the Mendoza College of Business, University of Notre Dame. Matt teaches courses on innovation, high-performance organizations, and creating inspiring workplaces. His research interests center on understanding well-being at work—what makes work a positive, meaningful, life-enriching experience. He explores topics such as what work is like when people experience it as a calling and what conditions help people to be at their physical, intellectual, and emotional best at work. Matt's research has been featured in business publications such as the *Wall Street Journal, New York Times,* and *Business Week,* and research journals including *Academy of Management Journal, Personnel Psychology, Strategic Management Journal, Research in Personnel and Human Resource Management,* and *European Business Review.*

Javier María Iguíñiz Echeverría is a professor at the Pontifical Catholic University of Peru in Lima and a former Kellogg Institute Fellow at the University of Notre Dame. He is author of numerous articles and several books, including *Decentralización, empleo y pobreza* (2001); *Desarrollo, libertad y liberación en Amartya Sen y Gustavo Gutiérrez* (2003), and *Homenaje a Máximo Vega Centeno* (2009).

Georges Enderle is John T. Ryan, Jr., Professor of International Business Ethics and a Fellow at the Kellogg Institute for International Studies and the Nanovic Institute for European Studies at the University of Notre Dame. He is the former president of the International Society of Business, Economics, and Ethics (2001–4). Recent publications include *Developing Business Ethics in China* (co-edited with Xiaohe Lu; 2006); "Wealth Creation in China and Some Lessons for Development Ethics" (*Journal of Business Ethics* 2010); and "Three Major Challenges for Business and Economic Ethics in the Next Ten Years: Wealth Creation, Human Rights, and Active Involvement of the World's Religions" (*Business and Professional Ethics Journal* 2011).

Stephen M. Fallon is John J. Cavanaugh Professor of the Humanities and professor of Liberal Studies and English at the University of Notre Dame. He is the author of *Milton among the Philosophers: Poetry and Materialism in Seventeenth-Century England* (1991) and *Milton's Peculiar*

Grace: Self-representation and Authority (2007), and he is coeditor of the Modern Library edition of *The Complete Poetry and Essential Prose of John Milton* (2007).

Paul Farmer is a medical anthropologist and physician, and a founding director of Partners in Health (PIH), an international nonprofit organization that provides direct health care services and has undertaken research and advocacy activities on behalf of the sick poor. He is the Kolokotrones University Professor and Chair of the Department of Global Health and Social Medicine at Harvard Medical School; Chief of the Division of Global Health Equity at Brigham and Women's Hospital; and the United Nations Deputy Special Envoy for Haiti, under Special Envoy Bill Clinton. He has written extensively on health, human rights, and the consequences of social inequality. His most recent book is *Haiti after the Earthquake* (2012). Other titles include *Partner to the Poor: A Paul Farmer Reader* (2010), *Pathologies of Power: Health, Human Rights, and the New War on the Poor* (2004), *The Uses of Haiti* (2005), *Infections and Inequalities: The Modern Plagues* (2001), and *AIDS and Accusation: Haiti and the Geography of Blame* (updated 2006).

Daniel G. Groody is a Holy Cross priest, a scholar, teacher, and an award-winning author and film producer. He is associate professor of theology and the director of the Center for Latino Spirituality and Culture at the Institute for Latino Studies at the University of Notre Dame. His books include *Border of Death, Valley of Life: An Immigrant Journey of Heart and Spirit* (2002) and *Globalization, Spirituality, and Justice: Navigating the Path to Peace* (2007). He is also editor of two books, *The Option for the Poor in Christian Theology* (2007) and *Gustavo Gutiérrez: Spiritual Writings* (2011), and co-editor of *A Promised Land, A Perilous Journey: Theological Perspectives on Migration* (2008).

Gustavo Gutiérrez, a Dominican priest and theologian from Peru, is widely recognized as one of the preeminent voices of liberation theology. His books include *A Theology of Liberation* (1988), *On Job* (1987), *We Drink from Our Own Wells* (2003), and *The God of Life* (1991). He is the John Cardinal O'Hara professor of theology at the University of Notre Dame.

Pat Maloney, Sr., was a personal injury and product liability trial lawyer for more than half a century. His numerous multimillion-dollar verdicts landed him on *Forbes* magazine's list of the nation's top money-making lawyers. Mr. Maloney is the coauthor of *Trials and Deliberations: Inside the Jury Room* (1992), and author of *Give Me Your Tired, Your Poor* (1998). He died at home at the age of eighty-one on September 11, 2005.

Mary J. Miller earned her Master of Arts degree in theology from the University of Notre Dame. She is a freelance writer and editor, and co-author with Daniel G. Groody of the JustFaith immigration course *Crossing Borders: Migration, Theology, and the Human Journey.*

F. Clark Power is a professor of Education in the Program of Liberal Studies at the University of Notre Dame. He is also the Program Director of "Play Like a Champion Today," a concurrent professor of psychology, and a Fellow at the Institute for Educational Initiatives at the University of Notre Dame. His publications focus on moral development and education, civic engagement, youth sports, and school climate. He is the co-editor of *Moral Education: A Handbook* (2007).

Robert E. Rodes, Jr., is the Paul J. Schierl/Fort Howard Corporation Professor of Legal Ethics in the School of Law at the University of Notre Dame. Recent publications include *Schools of Jurisprudence* (2011), *On Law and Chastity* (2006), and *Classic Problems of Jurisprudence* (2005). Professor Rodes is also the author of the liberationist volume *Pilgrim Law* (1997).

Stephen Bede Scharper is Associate Professor in the Department of Anthropology at the University of Toronto Mississauga and Centre for Environment, University of Toronto. He recently published, coedited with Ingrid Leman Stefanovic, *The Natural City: Re-Envisioning the Built Environment* (2011).

Kristin Shrader-Frechette is O'Neill Family Endowed Professor in the Department of Philosophy and the Department of Biological Sciences at the University of Notre Dame. Including 18 books and 380 scholarly articles, Shrader-Frechette's research has been funded for twenty-eight years by the U.S. National Science Foundation and has been translated into thirteen languages. Her recent books include *What Will Work: Fighting Climate Change with Renewable Energy, Not Nuclear Power* (2011); *Taking Action, Saving Lives* (2007); and *Environmental Justice: Creating Equality, Reclaiming Democracy* (2005). She and her students do pro bono scientific and environmental justice work in minority/poor communities throughout the world.

Gerard Thomas Straub is a documentary filmmaker and the founder and president of Pax et Bonum Communications, which produces films focused on the plight of the poor. He is also the author of six books, including *Thoughts of a Blind Beggar: Reflections from a Journey to God* (2007), and *Hidden in the Rubble: A Haitian Pilgrimage to Compassion and Resurrection* (2010). He speaks in churches and schools across the United States and in Europe.

Index